MEDICAL POWER AND SOCIAL KNOWLEDGE

MEDICAL POWER AND SOCIAL KNOWLEDGE

Bryan S. Turner

Ⓢ SAGE Publications
London · Beverly Hills · Newbury Park · New Delhi

SAGE Publications Ltd
28 Banner Street
London EC1Y 8QE

SAGE Publications Inc
275 South Beverly Drive
Beverly Hills, California 90212
and 2111 West Hillcrest Drive
Newbury Park, California 91320

SAGE Publications India Pvt Ltd
C-236 Defence Colony
New Delhi 110 024

British Library Cataloguing in Publication Data

Turner, Bryan S.
  Medical power and social knowledge.
  1.Social medicine
  I. Title
  362.1'042   RA418

  ISBN 0-8039-8087-6
  ISBN 0-8039-8088-4 Pbk

Library of Congress catalog card number 87-081057

Publishing services by Ponting–Green
London and Basingstoke
Photoset by Parker Typesetting Service, Leicester
Printed in Great Britain by J. W. Arrowsmith Ltd, Bristol

Contents

Acknowledgements

This study of medical sociology was originally a series of lectures at the Flinders University of South Australia. My understanding of medicine and modern society developed in response to valuable contributions from my students. The framework of this text was further extended through seminars at the Psychiatry Department of the Flinders Medical Centre and Glenside Hospital. Earlier versions of these chapters were presented at the University of Adelaide Conference on Illness Behaviour, the annual conference of the Society of Hospital Pharmacists of Australia and in the post-graduate seminars of the Sociology Department at Flinders University. I am grateful to Stephen Barr and Stephen Hill for their invaluable editorial advice. I would also like to thank Tony Parham, Joy Parham, Frank May, Lena Sudano and Kevin White for advice about doctors, pharmacists, nurses and patients. Karen Lane provided unlimited emotional support and intellectual companionship. I am grateful to Ina Cooper who typed the entire manuscript. Only the errors are my responsibility.

I
INTRODUCTION

1
Medical sociology

Text-books on medical sociology typically start with a critical evaluation of the discipline and its development. In this introduction to medical sociology, I largely follow a conventional set of criticisms of the subject, although I hope to come to radically different conclusions about the character and prospects of medical sociology. These criticisms of medical sociology are essentially concerned with the relationship between sociology and medical institutions. An examination of this relationship between medicine and sociology then leads eventually to a critical appraisal of the content and topics of medical sociology.

The alleged ambiguity of sociology in relation to medicine is conventionally expressed in terms of a dichotomy between sociology-in-medicine and the sociology of medicine. In this division, sociology-in-medicine is defined as dominated by medical values and professional needs, whereas the sociology of medicine (or sociology of health and illness) has traditionally been concerned with the nature of medicine as a profession, and embodies a shift away from the doctor's perspective on illness towards the client's view of their condition. The focus of the sociology of medicine has included the recruitment of doctors, their training, the development of the roles of doctors, paramedicals and patients, and the professionalization of medical and paramedical occupations. It also embraces the study of medical organizations with special reference to such institutions as the clinic, the asylum and the general hospital within the framework of a sociological study of bureaucracy.

In this book, I argue that the sociology of medicine should be more concerned to identify itself with the central theoretical problems of sociology as such; it is only by a shift towards the more theoretically formulated problems that the old dichotomy of sociology-in-medicine and the sociology of medicine will be finally surpassed. The sociology of medicine, like the sociology of religion or the sociology of law, is primarily a study in sociology, not a study in medicine.

Disease, illness and sickness
In this study of medical sociology, I shall be particularly concerned with the relationship between knowledge and power in the social distribution of health and illness, and as the basis for professional management of socially deviant individuals. That is, the argument will be concerned with the role of medical discourse as the foundation of medical power. In order to understand the character of this medical discourse, this book will be concerned in a variety of contexts with the distinction between deviance, illness and disease. Although Parsons' approach (1951) to the definition of sickness as involving choice and subjectivity within a system of social action was a radical departure from the medical model in the 1950s, it is now commonplace to recognize that social and psychological factors are crucial in the aetiology (causation) of illness. Certain text-books in medical sociology now propose a neat and economic classification of human disorders into three distinct categories, namely sickness, illness and disease. Whereas disease is a concept which describes malfunctions of a physiological and biological character, illness refers to the individual's subjective awareness of the disorder, and sickness designates appropriate social roles (Susser and Watson, 1971). It can be argued that this tripartite division of human disorders corresponds to a professional division of labour and to a prestige ranking of medical activity. For example, the physician is professionally trained to cure disease, the clinical psychiatrist to deal with illness and practitioners of clinical sociology are directed towards sickness. There is also a hierarchy of scientific status in which the analysis of sick roles is perceived to be the most under-developed aspect of medical practice from the point of view of precision, accuracy and reliability.

Disease is seen as a neutral and natural entity residing in nature, that is in the body of the patient. The division between physical and mental illness corresponds to a cultural division between mind and body, which is in fact philosophically and sociologically very problematic. In this study of medical sociology, it is argued that an adequate medical sociology would require a sociology of the body, since it is only by developing a notion of social embodiment that we can begin adequately to criticize the conventional divisions between mind and body, individual and society. A sociology of the body thus becomes an important theoretical basis for a medical sociology (Turner, 1984). Only by addressing the profound philosophical questions of sociology can we hope to develop a satisfactory medical sociology which will be geared into the central issues of sociology rather than of medical practice.

Issues in sociological theory

The central issues of sociological theory may be stated briefly. Firstly, sociology is concerned to understand the meaning of social action, that is the subjective perspective, emotions and feelings of human agents as social individuals. Secondly, sociology is concerned with the relationship between agency and structure. Sociology attempts to explore the relationship between human action and the structural determination of social relations by certain constraining elements which in general we can describe as power relations. Thirdly, classical sociology has been centrally organized around the problem of social order, that is the question of social integration through the presence of consensus and constraint in human life. Quite simply, sociology is concerned with the ultimate question of 'How is society possible?' Finally, sociology is about the analysis of the social processes and circumstances which constantly disrupt and disorganize the fragile order of social relations and social exchange. We can summarize this problem as the question of social inequality, because it is through an analysis of the unequal distribution of power (in terms of class, status and power) that we can begin to understand the de-stabilization of social relations and social systems through organized conflict and individual resistance.

A theoretically informed medical sociology would be concerned to criticize the idea of illness as mere behaviour by drawing attention to the role of choice, meaning and agency in the experience of illness. However, sociology is also concerned to draw attention to the role of social and natural constraints in the distribution and experience of health and illness. This approach involves a philosophical analysis of the idea of disease as a medical interpretation of reality (King, 1982). This enquiry leads to a critical evaluation of the facticity of 'nature' through a sociology of knowledge perspective on the categories of disease and illness. This type of medical sociology is a critical analysis of the history of medical discourse as a legitimation of medical power and practice. It is concerned with the character of the social construction of disease entities in the power relations of society. This sociology of knowledge project has become an important aspect of the critical history of medicine and the medical profession (Armstrong, 1983). Within a wider historical framework, this aspect of medical sociology would also involve the construction and transformation of discourses of illness in relation to social structure as legitimizing world-views. In particular, it would involve an enquiry into the relationship between the metaphors of the body, of society and of disorder (Sontag, 1978).

Finally, a theoretically informed medical sociology would address itself to the broader issues of social order and inequality by considering the role of medical values and institutions in the regulation of disease and disorder. Such an enquiry is concerned with the structural differentiation of religion, law and medicine as institutional forms of social control for the management of deviance and disorder in social groups. On the one hand, this involves historical studies of the institutional arrangements between various cultural patterns of sin, sickness and salvation. Within this framework medical sociology includes for example the study of the historical role of confession in religious and medical systems (Asad, 1983; Hepworth and Turner, 1982). The sociology of social order also involves an enquiry into the inequalities of power and wealth in human societies, since we may regard health as a resource which results in a hierarchical distribution of illness within a community. The analysis of inequality in health is especially concerned with the sexual division of labour in society, the problem of social classes and finally the relationship between aging and health.

In order to develop a general theory of health and illness in society, we will be concerned therefore with three levels of analysis. First, medical sociology can provide descriptions of the experience of illness from the perspective of the individual. In this study, it is argued that in terms of experience we can analyse disease as a form of alienation in which the body is experienced as an object or thing (Sacks, 1986). A variety of sociological perspectives – phenomenology (the analysis of everyday life to establish its underlying assumptions) and symbolic interactionism (the study of social life as a system of communication of symbols) – lend themselves to this task. At the second level, medical sociology would focus on the social construction of disease categories ('illness', 'sin' and 'deviance') whereby individuals are classified and regulated by professional groups. At this level we attempt to explore the emergence of institutions with a special responsibility for the sick and the deviant (asylums, hospitals and clinics). The concept of the sick role is crucial to this form of enquiry. The third level of analysis concerns the societal organization of health-care systems, their relationship to the state and the economy, and the problems of social inequality both within and between societies. The issues of macro-social analysis have been typically addressed by political economy and Marxist sociology (McKinlay, 1984). We can summarize these levels of analysis in Figure 1.

In order to understand the illness experiences of the individual, we require a general analysis of the social system in terms of inequalities of power. However, we also require a cultural study of disease categories which are variable over time and space. The linkage between the macro-analysis of social systems and the phenomenology of individual sickness is provided by the concept of the social role, and in particular by the idea of the sick role.

FIGURE 1
Sociology of health and illness

Level	Topic	Perspective
Individual	Illness experience	Phenomenology
Social	Cultural categories of sickness	Sociology of roles, norms and deviance
Societal	Health-care systems and politics of health	Political economy of illness

The history of medical sociology
The history of a discipline is frequently an important guide to its character and problems. This section provides an outline of the historical development of medical sociology in order to present an argument about the relationship between medicine and sociology. In an important sense medicine is (or ought to be) a form of applied sociology, since to understand the illness of a patient it is important (indeed necessary) to locate the patient in a social and personal environment. One major problem with technological medicine is the fact that it divorces the patient from this social context. It also follows however that, if medicine is applied sociology, then medical knowledge and medical history are of great interest and importance for the theoretical development of sociology itself. Medical problems force sociological theory to confront constantly the problem of the relationship between human biology, physiology and socio-cultural phenomena.

In reflecting on these issues, I want to criticize the conventional history of medical sociology in which the sub-discipline is regarded as a late comer to the sociological curriculum. By contrast, my argument considers Foucault's comment that sociology had its origins in nineteenth-century medical practices (in particular medical surveys), that sociology and medicine are inextricably linked together, and finally that modern medicine is in fact applied sociology, and sociology is applied medicine. Behind this historical sketch therefore there is the assumption that the contemporary importance of medical sociology is that it raises in an acute form the whole question of social ontology by asking what looks like a philosophical question: what is disease? Ontology is that branch of philosophy which is concerned with what can exist; the social ontology of disease considers the social constitutions of diseases. The issue of social ontology in its current form appears to be focused on a neglected issue in sociology, namely: what is the body? The history of medical sociology therefore is an outline of certain conceptual developments with respect to three issues, that is nature, society and embodiment.

In the conventional history of medical sociology, it is normally asserted that the institutionalization and development of medical sociology was relatively late in the modern evolution of sociology as an academic university subject (Badgley and Bloom, 1973; Gold, 1977). While early overviews of sociology as a discipline rarely contained any reference to medical sociology (Gurvitch and Moore, 1945), by the 1960s medical sociology had become a well established and formally recognized component of the sociology curriculum and appeared to be in some demand from medical faculties as a component of the medical curriculum.

One explanation for this alleged late development of medical sociology might be the absence of a classical statement from the founding fathers of sociology on the issue of health, illness and disease. If we compare the sociology of religion and medical sociology, it is self-evident that, while Marx, Weber, Durkheim and Simmel made major contributions to religion because the question of religious values was central to an understanding of rationality, the founding fathers of sociology apparently made little or no contribution to the development of a sociological perspective on medicine and health. Because no classical sociologist was overtly interested in health and illness, no real theoretical groundwork for medical sociology was established with the foundation of the discipline as a whole. The principal exception to this argument may be Durkheim's study of suicide in 1897. It is certainly the case that Durkheim's view of the importance of social regulation and integration in relation to suicide rates in European societies created the theoretical basis for subsequent studies of suicide behaviour and these studies came to provide a framework for the modern sociological analysis of depression (Brown and Harris, 1978). However, the main issue in Durkheim's sociology was not suicide behaviour as such, but the argument that sociology was an autonomous and independent subject which did not depend upon psychological explanations or assumptions about individual behaviour. Durkheim selected suicide as a topic partly to demonstrate that sociology could provide an explanation of the variation in suicide rates without recourse to psychological or philosophical assumptions.

We might also argue that classical sociology did not engage with the issues of medicine and health partly because sociology grew up in opposition to the widespread predominance of biologism and Social Darwinism in social thought in the nineteenth century. For example, Weber's emphasis on interpretative sociology can be seen as a neo-Kantian response to the relationship between nature and culture, which gave a special emphasis to the importance of cultural interpretation of meaningful behaviour. In Weber's sociology, any notion of the social actor as a biological system was removed by this emphasis on meaning and interpretation. It is also the case that Marx and Engels rejected Darwinism on the grounds that the concept of the 'survival of the fittest' was simply an ideological distortion of social relations giving expression to the competitive quality of capitalist society.

The standard history of medical sociology takes note of the fact that in the twentieth century the main theoretical contribution to the emergence of a specific sub-field came from Parsons (1951) through an analysis of the role of motivation in illness and the sick role. Through his interest in Freud, Parsons had become interested in the question of detachment and involvement in the doctor–patient relationship and this issue had been the focus of the concept of the sick role in his analysis of the social system. In addition, Parsons had made a number of significant contributions to the debate about the professions and the role of professional values in capitalism; these early analyses of professionalism contributed in an important way to the development of an interest in the medical profession as a crucial element in the modern system of occupational hierarchies (Parsons, 1939). It would however be misleading to call Parsons a medical sociologist, since his analysis of sickness and the medical profession was simply one component within a broader enquiry into social deviance, general values and professional ethics.

There is some agreement that, regardless of the contribution of Parsons, medical sociology did not achieve any significant development until the 1960s. The conventional account of the history of medical sociology normally concludes by noting that there are many indications that, having had a late start and having been dominated by a managerial bias, medical sociology is at last beginning to emerge as an area of study which is recognized as valid in sociology, and also increasingly acceptable within the medical profession. It is felt that sociology can make an important contribution to the medical understanding of the social causes of disease, can provide an insight into the patient's experience of illness, can improve the skills of interviewing of general practitioners, and finally that it can provide a new perspective on the character of bureaucracy in medical health-care systems.

Changes in the nature of disease
This view of the growing alliance of medicine and sociology is also the product of the changing nature of disease and illness in contemporary industrial societies. For example, in the nineteenth century doctors in the USA were mainly confronted with a range of diseases and illnesses which were acute, life threatening and often contagious. The leading causes of death in 1900 in the USA were influenza, pneumonia, tuberculosis and gastroenteritis, whereas in the 1980s the principal causes of death are diseases of the heart, malignant neoplasms (cancers), vascular lesions of the central nervous system and accidents. Other causes of disease in the twentieth century are related to the aging of the population and changes in lifestyle. For example, while in the nineteenth century diabetes did not appear in the list of leading causes of death, diabetes mellitus has become increasingly important in societies characterized by their affluence and their aging populations. In the second half of the twentieth century therefore doctors in western industrial societies will be mainly confronted with long-term chronic disorders which prevent the patient from functioning socially. To some extent stress has replaced the germ as the major explanation of modern illness; the concept of cure will be increasingly replaced by concepts of rehabilitation and care. The result is that the general practitioner will come to depend more and more on sociological skills as their education in the physiological, chemical and biological aspects of disease and illness becomes increasingly less relevant in the treatment and management of patients. The age of heroic medicine has been replaced by the mundane medical management of chronic as opposed to acute illness. The problem of long-term illness and its management will be addressed more effectively by sociological perspectives than by purely bio-medical perspectives.

The changing character of disease and illness has given rise in sociology and in clinical medicine to a new conception of holistic medicine. It is suggested that sociology is concerned with the whole person in the context of their social environment and therefore sociology can make a direct and important contribution to the medical perception and understanding of illness in modern society. Mangen (1982:2) has suggested that 'the sociological perspective encourages us to consider not only the patient but the staff member too as "whole persons"'. The sociological perspective encourages medical professionals to approach the person and not the patient as the focus of an enquiry into illness.

There appears to be some evidence of a convergence between the holistic critique of allopathic medicine, the sociological critique of the medical model and the neo-Marxist emphasis on social–environmental factors in capitalism as the cause of modern illness via stress, poor housing and poverty. The medical model in the medical explanation of disease has a number of important features. Disease is regarded as the consequence of certain malfunctions of the human body conceptualized as a biochemical machine. Secondly, the medical model assumes that all human dysfunctions might eventually be traced to such specific causal mechanisms within the organism; eventually various forms of mental illness would be explicable directly in terms of biochemical changes. The medical model is reductionist in the sense that all disease and illness behaviours would be reduced causally to a number of specific bio-chemical mechanisms. Furthermore, the medical model is exclusionary in that alternative perspectives would be removed as invalid. Finally, the medical model presupposes a clear mind/body distinction where ultimately the causal agent of illness would be located in the human body (Engel, 1981).

The sociological model of illness takes a critical and opposed position on the biochemical model of disease. It treats the concepts of medical science as products of cultural changes, by denying the mind/body distinction through the development of a concept of embodiment, by arguing against reductionism and exclusionary frameworks in suggesting that disease, like crime, cannot have a single causal framework, and finally by asserting that the sickness of the patient cannot be understood outside the historical, social and cultural context of the person. It has been suggested that a progressive and humanistic medical practice will concern itself with the total person and will inevitably become a sociological medical practice. The implication of this view of medical sociology is that sociology is at last equipped to enter the clinic where the sociologist will begin to take his place alongside the physician, the psychiatrist and other professional health agents.

Foucault and medical sociology
In this introduction to medical sociology, I shall be particularly concerned with the work of the French philosopher Foucault because he raised the issues which I see as central to medical sociology. Foucault was concerned to examine the relationship

between certain medical discourses and the exercise of power in society, that is the development of alliances between discourse, practice and professional groups. This Foucaultian enquiry into knowledge/power was organized around an enquiry into the body (of individuals) and bodies (of populations). Foucault saw the medical struggle around the body historically as the origins of a bio-politics of populations in modern society. These professional and medical discourses evolved in relation to the growth of the surveillance of societies through the exercise of discipline over the body and populations. In particular, Foucault (1971, 1973, 1977) was concerned to trace the development of a form of surveillance which he called 'panopticism' through the clinic, the asylum and the prison. A number of interpretations are now available of Foucault's work; they provide a general overview of his work and locate his contribution within modern social theory (Cousins and Hussain, 1984; Dreyfus and Rabinow, 1982; Lemert and Gillan, 1982; Smart, 1985). Foucault's interest in the relationship between the discourse of scientific knowledge and the exercise of professional power, the development of a political struggle around the body, the history of sexuality in relation to medical institutions, and finally the development of various forms of discipline and surveillance under the general notion of panopticism provide a powerful framework for the development of a theoretical medical sociology addressed to the central issues of meaning, structure, social order and power.

In providing a brief outline of Foucault's work, I shall consider his approach under four headings: epistemology, power, history and the sociology of the body. Epistemology as a branch of philosophy is the theory of knowledge; it is concerned with what can be known. The scientific revolution of the seventeenth century was associated with the empiricist epistemology of philosophers like René Descartes in France and Francis Bacon in England. Empiricism suggests that what we can see (or more generally, the evidence of the senses) is real and that science can only advance by empirical investigation and experiment. Empiricist scientists were, therefore, particularly concerned to improve our ways of seeing through, for example, improvements in optics. By contrast, twentieth-century philosophers who have been influenced by writers like Friedrich Nietzsche tend to argue that we cannot, as it were, trust the seeing–knowing subject whose gaze extracts evidence from the world (Jay, 1986). For Foucault we know or see what our language permits, because we can never naively apprehend or know 'reality' outside of language. Like all forms of human knowledge, scientific discourse is simply a collection of metaphors. Scientific knowledge of the world is a form of narrative (a story) and like all narratives science depends on various conventions of language (a style of writing, for instance). Narrative is a set of events within a language and language is a self-referential system. Nothing occurs outside the language. Therefore, what we know about 'the world' is simply the outcome of the arbitrary conventions we adopt to describe the world. Different societies and different historical periods have different conventions and therefore different realities.

This epistemology associated with the works of Foucault has radical implications for medical sociology. We can no longer regard 'diseases' as natural events in the world which occur outside the language with which they are described. A disease entity is the product of medical discourses which in turn reflect the dominant mode of thinking (the episteme in Foucault's terminology) within a society. For example, homosexuality was regarded as a sin under Christian therapy, as a behavioural disorder by early psychology and as merely a sexual preference by contemporary medicine. Similarly, madness was treaded as naughtiness before the emergence of Tuke's moral remedy, as Foucault was concerned to illustrate in *Madness and Civilization* (1971). Is anorexia nervosa a form of behavioural disorder of the hormonal system in young women, or a spiritual quest for perfection? Alternatively, is anorexia a product of modern consumerism employing patriarchal attitudes to promote a particular body image? What things are depends on how they are defined; how things are defined depends on how the general culture allocates phenomena within the spaces of convention. If we adopt this theory of knowledge, then disease is not a pathological entity in nature, but the outcome of socio-historical processes. This epistemological argument was presented by Foucault in *The Order of Things* (1974).

Foucault was not in his epistemology adopting an idealist position, which would suggest that either ideas are the only existing phenomena, or that material events are caused by ideas. On the contrary, he wanted to observe a very close relationship between power and knowledge. For example, access to a 'scientific' body of knowledge gave doctors towards the end of the nineteenth century enormous social prestige and influence. The clinical gaze (as Foucault called medical power in *The Birth of the Clinic*) enabled medical men to assume considerable social power in defining reality and hence in identifying deviance and social disorder. In Foucault's history of western rationality the medical men and the police replaced the priests as the guardians of social reality. Indeed, Foucault thought that the interpenetration of knowledge and power was so profound that he typically used the expression 'knowledge/power' to express this unity. He suggested that

We should admit rather that power produces knowledge... that power and knowledge directly imply one another; that there is no power relation without the correlative constitution of a field of knowledge, nor any knowledge that does not presuppose and constitute at the same time power relations. These 'power–knowledge relations' are to be analysed, therefore, not on the basis of a subject of knowledge who is or is not free in relation to the power system, but on the contrary, the subject who knows, the objects to be known and the modalities of knowledge must be regarded as so many effects of these fundamental implications of power–knowledge and their historical transformations. (Foucault, 1977:27–28)

Foucault was fascinated by the paradox that in modern societies and contemporary history human beings ('Man') are simultaneously the subjects of history (as active agents) and objects of history (as topics of discourse). In particular, what we understand by 'Man' is the effect of knowledge–power relations in which medicine and social science have played an important part as agents of control. The modern penitentiary, hospital, prison and school are elements within an expanding apparatus of control, discipline and regulations (a panoptic system of surveillance) which have secured order not through overt violence but through a micro-politics of discipline whereby people have been morally regulated into conformity. This system of control has been, at least in part, made possible by 'advances' in scientific medicine and by the emergence of new forms of knowledge: criminology, penology, sociology, psychology and so forth. The architecture of discipline is not simply a question of designing new buildings, but of redesigning human beings through the aid of social science. For Foucault, sociology is merely a branch of social medicine.

These views on knowledge and power were associated in Foucault's work with a distinctive approach to history and the writing of history. In general, he was critical of what we might call 'official histories'. Professional bodies, rather like whole societies, legitimize their social power by developing historical accounts of their emergence which emphasize their altruistic contribution to mankind and their opposition to cruelty and violence. In part, Foucault has been concerned to demystify these official histories, by showing that history is always discontinuous history. This critique of the use of history was particularly important in his study of madness. Firstly, he noted that we tend to write about madness from the standpoint of sanity (implying thereby the question of whether we can ever know madness without already giving a privileged status to reason). Secondly, he rejected the assumption that madness was a unitary phenomenon with a continuous history. Finally, he observed that while we no longer chain up our 'lunatics' and pour water over them, we have devised new, subtle and indirect systems of detailed and precise regulation.

While Foucault characteristically emphasized breaks, ruptures and fissures in history against the false unities of the history of science and the professions, it is possible to detect in his work a study of rationalization which is parallel to the rationalization theme in Max Weber's historical sociology. For Foucault, western society has been increasingly regulated (by the state, the police force, professional associations and social workers); it has been more and more dominated by the standards of reason (through the applications of science to everyday life). It has as a result become increasingly uniform and standardized, because we cannot or will not tolerate ideas and lifestyles which diverge too far from the 'normal' (as defined primarily by medicine). At least part of this standardization is brought about by the apparatus of the state and its local agencies. This principle of regulation, he called panopticism; the society it creates, he called the carceral. In short, medicine is part of an extensive system of moral regulation of populations through the medical regimen. Finally, therefore, we can see Foucault's philosophy and history as a contribution to a sociology of the body. Such a sociology is concerned to understand how human feeling and emotion are subordinated to normalization through medicine which establishes acceptable criteria of 'normal emotion'. It would analyse how sexuality becomes the target of medical technology, whereby the very reproduction of the species falls into the hands of medical men. For Foucault, life itself is now being occupied by medicine; the result is a new stage in the political history of society, namely 'the anatomo-politics of the human body' and 'a bio-politics of the population' (as he described this process in *The History of Sexuality*). Modern disciplines, systems of surveillance and control, and contemporary forms of knowledge about man are focused on the body and its reproduction. It is for this reason that sociologists have become especially interested in medicine and the medicalization of social relations as an aspect of moral regulation; it is also for this reason that we should take the work of Foucault seriously.

There are, however, a number of problems with Foucault's theory. Firstly, given the power of discipline and surveillance, it is difficult to know how one would explain or locate opposition, resistance and criticism to medical (or any other form of) dominance. Secondly, because Foucault gave such a powerful emphasis to the effects of language, it is difficult to understand how deviance develops and is sustained. Thirdly, he failed to grasp the paradoxes and unintended consequences of action: do we wish to imply that every aspect of modern medicine is a contribution to surveillance?

Fourthly, Foucault's epistemology makes it difficult to provide grounds for alternatives. Many of these criticisms are now well known (Hoy, 1986). Despite the criticism, Foucault's studies of medical history and his general perspective provide a powerful framework within which to develop medical sociology.

Although in this study of medical sociology, the principal emphasis will be on the analysis of the body, the self and society from the perspective of Foucault, I do not wish to suggest that previous research or perspectives are wholly undermined by this new paradigm in medical sociology, nor to suggest that previous research can be conveniently ignored and abandoned. The point of this study is to present a general and coherent view of medical sociology which is broad, catholic and eclectic, but organized around a number of issues from the perspective of contemporary social theory. The point is to use theory creatively and constructively, rather than to generate narrow and exclusive positions which in a ritualistic fashion attempt to expurgate all previous analyses and conclusions.

There are in any case a number of reasons for believing that, given the complexity of health and illness in contemporary societies, various theories and methodologies will be necessary for medical sociology to develop an adequate perspective on medical phenomena. Illness, rather like crime, will not be explained satisfactorily in sociology by a narrow, unidimensional approach. Given the social character of chronic illness in advanced societies, a broad, multidisciplinary approach is necessary. We can illustrate this argument for eclecticism and theoretical breadth in medical sociology by examining a curious illness which has reached 'epidemic' proportions in Australia, namely repetitious strain injury (Stone, 1983), or RSI.

In the 1980s RSI or tenosynovitis has become a prominent problem, especially among office workers using modern office technology. RSI, which is primarily pain in the upper extremities associated with repetitious work practices under modern office conditions, has been referred to as the new industrial epidemic of Australia (Ferguson, 1984), resulting in widespread compensation claims, transformation of work practices, and extensive media coverage. The 'disease' has also been the topic of much medical controversy, since its apparent specificity to Australia led some doctors to regard it as a myth which excused malingering at work. Some diagnosticians believe the disease does have an organic base; others hold that it is a form of occupational neurosis. RSI has also become a topic of considerable interest to trade unionists, insurance companies, industrialists and various government committees.

While there is no consensus in medical circles concerning the nature and treatment of RSI, it is felt by some observers that a variety of factors contribute to its prevalence. First, there may be certain psychological factors which predispose some workers to suffer from this muscular problem, since it is clearly the case that not all workers exposed to the same set of circumstances claim to experience pains in the upper part of the arm. These factors of vulnerability may be related to anger and stress. Secondly, there are probably work conditions and practices which contribute injuries related to over-use. These conditions may also include the nature of modern office equipment and office architecture. RSI is also related to a political struggle between management, unions and insurance companies to have the 'disease' recognized, or alternatively to have it rejected as a myth or excuse. Finally, we would need to consider why RSI appeared in Australia at the particular time it did, why it achieved epidemic proportions in the early 1980s, and why it was contained within certain states and work areas. The point of this argument is to recognize that, in one sense, RSI is a social process by which a 'disease' entity was recognized by certain experts (Willis, 1986). It is possible to find parallels to RSI in previous periods where recognition of a disease was the outcome of socio-political processes (Figlio, 1982).

RSI is a typically 'modern' disease; it is chronic and it is difficult to diagnose and to treat, partly because it has a complex and uncertain aetiology. In addition, the disease is the focus of a certain amount of professional and political controversy: does it exist? There are certain moral overtones to the disease: is it an excuse for malingering? In this respect, RSI as a medical category would share certain features with AIDS (acquired immune deficiency syndrome), anorexia nervosa, the hyperactive child syndrome and Munchausen's syndrome. These 'diseases' are often highly contested (morally and politically); they are not easy to treat; indeed, for some modern conditions such as anorexia, the sufferer often regards treatment and cure as a personal defeat. Certainly the treatment regimens for these diseases require various approaches (psychological, sociological and medical). The response to RSI involved a reconsideration of office ergonomics, work practices and worker motivation, including a specific medical response to the pain itself.

The point of this illustration is to suggest that sociological eclecticism is not only desirable but necessary. A sociology of RSI (as well as anorexia, Alzheimer's disease, diabetes and many other chronic conditions) would require: (1) a phenomenology of pain with a specific inquiry into the sufferer's interpretations and perceptions of the disorder; (2) an analysis of the social processes by which the 'disease' is constituted as a topic by conflicting professional groups with their own vested interests in the existence or disappearance of the problem; and (3) a political economy of the conditions of white-collar employment in modern capitalism which, through pressure on the worker, create work processes which produce occupational injuries. In order to achieve these different levels of analysis (the individual, the social and the societal) we require a high degree of theoretical continuity between different explanatory paradigms in contemporary sociology.

This argument for both continuity and eclecticism is also associated in this study with the argument that an intellectually satisfying medical sociology will also have to be comparative and historical in its approach. It is only through a perspective which gives prominence to historical sociology that we can get a grip on the profound contextualisation of illness categories as products of social conditions and processes. In turn, this commitment to comparative and historical sociology brings us to appreciate the fruitful overlap between the history of ideas, the sociology of knowledge and the philosophy of medicine. In part, this recognition is a further justification for taking seriously the contribution of Foucault to medical sociology.

It is important to note that Foucault's own work forces us to reflect creatively on the history of the social sciences, especially the history of social medicine and sociology. For example, in an interview Foucault (1980:151) reflected on the history of sociology by arguing:

> countless people have sought the origins of sociology in Montesquieu and Comte. That is a very ignorant enterprise. Sociological knowledge (*savoir*) is formed rather in practices like those of the doctors. For instance, at the start of the nineteenth century Guepin wrote a marvellous study of the city of Nantes.

Foucault's argument was that the human and social sciences had in part emerged as a response to the pressure of population in the industrial cities of the nineteenth century, where the new forms of knowledge were important for the surveillance and control of urban populations. Social medicine has to be seen as an aspect of this general response to the crisis of population as a problem of political control and social surveillance. According to Foucault, both sociology and social medicine were formed in response to these issues. The implication of this viewpoint is that medical sociology is not a late starter or marginal to sociology as a whole, but its very foundation was to be seen in the practices of clinical investigation and the social survey of disease as a form of deviance. Sociology and medicine in this framework have not combined in a recent marriage; rather medicine can be regarded as a form of clinical sociology and the origins of sociology lie in post-Revolutionary French medicine rather than in the social science of Comte and Durkheim.

Once we recognize the intimate linkage between social medicine and sociology in the first half of the nineteenth century, then the neo-Marxist and political-economy approaches no longer appear so radical or innovative (Stern, 1959). Engels and Marx clearly recognized the connection between poverty, disease and social deviance in the nineteenth-century working class. This concern for the social causes of disease and social anomie was also shared later by British social scientists such as Booth and Rowntree. As Rosen (1979:23) has observed:

> Social scientists tend to emphasize the newness of medical sociology, but viewed as the study of the relationship between health phenomena and social factors and context, medical sociology has deep historical roots.

The real division therefore is not between sociology and medicine, but between those paradigms which see illness and disease as social facts in the Durkheimian sense, and those who regard illness and disease as conditions of the individual, especially the isolated organism invaded by germs and disorder. The main thrust of this study is that the concept of the isolated, separate human organism is itself a cultural product, since the body cannot be regarded simply and exclusively as an entity inside nature. The importance of Foucault's perspective is precisely to see the body of individuals and the body of populations as products of power and knowledge.

2
Religion and medicine: from sin to sickness

Introduction
In the opening sections of this study, it has been argued that medical sociology needs to incorporate a sociology of knowledge approach to medical categories, since what it is to be sick will depend upon the available cultural categories by which behaviour can be described and understood. Just as the sociology of religion has to ask what is religion, so medical sociology has to concern itself with the historical and comparative constitution of health and disease as social phenomena. It is well known for example that western categories of health and therapeutics are in important ways vastly different from those which have operated historically in China (Unschuld, 1985). This question is not simply an academic issue, because much of the claims of professional expertise in medicine rest on 'knowledge' of disease where this knowledge is socially produced rather than objective, and has significant effects in terms of the distribution of power and authority. Sociology cannot be content with medical definitions of illness, health and disease any more than sociology can be content with legal categorization of social deviance. There is throughout sociology a profound problem of relativism which cannot be ignored in the area of medical enquiry. It is simply the case that different types of society have different types of disease and different approaches to therapy; these variations are the products of culture and social organization.

This perspective from the sociology of knowledge leads us into the history of medical classifications. To say that diseases have histories is a socially liberating claim in that it challenges the authority of the medical model, but it is also highly problematic. Are diseases merely the products of different types of classificatory procedure? Or are diseases the effects of our biological and physiological constitution? In this study I argue that diseases are indeed socially constructed products of cultural and social arrangements, since I wish to treat the body itself as the product of cultural practices. The body is not simply a physical entity; it is ambiguous and problematic in human cultures and especially in the context of the Judeo-Christian tradition.

To understand the nature of modern conceptions of disease, we need to look at the historical emergence of medical categories as separate and distinctive forms of discourse. In this chapter I will trace the emergence of various aspects of medicine through a study of diet and anatomy as a discourse about the body. Furthermore, it is argued that medicine has its historical roots in the institutional apparatus of social control, and that medicine is an important part of what Foucault had in mind by the notion of micro-politics, that is forms of political practice which are decentralized and operate locally through various institutional settings such as the anatomical theatre and the medical clinic.

Mastery of the flesh
Following Weber, we can regard the history of western culture as a set of variations on the relationship between mind and body, spirit and flesh, culture and nature. Weber regarded the development of asceticism, rationalization and world mastery as in part the consequences of a tension or contradiction in Christian theology between the life of the spirit and the existence of the world. In this division the world embraced a range of issues (pleasures, enjoyments and the luxury of the body); the major component of this concept of the world can be seen in terms of the problematic of embodiment. That is, the problem of the world implies a sociology of the body, an issue which has remained implicit and under-developed in sociology as a whole (Turner, 1984). The peculiar features of human embodiment may be best signified by the use of the term 'flesh'.

Western culture, and to some extent human culture as a whole, has managed the unusual features of the flesh through three crucial institutional arrangements, namely religion, law and medicine. Human societies can be conceptualized in terms of these institutional arrangements for the management of human embodiment; law, religion and medicine regulate and control human embodiment. Religion, through a variety of ritual practices, regulated and constrained the human body with the aim of developing our spiritual existence. The law has been concerned especially through criminal law with the management of crime and in particular with the urban surveillance of populations. Finally, medicine can be seen as a powerful form of regulation, restraint and representation of the body as flesh. In the terminology of Foucault, we can suggest that law, religion and medicine were three discursive formations for the rational and disciplined management of the body and populations. This model for the analysis of the body as flesh follows from Weber's (1966) discussion of the various contradictions between the Christian ethic of asceticism and secular life, especially as the world was represented in sexuality, art and knowledge.

The critical core of this ethic was the doctrine of the seven deadly sins which had their ultimate root in the fleshliness of human existence. Protestantism sought not only to reject the world but to master it through the imposition of discipline, regulation and the creation of a systematic lifestyle. These disciplines attempted to subordinate the passions by the cultivation of conscience and the regularization of everyday existence. Protestantism also took over the religio-medical management of the body which was handed down from medieval monastic practice. There appears to be as a result an important convergence between Weber's analysis of the origins of asceticism in military discipline and monastic activity, and Foucault's cultural study of the origins of disciplinary practices in the modern historical period. Following both, we can argue that ascetic disciplines formed part of a this-worldly mastery involving forms of personal surveillance and social regulation. This collection of disciplines, practices, institutions and knowledge can be more broadly described as the ethic of world mastery. This ethic was crucial to the development of scientific medicine.

This chapter is concerned to study the historical development of these disciplines of the flesh, primarily through the study of medical knowledge and practice. The connection between religion and medicine is an ancient one and we may draw a connection between these two domains by considering the verbs to *save* the soul and to *salve* the body. The ultimate notion of salvation was 'salus' or health. While religion and medicine were connected, there were also certain tensions between medicine and religion. The Church regarded the payment of a fee as problematic, since the Christian tradition regarded medical intervention as a form of charity. These complicated relations between religion and medicine can be studied through a number of empirical illustrations in western history.

The Greek legacy: melancholy and diet
Europe inherited a traditional Greek medical system which was essentially secular in the sense that illness was seen to be the effect of natural causes. Onto this Greek base, Christianity moralized medicine because illness was, within a Christian framework, often seen to be either a punishment by God or a form of instruction to the soul. There was considerable conflict between the secular assumptions of Greek medicine and the spiritual aims of Christian religious practice. We may note in any case that many of our everyday descriptions of disease and illness carry these moral implications. For example, the notions of malady and malignancy are derived from the Latin 'malus' (evil).

The Church argued that healing the sick was an act of Christian mercy for which no monetary reward should be expected. We can claim that professional ethics in medical history were in part an apologetic response to this religious critique. Law, medicine and religion are three institutional responses to the problems of human deviance, but these three areas have become increasingly structurally separate. However, medicine still embodies a moral discourse. In order to illustrate some of these points, we may turn initially to the question of melancholy and obesity.

In order to grasp the force of these two illustrations, we need to keep in mind that, prior to the dominance of the germ theory with the growing authority of Lister in the 1880s, traditional European medicine was dominated by practices which went back to the Greek medical tradition. For example, blood letting had been a technique which was common in Greek medical practice. It was still in use in Europe in the middle of the nineteenth century, although the theoretical justification for it had changed considerably (King, 1982). Furthermore, the humoral theory of disease was a basic framework of western medicine deriving from Hippocrates, Empedocles and Galen. These humoral theories conceived the world in terms of four basic elements (fire, earth, air and water), four qualities (heat, cold, dry and dampness), four humors (blood, phlegm, yellow bile and black bile), and four personality types (sanguine, phlegmatic, choleric and melancholic). For instance, melancholia was analysed as an excess of black bile, but melancholy was also derived from the seven deadly sins as established by Gregory the Great (540–604). The Gregorian list included vainglory, anger, envy, dejection ('acedia' or 'tristitia'), covetousness, gluttony and fornication.

In traditional medicine the body was conceptualized as an organic system which tends towards equilibrium. Illness was thus the effect of too much or too little humoral activity and therapy consisted in attempts to restore a balance. These practices were limited to diet, exercise, bleeding and rest. In order to understand melancholy as simultaneously a moral condition and a physical deviation from organic equilibrium, we need to keep in mind this Greek legacy in which the body is a hydraulic system.

Melancholy was initially a condition of monks and was variously described as 'tristitia' (dejection and sorrow), 'desperatio' (despair), 'acedia' (apathy and sloth) (Jackson, 1981). Cassian associated acedia with sin, namely the spiritual dejection of monks. Acedia was a spiritual failing which could be treated religiously through the use of the confessional. In the twelfth century, the new penitential handbooks in the Church increasingly associated acedia with sloth, in particular with the neglect of certain religious duties and the antidote was sought in prayer and activity. Through the medieval period two models emerged whereby sorrow was associated with internal spiritual conditions of dejection and despair. Secondly, there was a behavioural state of affairs associated with neglect, idleness and indolence. Traditional Catholic teaching on acedia was eventually replaced by Protestant secular medical views. Given the Protestant emphasis on activism and achievement, idleness was regarded as especially dangerous in leading to moral decay. In medical circles, tristitia and acedia disappeared as concepts, but they were replaced by a new emphasis on melancholia as a disease.

The melancholic condition was important in the development of Shakespeare's conceptualization of Hamlet as a melancholic character and featured in a prominent fashion in Burton's *Anatomy of Melancholie*. Idleness was a problem of great significance in aristocratic women, especially those who were not married, and Burton recommended prayer and pregnancy as the most efficacious treatment of despair. By the eighteenth century, melancholy had become a complaint particularly associated with the English, and hence this form of madness was often called 'the English Malady' and was viewed as the cause of the unusually high suicide rate amongst the English (Skultans, 1979). Melancholy had ceased to be the peculiar problem of the spiritual dryness of monks, being transformed gradually into a secular category for the description of the propensity of the English upper classes to commit suicide. The old medieval framework of sorrow had been replaced by an increasingly secular view of the causes of depression. It is interesting that by the eighteenth century one cause of depression was obesity and medical practice began to embrace dietetics as the basis for the medical treatment of the sorrows of the upper classes.

We should note that diet had always been a major part of both religious and medical practice. In Greek medical regimes diet was associated with 'diaita', that is with a mode of living in which the regulation of food was simply a part of a broader regimen, that is a set of rules or government of the body. To ration was to reckon and to limit the body by the application of power in the form of dietetic knowledge. Traditionally, monastic diets were aimed at regulating human passion by controlling the digestion through the restrained use of red meat and wine in order to avoid inflaming the sexual appetite.

Although medical instruction on appropriate diet has had a long history in western medicine, treatises on dietary management, particularly when combined with a religious perspective, became particularly important in the seventeenth and eighteenth centuries in western Europe. One doctor in this area who exercised considerable influence was George Cheyne (1671–1743) whose practice embraced the aristocratic and professional classes of London and Bath. Cheyne is well known for his *The English Malady* of 1733, which recommended diet as the principal method for the management of melancholy, and included amongst his clientele David Hume, Samuel Richardson, Samuel Johnson, Alexander Pope and John Wesley. Cheyne's writing on the general benefit of an appropriate diet for mental stability and longevity was the outcome of a personal crisis which had been brought about by chronic obesity at the beginning of his medical profession and career. Arriving in London at the peak of the popularity of coffee houses and taverns as meeting places for professional people in the reign of Queen Anne, Cheyne fell into the company of loose-living persons with the result that his own weight rose to 448lb. Having diagnosed himself as the sufferer of English melancholy, Cheyne, after a considerable period of experimentation, arrived at a diet of milk and vegetables combined with regular exercise, systematic patterns of sleep and self-imposed temperance. As a consequence he was blessed by a long life of personal tranquility and mental stability.

The theoretical foundation for Cheyne's own medical views was derived from Descartes's mechanistic framework for the analysis of the body, the rationalism of the medical school of Leyden and the iatromathematical tradition (that is, the application of mathematical principles to medicine) of Herman Boerhaave (1668–1738). Descartes's view that the body is nothing other than a machine of clay and Harvey's work on the circulation of the blood laid the foundation for Cheyne's argument that the body is 'an hydraulic machine filled with liquor'. The health of this system of pipes and pumps could only be maintained as the outcome of a regular supply of food and liquid determined by clinical experience and scientific medical knowledge. The employment of drugs and surgery was secondary to this dietary management in controlling disease and in promoting long life. These iatromathematical principles were combined with a religious outlook on the health of the body as the duty of Christians; gluttony was regarded as equivalent to suicide. Cheyne's dietetic management was part of a wider religio-moral tradition in which the management of the body was an aspect of a religious calling.

Cheyne's ideas on diet were influenced by Leonard Lessius (1554–1632) and by Luigi Cornaro (1475–1566). Cornaro (1558) had argued that the social disturbances of his time were linked with the disorders of the human body; in particular, he suggested that the social malaise of Italy was brought about by bad customs, namely flattery, Lutheranism and intemperance. The solution for these social and physical disorders was to be sought in the disciplined, regular and sober lifestyle. Cornaro recommended a limited use of meat, wine and rich food. For Cornaro, dieting would bring about a number of important social and medical changes; in particular mental stability was to be achieved through the regulation of passions and a moral order which was regulated and stable. Cornaro treated diet as part of a wider religious framework which would be a defence against the temptations of the flesh. It is clear from Cornaro's treatise that no clear conceptual separation was attempted between morality, religion and medicine; these formed part of a uniform and general system of social regulation. The disturbance of the body was simply a reflection of a wider instability in the social system. Therefore, the medical regimen could not be practised without a concern for this broader moral and social environment.

We can see Cheyne as part of a medical tradition which combined moral and medical views in a system of diet which was intended to bring about longevity. In addition, there is some evidence that Cheyne's views of dietary management became socially influential as a result of their impact on the Methodist movement of the eighteenth century. John Wesley adopted many of Cheyne's views which he published eventually in *Primitive Physick*. Wesley found Cheyne's views on the Christian importance of maintaining the body attractive and obviously compatible with his own version of asceticism. The medical views of Cornaro and Cheyne continued to be influential in the evangelical movement of the nineteenth century when we find Christian ministers recommending diet and exercise as a useful lifestyle for young ladies; there was thought to be a connection between physical health and Christian wellbeing (Turner, 1982).

The main issue behind these religious dietaries was an attempt to control the inner body as the arena of passion through medical restraint in order to bring about a discipline of desire in the interests of social stability. Modern systems of health care by contrast are more overtly concerned with the secular issues of longevity, health and sexuality. We diet in order to live longer in order to enjoy the benefits of good health and longevity, where our sexual expectations have increased significantly. It is no longer thought to be the case that sexual desire declines with age but rather that our bodies can be made youthful by the discipline of secular medicine and diet. Whereas the diets of writers like Cheyne attempted to control the inner body to promote a religious state of affairs, modern diets, cosmetics and other systems of body maintenance are aimed at the outer body: looking good is equivalent to feeling good in a society based upon the dominance of the representational self (Turner, 1985a).

A number of rather complex causes transformed diet in the late nineteenth century into a secular science for the rationalization of the body. For example, the insanitary condition of the poor districts of congested cities in the second half of the nineteenth century constituted a medical threat to the middle classes, especially with the spread of contagious diseases. An interest in the diet of the working class can be seen as part of a broader environmental movement whereby the middle class sought to protect itself from contagion. In addition, high levels of unemployment represented a tax burden on local authorities which were held responsible for maintaining work houses under poor law legislation. This situation provided an incentive for inspecting the health of the working class in the interests of the management of asylums and work houses. More importantly, conscription into the army revealed extensive illness and incapacity in the male population as a result of disease, sickness and unemployment. These military surveys of health raised questions about the capacity of the nation to defend itself in conditions of mass warfare. During the period 1850–1939, cholera epidemics increased public awareness about the importance of sanitation and ventilation. The Crimean, Boer, First and Second World Wars exposed the inadequacy of military administration of hospitals and medical supplies, and also reinforced the realization that the male population as a whole was too sick to provide the basis of a modern army. The result was a movement to promote discipline amongst the working class through training, temperance and military service. In this respect the rise of the Boy Scout Association can be seen as simply one facet of a general interest in the fitness of young men through proper diet and environmental reform. Here again we can see the force of Foucault's argument that medicine is social medicine and that sociology had its origins in a disciplinary movement to manage the social environment on the basis of new forms of knowledge.

The trend towards a scientific analysis of diet was the outcome of debates about urban poverty, efficiency and the management of prisons and asylums. Food consumption became the basis for a measurement of poverty in the work of Booth (*The Life and Labour of the People in London*) and Rowntree (*Poverty, A Study of Town Life*). Rowntree was particularly interested in the problem of obtaining accurate measurement of the energy requirements of the average working man in terms of calories. The scientific advance of dietetics therefore came to depend upon the development of the principles of thermodynamics. However, even in Rowntree's empirical social science, we can observe a Quaker concern for temperance and discipline which was developed alongside the metaphor of the body as a thermodynamic system. Furthermore, we should see these developments in social surveys of the poor and the management of prisons as part of a general concern in political life for an appropriate genetic policy for the control of populations. The theoretical developments of dietetics, biology, demography and eugenics were associated with a growing social and political concern about the impact of the working class on nineteenth-century democracy which was still based upon property ownership. Within the framework of Foucault's historical analysis of discipline, it is possible to see that the criminal, the working man and the soldier became the targets of scientific discourse and political institutions.

In twentieth-century popular and consumer culture, the thin body has become the symbol of youthfulness, activity and health. Thinness has become a norm of beauty in a society where the thin body is socially constructed by training, diet and discipline. Whereas the monastic practices of earlier centuries were concerned with the management of the inner body, consumerism points to a discipline of the surfaces of the body in which the self is enhanced and displayed by the absence of flesh. To be fat is to be out of control and to lack a consumer asceticism. However, within medical discourse, the body still has an ambiguous location despite the secularization of medical viewpoints. While obesity is stigmatized in popular culture (Cahnman, 1968) it is also the case that in the 1950s obesity was increasingly defined as a medical problem, being associated with heart disease. In the post war period of affluence, obesity, alcoholism and diabetes came to be regarded as the new diseases of civilisation (Callen and Sussman, 1984). While the current medical view is less dogmatic about the negative effects of obesity, especially in relation to stress and heart disease, there is still a widespread moral condemnation of obesity as indicative of an absence of personal control. There is also a large consumer market for dietary schemes and approximately twenty million Americans are seriously dieting at any given time and ten billion dollars are spent annually on slimming aids. For reasons which I shall consider in Chapter 5 we can argue that anorexia nervosa is characteristically a disease of the new discourse of bodily management and regulation, in many ways resembling the religious practices of medieval saints.

I have attempted to illustrate the idea that the body as flesh is problematic in western cultures by a consideration of the history of dietary management. It has been suggested that diet in a religious framework is the management of the interior body while in a secular medical practice, it becomes increasingly the organization of the exterior body in the interests of longevity and sexuality. The point of this illustration is to suggest that the categories of sin and sickness

have evolved into separate and specialized components as the outcome of a process of secularization, although it is also recognized
that medical discourse still contains a moral viewpoint on individual
and social organization. In medieval European culture, these distinctions did not exist and Christian sacramentalism retained the
notion that the cure of souls and bodies could be brought about
through the rituals of penance. It was traditional in Christian cultures to recognize a parallel between the work of the priest and that
of the physician. For example, in the early thirteenth century the
relationship between health and salvation was a common motif of
religious manuals. The connection between the sinner/confessor
and patient/physician was clearly recognized by theologians like
Grosseteste who identified a connection between moral vices and
physical sins. In popular medieval culture, shrines and pilgrimages
were a traditional feature of medical cure. Diseases were cured
through the religious relics which were contained in shrines along
the routes which were followed by pilgrims. While the role of the
secular physician was recognized, it was also assumed that certain
forms of illness were the special monopoly of priests. The miracles
of Jesus were employed as a theological guarantee for the ability of
priests to exorcise demons. It was Aquinas who clearly established
in *Summa Theologica* the care of the sick as a critical feature of
Christian charity.

Although there was a certain parallelism between religion and
medicine, there was also a long tradition of conflict and critique
whereby the Church sought to regulate the practice of medicine in
the interests of Christian charity. There were broadly three areas of
conflict. First, since healing was part of Christian charity, there was
a religious opposition to the practice of physicians charging a fee.
The solution to this problem was the development of a more
articulate professional set of ethical standards whereby medicine
came to be regarded as a calling equivalent to that of religion; the
economic aspects of the contract between physician and client were
played down in the interests of a stronger conception of the moral
responsibility of the physician to the patient. The second area of
conflict was that if illness is regarded as part of God's design for the
individual (bringing training and a sense of God's mercy) then the
intervention of the physician is incompatible with the notion of
God's purpose. That is, medicine is seen to interfere with a religious
plan. In any case, the Christian theologians often regarded human
maladies (especially madness) as charged with spiritual powers
(Screech, 1985). The solution to this problem was to develop a
theodicy of pain in combination with a professional ethical code for
the physician; by stressing the educative aspect of sickness, the

Church was able to accept the role of the physician as compatible with these Christian principles. The third area of conflict lay in the fact that medieval medical practice was derived largely from Greek science and Hippocratic medicine was essentially secular in its attitude towards illness. Classical Greek medicine had developed as a secular explanation of the natural causes bringing about health and illness. The secular physicians of Greek classical society looked to a rational medical model as the basis for distinguishing their practice from the popular remedies of leech craft and magic. There was a profound professional hostility to superstition and popular belief which the Hippocratic treatise on *The Sacred Disease* made plain by arguing that epilepsy was not brought about by divine or sacred causes. The legacy of Galen and Asclepius allowed little space for sacred causality especially in the doctrine of the four humors.

Clearly the relationship between religious and secular values and institutions and the history of medicine is complex and ambiguous. Although I have suggested that a general trend of secularization can be detected, this trend is by no means a simple evolutionary development. The general point is that while medicine and morality became separated at a formal level, medical practice continued to assume implicitly certain important moral and indeed religious assumptions. The ambiguity between religion and medicine is rather well illustrated by the development of anatomy.

The anatomy lesson
Since medieval times the human body has been seen metaphorically as the microcosm of the macrocosm, thereby linking our intimate life to the structure of the universe. Indeed, the body has been seen as the centre of a set of relations which provide the link between embodiment and the natural order. For example, in the humoral theory of disease we find a good illustration of how the human body was directly connected to the world of the stars. There are in addition important historical connections between the pseudo-sciences of physiognomy and somatomancy (Shortland, 1985).

Within a broader study, it would be possible to show the cultural linkage between the colonial exploration of the sixteenth and seventeenth centuries and anatomical discoveries. Through the work of Merton (1970), we have access to research and argument which would provide some plausibility for this broader project. At least one intriguing connection between colonialism and the exploration of bodies in anatomy is provided in the seventeenth century by the development of travelogues and advertisements for capitalist investment in distant and exotic lands. These pictorial advertisements of recently discovered lands were particularly concerned with the question of cannibalism as a practice separating civilized society from primitive societies. Bucher (1981) has attempted through a structural analysis to decode de Bry's *Great Voyages* (1590–1634) in order to explore the symbolic significance of monsters and cannibalism in the popular mythology of the seventeenth century. The opening up of continents was connected with the opening up of bodies in the savage practice of cannibalism. A rather parallel argument can be drawn from Foucault (1973) who has made great play with the slogan of Bichat in *Anatomie Generale* in 1801 where Bichat claimed that the discoveries of pathological anatomy had caused a revolution in clinical medicine simply on the basis of opening up a few corpses. The role of anatomy was to dissipate the darkness which had surrounded observation of the body. In a similar fashion, colonialism used the metaphor of opening up to light the dark continent of Africa as a consequence of western civilization. We can suggest therefore that colonialism represents a geographical anatomy of the exterior world analogous to the pathological anatomy which sought to expose the structure of the inner world of bodies.

In summary, the ethic of world mastery sought firstly the exploration and elevation of mind (consciousness) over the life of the senses which were rooted in bodily functions. This ethic sought therefore to subordinate feeling to reason, body to mind. The central challenge to this mastery of the sensual world by reason was madness itself. As Foucault (1971) has argued, the emergence of the modern world view was forced to exclude the possibility of madness in order for rational thought to remain permanently secure. Secondly, this ethic of world mastery sought the subordination of the body (flesh) through religious discipline with the aid of medicine. This regulation of the body by religion was gradually expanded to include a wide range of practices which again following Foucault we might simply call 'panopticism'. The central challenge to this system of disciplinary practices was the irrationality of sexuality. Thirdly, the ethic involved the exploration of space, that is the outside world as opposed to the inside world of mind and senses. This outside space was appropriated and regulated by the emerging culture of colonialism. The central challenge to this system was the insurrection and insubordination of local aboriginal populations who were seen as an irrational eruption against systematic regulation and control.

It is difficult to separate the history of anatomy from an understanding of the role of surgery and surgeons, especially within the medical tradition of Greek medicine. It is important to note that word 'surgeon' derives from the Greek word 'kheirourgia' meaning handiwork. The surgeon was literally someone who undertook manual work as opposed to the mental labour of the physician who was a sort of medical philosopher. The surgeons of classical Greek medicine were itinerant practitioners of minor external surgery whose trade was associated with market places. In later centuries, the surgeons were typically associated with the barbers, since it was the barbers who possessed sharp instruments and typically sought their custom amongst the military. Therefore, the barber–surgeons were manual medical labourers who followed in the wake of armies. It was war and military injury which stimulated the development of modern surgery.

The main legacy of Greek anatomy and medicine generally is associated with the name of Galen (129–199 AD). Galen's text *On the Conduct of Anatomies* became the definitive source for medical understanding of the structure and function of the human body until it was successfully challenged in the late sixteenth century by the growth of pathological anatomy. An important issue with respect to authority of Galen's text centres on the fact that Galen never conducted an anatomical dissection of a human corpse. Galen's dissections were carried out on the bodies of monkeys and there is also some evidence that he undertook dissections of marine animals. In short, the Galenic tradition and its authority was not based upon the anatomy of human beings.

The late development of anatomy and the general reluctance to conduct anatomical dissections on human bodies is an important issue in medical and cultural analysis. The respect for the human body was closely associated in the West with Christian and popular attitudes towards the status of the body. There does not appear to be a definitive Christian document or law precluding anatomy. However, the doctrine of the resurrection of the body meant that anatomical dissection would be a particularly grievous and punitive exercise on human beings since it was thought that anatomy would rule out resurrection. As a consequence anatomy was always associated with the punishment of criminal bodies following a civic execution. In fact the dissection was an essential part of the whole process of legal punishment and juridical execution (Foucault, 1977). One may also suggest that there was a general public dislike of anatomy, because it was associated with malpractice and with the snatching of bodies. There was always considerable doubt about the source of cadavers for anatomy.

While there were certain semi-official norms prohibiting anatomical dissection, anatomies were carried out in Europe from an early period. For example, anatomies were conducted by Mundinus in 1316 and by Vigarano in 1345, but these anatomies were not strictly focused on an enquiry into the corpse. Basically there were two forms of anatomy. First, there were private anatomical inspections of the dead within aristocratic groups where there was a suspicion of unnatural death brought about for example by poisonings. Secondly, there were irregular public anatomies of criminal corpses throughout medieval times, but these dissections were not guided by a significant medical interest in discovery and experimentation. The emergence of pathological anatomy is associated with the growth of a professional training in medicine which was increasingly regarded as a science. Furthermore, the development of a scientific approach to anatomy was connected with the professional separation of the surgeons from the barbers.

The most important location for the development of anatomy into a medical scientific practice was the northern universities of Italy in the middle of the sixteenth century. It was in 1543 that Andreas Vesalius Bruxellensis published his famous *De Humani Corporis Fabrica*. The importance of the *Fabrica* was that it was based upon real anatomical dissections of human corpses and secondly this text was illustrated. Vesalius's dissections of human bodies brought him eventually to challenge the whole Galenic legacy. There were however a number of important precursors of Vesalius. For example, it was Berengario da Carpi (Bologna) who critically examined every part of the body, making a number of anatomical discoveries. He worked independently of the Galenic tradition and published his results in *Commentaria Cum Additionibus Super Anatomian Mundini*. Berengario carried out over one hundred dissections and some apects of these enquiries were published in 1530 in his *Isagoge Breves*. Berengario's slogan was 'the experience of my eyes is my guiding star'. Despite this apparently empirical slogan, he was reluctant to challenge the Galenic tradition directly and he, like other surgeons and anatomists, tended to regard deviations from the Galenic anatomical atlas as monstrous or unnatural anatomical phenomena, thereby leaving the Galenic tradition intact. A variety of books related to problems of anatomy were published between 1500 and 1543 in Italy and France. For example in France, Estienne in his *De Dissectione Partium Corporis Humani Libri Tres* (1539) argued the importance of direct experience for medical science and the development of clinical practice.

The importance of Vesalius was his willingness to question the Galenic tradition, to publish his results and to illustrate his findings so that his ideas could be widely communicated. He had as a consequence a widespread influence on the development of medicine, particularly pathological anatomy in Northern Europe. One of his most famous disciples was Gabriele Fallopio who published *Observationes Anatomicae* in 1561 (Rath, 1961; Singer, 1925). Other professors of medicine who in this period developed anatomy included Columbus (1516–1559) and Fabricus (1537–1619). There were also significant developments in surgical techniques advanced by practising military surgeons such as Ambrose Paré (1510–1590), who worked at the Hotel Dieu in Paris from 1529 and followed the French army in the Wars of Religion. Paré devised various new methods for the treatment of wounds and generally raised the status of practical surgical technique.

It was the anatomy of the heart which laid the basis for an understanding of the circulation of the blood. Michael Servetus (1511–1553) was particularly influential in the development of the ideas of Harvey (1578–1657) in establishing the theory of the circulation of the blood in 1628 in *On the Motion of the Heart and the Blood*. As a young man Harvey had studied medicine under Fabricus at Padua and it was Fabricus who had discovered the valves in the veins permitting the blood to flow in one direction. Harvey used a variety of metaphors for the body which were essentially political and based upon the concept of monarchy. In short, his discovery of the motion of the blood was very much influenced by his own political perspective in which the monarch was the heart of the body politic (Hill, 1964).

The rise of pathological anatomy as a necessary part of the medical curriculum was simply one aspect of a broader social movement of empiricism in science, especially in clinical medicine as a revolt against Galenic deductivism of the traditional physicians. This trend of empiricism was especially strong in England where the work of Francis Bacon (*The Advancement of Learning* in 1605 and *The Great Instauration of Learning* in 1620) and Robert Boyle's scientific experimentation were particularly influential. This empiricism was noticeable in the clinical methods of Thomas Sydenham and John Locke (Cranston, 1957; Payne, 1900). For writers like Bacon and Boyle, notions of dissection and anatomization were equivalent to experimental analysis. Bacon argued strongly the case for comparative anatomy, that is the systematic comparative study of different organs in different persons (Crowther, 1960). Comparative anatomy was given its first rigorous meaning in Nehemia Grew's *Comparative Anatomy of Stomachs and Guts* begun in 1676 and the whole trend towards a more experimental approach was stimulated by the publication of Boyle's *The Usefulness of Experimental Philosophy* in 1663.

However, we should be careful not to exaggerate the importance of experimental anatomy in the clinical methods of Sydenham and

Locke. Both of these men saw that anatomical science on a comparative basis had a rather limited practical usefulness. While Boyle had said that he got more pleasure from a skilful anatomy than from looking at the famous clock at Strasburg, Sydenham and Locke were sceptical about the practical utility of systematic anatomical enquiry. They associated comparative anatomy with an emphasis on book learning and abstraction, arguing that anatomy should be significantly subordinated to clinical practice. As in other aspects of their work, they emphasized the central value of direct observation of the sick patient over a long period of time. Their objection was also associated with a puritanical commitment to practical utilitarian knowledge acquired through experience and observation. Both were somewhat opposed to the practical value of the search for ultimate causes in the structure of the human body. They associated dissection with this impractical quest for final causes whereas the clinical method depended upon knowledge of proximate causes (Dewhurst, 1958; King, 1970; Wolfe, 1961). While these practitioners were dubious as to the value of a systematic anatomy, the gradual development of pathological anatomy appears to be associated in the English case with the development of puritanism, the establishment of the Royal Society and the spread of a scientific attitude towards experimentation and observation.

In France rather similar developments took place in the emergence of the surgeons as a professional group and the evolution of a scientific pathological anatomy. The first recorded dissection was performed in Paris in 1407 and the next recording was 1478 when an executioner was paid for the delivery of a body to the surgeons. In 1493 there is a record of a public dissection in Latin to the barbers from a book on surgery which was read out by the physician. The evidence from the fifteenth century suggests that there was considerable conflict between the barbers, surgeons and physicians; the evidence points to a somewhat irregular practice in the obtaining of bodies and there were difficulties in the disposing of dissected bodies in an acceptable fashion. Despite these difficulties, the practice of public and regular dissection appeared to be commonplace by 1510. However, in these dissections, the anatomy of the abdomen was the basis of the public demonstration. The surgeon dissected while the physician read from his chair with authority (that is *ex cathedra*). While anatomy had become regular, it was simply an illustration of Galen's principles from his book on the *Conduct of Anatomies*.

In conclusion, the emergence of pathological anatomy as a crucial part of the medical curriculum was an outcome of the struggle between barbers, surgeons and physicians for social recognition.

The social status of the physicians was marked by their book learning in which the Galenic text was the indicator of their social position. There was within medieval times considerable religious and popular opposition to dissection and therefore anatomy tended to be an irregular and somewhat illegitimate practice. The growth of a more systematic approach can be dated from a publication of Vesalius' *Fabrica* in 1543. Before this period it is clear that artists like Leonardo De Vinci (1452–1519) and Michelangelo (1475–1564) had access to anatomical dissections, since their sketches of the interior structure of the human body indicate a rather advanced knowledge of the human anatomy. The conditions for the development of dissection as a significant medical activity would appear to include empiricism, professional conflicts and the technical impact of military surgery. With respect to this final condition, it is interesting to note that the Civil War in England in the seventeenth century was closely associated with a burst of activity in surgical practice enquiry and publication.

The advancement of anatomical dissections appears to be associated with the decline of religious prohibitions on public dissection and with the growth of empirical science under the general cultural influence of Puritanism. The public dissection was always performed on a criminal body and the public anatomy lesson therefore was part of a juridical punishment of the criminal. Furthermore, these public dissections continued to have a moral and religious purpose indicating the frailty and finitude of human mortal flesh. This religio-moral character of the public dissection can be illustrated from a consideration of Rembrandt's famous painting of the anatomy lesson in 1632. Rembrandt's painting is a particularly important illustration of this union of moral and medical ideas in the regulation of criminal bodies (Heckscher, 1958). From the perspective of Foucault's analysis of punishment, we can regard the public anatomy as part of a discipline of bodies in the interests of social order.

From punishment to the examination
In this chapter I have been concerned to trace two related developments. The first process involves the secularization of the human body as an object of science rather than as a feature of Christian theology and confessional practice. As the Church became structurally differentiated from other institutional areas of society (especially from the state), there was a gradual but uneven differentiation of categories of disorder. There emerged more clear and precise notions of sin, disease, deviance and crime. As a result, the Christian confessional was first copied and then replaced by

psychoanalytical investigations. Through this process of secularization, the human body was forced to give up its mysteries, becoming
open to the anatomical gaze. Through death the anatomized corpse
gave up its secrets to the living. The anatomy lesson became eventually less overtly a moral lesson, instructing the onlookers in the
frailty and finitude of life. The first process therefore concerns the
secularization of disorder, permitting the evolution of differentiated
practices (law, penology and medicine).

The second process concerns the evolution of a rational and
bureaucratic management of the body and populations as a consequence of modern secular institutions and practices (the hospital,
asylum and clinic with their attendant professional bodies and associations). The growth of modern medicine is one aspect of contemporary forms of social regulation and control. Within the framework
of Foucault's approach to medical history and institutions, we can
regard the secularization of the body and its maladies as a component within a broader social process, namely the emergence of
the modern state and its localized institutions. We can trace this
development through the reorganization of systems punishment.

Foucault (1977) was concerned to follow the history of different
types of punishment. Until the reforms of the eighteenth and nineteenth centuries, the aim of punishment was to inflict pain on the
body of the criminal in order to create a spectacle of violence.
Public terror was used to teach a very simple lesson: the superiority
of the power of the king over the enemies of the social order.
Because society was thought to be an extension of the king's body,
any attack on the body of the king was an attack on the society as a
whole. Therefore, the aim of punishment was to destroy the body of
the criminal in order to create a public drama of revenge. This logic
was the basis of the public execution and torture of the criminal on
the scaffold.

When the criminal's body was eventually removed from the scaffold, it was often then transferred to the operating table of the local
anatomy theatre. The anatomical theatre was part of the same
drama of public humiliation which had started on the scaffold.
Hence in Rembrandt's painting of the anatomy lesson, the body of
the dead man is simultaneously an object of judicial and medical
investigation. The painting shows Doctor Nicholaas Tulp perform-
ing a dissection surrounded by the Amsterdam Guild of Surgeons
during the annual public dissection. The body of surgeons was
taking a form of revenge on the body of the criminal in the interests
of public authority. The body of the criminal was being slowly
destroyed as part of the legal system of revenge.

Why did the scaffold and the public execution disappear? The use of the scaffold often provided an excuse or an opportunity for public disorder, because the drama typically involved a public holiday during which considerable alcohol would be consumed. The execution often had the opposite effect of defending the king, especially where the sympathy of the crowd was on the side of the victim. With the political changes which eventually swept away the absolutist monarchies of the *ancien regime*, the concept of sovereignty became more abstract; it was no longer directly associated with the body of the ruler. There was also a profound change in attitudes towards crime and its treatment as a consequence of the Enlightenment in Europe. A leading representative of this new perspective was Cesare Bonesana, Marchese di Beccaria who published *Of Crimes and Punishments* in 1764. Beccaria argued that the punishment had to fit the crime exactly and that imprisonment made possible an exact calculus of juridical pain (Weisser, 1979). This apparently simple proposal laid the foundations for a new regime of punishment and a new science of precise retribution and training, namely penology. Whereas under the old system of violence, the body of the criminal was given over to the king; in the new system of imprisonment, detention, convict settlement and re-training, the body of the criminal was given over to society as a whole. Furthermore, it was to become a useful body through labour and through providing specimens for medical science.

In order to make the bodies of criminals useful, they had to be first rendered docile. To make men conformable to a new system of regulations, it was necessary to have disciplines and an essential feature of discipline was the examination. Foucault has asked the question in relation to the history of the experiment:

> who will write the more general, more fluid, but also more determinant history of the 'examination' — its rituals, its methods, its characters and their roles, its play questions and answers, its systems of marking and classification? For in this slender technique are to be found a whole domain of knowledge, a whole type of power. (Foucault, 1977:185)

The examination is of considerable interest to the historian of medicine and to the medical sociologist, because it is closely associated, as Foucault (1973) shows, with the rise of the hospital as a teaching institution rather than as a general dumping ground for the poor and destitute. One of the basic changes in eighteenth-century French medicine was the development of the hospital as an apparatus of examination. The focus of this examination was the body, now rendered into the profane object of a secular science.

Foucault has traced the development of the hospital examination of sick patients over a number of centuries within the French hospital system. He noted that, while in the seventeenth century the doctor's visit was casual and irregular, by the end of the eighteenth century it had turned into a regular, organized rotation of inspections by physicians. Furthermore, the physician had become an established member of the hospital staff, eventually replacing the religious staff who increasingly assumed a subordinate position. The hospital as the place of the medical gaze became the institutional representation of medical disciplines and regimens. The discipline implied within the medical examination of sick patients is an invisible form of power which renders the patient visible. The examination also involved a detailed registration and administration of the patient. This disciplinary individuation of patients within the hospital bureaucracy permitted the medical staff to 'follow the evolution of diseases, study the effectiveness of treatments, map similar cases and the beginnings of epidemics' (Foucault, 1977:189). These disciplinary methods subordinated the individuality of the patient under the routine of description, administration and control. These practices made possible a new micro-power of medical professions, but for Foucault the medical examination has to be seen as simply one small component of a transformation of traditional society by a new system of societal surveillance.

Conclusion

The growth of western rationality can be approached in terms of different dimensions. First, there has been a general secularization of culture, whereby religious symbols and beliefs lose their public dominance; activities previously undertaken within a sacred sphere are now subsumed under profane institutions and practices. Secondly, there is a corresponding intellectualization of the mundane world, whereby scientific procedures and beliefs become in principle the criteria for action. Thirdly, rationalization involves the increasing importance of systems of individual discipline and regulation by bureaucratic agencies related to the nation–state.

In this chapter I have examined various features of rationalization within the medical sphere. The general argument is that the emergence of medical classification of deviance, the growing importance of the doctor as a professional man, the development of medical institutions around the hospital, the clinic and the examination, and the organization of a medical surveillance of society represent components of a secularization of western cultures. Put simply, the doctor has replaced the priest as the custodian of social values; the panoply of ecclesiastical institutions of regulation (the ritual order of sacraments, the places of vocational training, the hospice for pilgrims, places of worship and sanctuary) have been transferred through the evolution of scientific medicine to a panoptic collection of localized agencies of surveillance and control. Furthermore, the rise of preventive medicine, social medicine and community medicine has extended these agencies of regulation deeper and deeper into social life. This study of medical power and social knowledge is concerned to understand the origins and maintenance of these systems of benign regulation.

II
CONCEPTS OF DISEASE AND SICKNESS

3
On being sick

Introduction

The basic position in the sociological approach to illness and disease is that being sick is a fundamentally social state of affairs rather than being a narrowly defined biochemical malfunction of the organism. Sociology is concerned to explain the social causes of sickness, the character of sickness as a social role and the human response to sickness in terms of feeling, language and social action. The notion of sickness as a social role is very closely associated with the sociology of Parsons (1951) who first conceptualized the notion of the sick role. Parsons's contribution to medical sociology has been extensive, although unfortunately the evaluation of Parsons's contribution is often confined to commentaries on the sick role. Although there has been extensive evaluation of Parsons's formulation of the sick role (Levine and Kozloff, 1978), the general character of Parsonian medical sociology has been somewhat neglected (Holton and Turner, 1986).

There were four areas to Parsons's contribution to medical sociology broadly conceived. First, Parsons was interested in the ethical character of the professions in relation to the profit motive of capitalist society. He sought to argue that there was a distinctive feature to the learned and caring professions, namely that they were organized in terms of service to the community which did not reflect the dominant values of capitalist society. Secondly, he was concerned to analyse the effect of the social structure and culture on the general features of health; Parsons's work on the family in relation to stress would be one illustration of this component of his sociology. Thirdly, Parsons analysed the relationship between death, religion and the gift of life which he saw as part of a more general problem of meaning. Fourthly, Parsons developed the concept of the sick role as implicitly a critique of biologism in the conceptualization of illness. In this latter respect Parsons's concept of the sick role provided a major alternative to the medical model. The Parsonian approach to medical sociology may be regarded as an action-system theoretical orientation. The approach is functionalist (funcionalism analyses social activities in terms of their contribution to the maintenance of a social system or institution) in that Parsons argued that if the definition of sickness and disability were too lenient or general, then severe social strains would be exerted on the social system bringing about considerable dysfunction in the achievement of general goals (Mechanic, 1968). The social control and regulation of sickness is brought about by what may be termed the sick-role mechanism. The consequence is that in western societies general practitioners are concerned with clinical situations where they are professionally obliged to certify illness in order to explain the patient's failure to comply with social expectations.

The sick role can be defined in terms of four components. The first aspect is that the sick role legitimates social withdrawal from a number of obligations, such as those relating to work and family duties. The idea is that a sick person ought to stay at home and take rest in order to facilitate recovery. The second feature of the role is that a sick person is exempted from responsibility for their medical condition; the assumption is that they cannot get better without professional help and support. The third component is that the person has a social obligation to improve and get better; the legitimation of sickness as a basis for social withdrawal from roles is conditional on the patient's full acceptance of an obligation to get better by co-operating with the professional recommendations of a competent doctor. The fourth element within the sick role is therefore an expectation that the person will seek out competent health care from a trained physician. As a consequence, the sick role describes the role-set or social system of the doctor–patient relationship which is structured in terms of the pattern variables, which Parsons had outlined in a discussion of professionalism.

The concept of the sick role was elaborated by Parsons against a background in which the American medical profession was beginning to take some notice of the idea of psychosomatic illness and to realize that the emotional connection between the doctor and patient was an important aspect of both the diagnostic and therapeutic processes. Parsons had also become aware of the relevance of Freudian psychoanalysis for the study of sickness, especially Freud's notion of transference. These intellectual influences brought Parsons to a realization that there was a significant issue of motivation in the process of becoming sick and getting better. Given the concept of the action frame of reference with its voluntaristic premises in Parsonian sociology, there was an important sense in which the social agent decides to be sick. Voluntarism was important because sickness could not be considered merely as an objective condition of the organism without some discussion of the motivation of the individual in relation to the social system. To be sick required certain exemptions from social obligation and a motivation to accept a therapeutic regime. It was for this reason that Parsons classified sickness as a form of deviant behaviour which required legitimation and social control. While the sick role legitimizes social deviance, it also requires an acceptance of a medical regime. The sick role was therefore an important vehicle for social control, since the aim of the medical regime was to return the sick person to conventional social roles. In some respects, Parsons's analysis of the sick role anticipated a variety of deviancy models of mental illness which subsequently became influential in sociology in the work of Lemert (1967) and Scheff (1966).

In terms of Parsons's pattern variables, the doctor–patient relationship is characterized by its affective neutrality, universalism, functional specificity and orientation to collective norms. The point of this description is to show how the doctor and patient are committed to breaking their relationship rather than forming a social connection as a stable and permanent system of interaction. The sick role is to be a temporary role and it is important that the patient does not become emotionally dependent on the doctor or the doctor become involved in a particularistic relation with the patient. The whole aim of the exercise is to get the patient out of a sick role and back into a social environment involving activism and obligation. A typical sickness episode would be an attack of gastroenteritis where the patient is forced to stay away from work for a limited period of time in order to undertake appropriate medication. The sickness has a limited duration and, where the sick role is successfully occupied, the patient returns to normal expectations after a brief respite from major social duties.

Abnormal illness
We might, however, identify a deviant form of sick role, where the sick role becomes a more or less permanent state of affairs. For example, Merton (1957) outlined a theory of deviance in the context of American values which give a special emphasis to achievement and worldly success. Merton argued that in a society where a significant proportion of the population would be unable to achieve material benefits through legitimate means, then one might expect considerable deviancy whereby people attempted to manipulate the means or ends of an achievement culture for illegitimate purposes. In such a society, Merton suggested that retreatism or escapism might become a permanent orientation to the social structure, where the deviant rejected both the ends of the society and the

means for achieving those ends. Merton suggested that drug addiction would be a compelling illustration of such retreatism representing a deviant but permanent adaptation to the social structure. We can suggest, following Merton, that an alternative version of the sick role would be for the sickness to become a permanent solution to the structural contradictions of contemporary society. In short, there may be important secondary gains from being sick whereby the individual avoids responsibility for their sickness and is able to retreat from the demanding requirements of an industrial society based upon an activist culture and a norm of achievement. In this context the doctor would provide a gateway for legitimized withdrawal from social roles and social responsibility. This situation may well lead to obvious conflicts between a doctor's commitment to the idea of the patient getting better and the patient's commitment to staying sick.

The possibility of systematic disagreement between patient and doctor as to the character of the illness has led some commentators to develop a classification of 'abnormal illness behaviours' (Pilowsky, 1978). Abnormal illness behaviour occurs when the doctor does not believe that the sick role is appropriate given the objective pathology detected during the clinical interview; that is, there is a conflict between the patient's presentation and claims to a sick role, and the doctor's diagnosis of this condition. More technically, this form of behaviour may be defined as

> the persistence of an inappropriate or mal-adaptive mode of perceiving, evaluating and acting in relation to one's own state of health, despite the fact that a doctor (or other appropriate social agent) has offered a reasonably lucid explanation of the nature of the illness and the appropriate course of management to be followed, based on a thorough examination and assessment of all parameters of functioning (including the use of special investigations where necessary), and taking into account the individual's age, educational and sociocultural background. (Pilowsky, 1978:133)

Pilowsky went on to argue that it would be appropriate to distinguish between illness-affirming behaviour and illness-denying behaviour. For example, an illustration of conscious illness-affirming behaviour irrespective of a doctor's objective diagnosis would be Munchausen's Syndrome (Asher, 1951), in which the patient consciously enters the sick role against the instructions or recommendations of a doctor by knowingly inflicting suffering upon themselves. Alternatively a doctor may diagnose an objective disease which the patient systematically denies. Possibly because of a fear of the appropriate therapy, the patient adopts a 'flight into health' which involves a complete non-compliance with the recommendations of a physician. By developing Pilowsky's argument, we can suggest four logically possible relationships between a doctor's and a patient's perception of the presence of illness. Representing these diagrammatically:

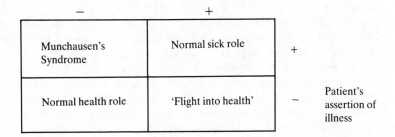

FIGURE 2
Normal and abnormal illness behaviour

Doctor's perception of illness

	−	+	
	Munchausen's Syndrome	Normal sick role	+
	Normal health role	'Flight into health'	−

Patient's assertion of illness

Three boxes in this property space representation are immediately intelligible. Munchausen's Syndrome, or in psychological terms hypochondriasis, would represent a situation where the patient's assertion of an illness was not confirmed by a doctor's diagnosis. Secondly, the normal sick role would represent an agreement between doctor and patient as to the presence of a diagnosed problem. Thirdly, 'flight into health' would be represented by the doctor's perception of an illness which is denied by the patient. One illustration of this would be a patient who rejected the diagnosis of a malignant cancer in a situation where the patient feared the therapy required. The fourth situation might be described as a normal health role. A situation might arise where a patient, referred to a doctor for a routine examination for a job or insurance policy, is given a clean bill of health; both doctor and patient agree that no disease is present. This typology for the analysis of doctor–patient relationships is useful, but one problem in the notion of abnormal illness behaviour is that it implicitly gives prominence to the doctor's perception, namely what characterizes abnormality is the patient's failure to submit to the doctor's analysis. Existing theories of abnormal illness behaviour do not adequately take into account a situation where a doctor might fail to analyse a disease or misclassify a disease. One further complication in this model is the problem of medical uncertainty in prognosis and diagnosis.

Even where the diagnostic tools available to the doctor are very sophisticated, there is always an element of medical uncertainty in which a doctor may misdiagnose an illness or fail to detect the presence of an illness. It has been suggested that much of the informal education of medical students is concerned with the problem of coping with uncertainty (Fox, 1957). In the clinical situation, the doctor is faced with the problem of deciding whether to communicate his own uncertainty, thereby reinforcing the anxiety and uncertainty of the patient (Davis, 1960).

In statistical theory, we can distinguish between rejecting a hypothesis which is true (type one errors) or accepting one which is false (type two errors). The same problem faces a doctor, namely whether to accept the possibility of the presence of an illness or risk the problem of accepting one which turns out to be false. On balance a doctor is more likely to accept the hypothesis that there is an illness rather than rejecting such a proposition, since the imposition of the therapy where a disease is not present is unlikely actually to kill the patient, although it may well cause the patient considerable discomfort. This course of action is more likely, since to reject the hypothesis that an illness is present may result in the patient's death, because therapy is not recommended at a sufficiently early period. Scheff (1963) has employed this statistical argument as a method for explaining why doctors are more likely to over-prescribe than under-prescribe in a context of permanent uncertainty. Quite simply, doctors are more likely to intervene than to abstain from medical action, since it is better to be wrong in a situation where the therapy will not kill the patient than to be wrong by failing to recommend therapy in a situation where the disease may well kill the patient.

Some evidence for this argument can be derived from Bakwin (1945) who studied physicians' judgements regarding the advisability of tonsillectomy for a sample of 1000 school children. Of these children, 610 had their tonsils removed after a preliminary investigation. The remaining children were then examined by another group of physicians and 174 were selected for tonsillectomy. Another group of doctors were then asked to examine the remaining group of children and of these 99 were judged to require tonsillectomy. Yet another group of doctors were employed to examine the remaining children and nearly one-half of these were recommended for the operation. This procedure left 58 children with their tonsils still intact. Since tonsillectomy is not life-threatening in any serious sense, the implication of this procedure is that it is better to be safe than sorry, namely it is better to intervene where the outcome is not serious.

The implication of this argument for the study of normal and abnormal illness behaviour is that one might expect a considerable amount of disagreement between doctor and patient as a consequence of the uncertainty of correct diagnosis. That is, a doctor is more rather than less likely to accept a patient's assertion of illness since medical intervention may be unnecessary, but a physician would prefer to guard himself against an inaccurate diagnosis. Despite the pressure to diagnose the presentation of a symptom as real, studies of doctor–patient interaction, at least in the British context, have suggested that the majority of doctors will typically regard the presentation of the symptom as a trivial grievance. In one study as many as 26 percent of general practitioners felt that over half of their consultations were trivial (Cartwright, 1967).

A number of complications have been considered with respect to Parsons's sick-role theory. In particular, there is the problem of disagreement between doctor and patient as to the character of the symptoms, namely whether they are true or false. These complications represent an implicit critique of Parsons's sick-role model; we are now in a position to consider a range of overt criticisms of the sick-role concept.

Criticisms of the sick-role concept
The first major criticism of the Parsonian model is that going to see the doctor may be the end process of a complex system of help-seeking behaviour (Mechanic, 1968:268 ff.). Freidson (1961, 1970) has discussed the importance of the so-called 'lay referral system' in the social process by which lay people consult the physician. Freidson has argued that the lay person only consults the doctor after a series of consultations with significant lay groups. It is the lay culture, not the professional values of the physician, which defines the meaning of illness in a social context. If a person perceives himself to be sick and in need of specialized help, he is likely to find support within his own cultural context only if 'he shows evidence of symptoms the others perceive to be illness and if he interprets them the way the others find plausible' (Freidson, 1970:289). Once the requirement for specialized health care is acknowledged by the lay culture, then help-seeking behaviour is organized in terms of the lay referral system. The lay referral system has two components: the lay culture and a network of personal influence which is the lay referral structure. A variety of sociological studies (McKinlay, 1973; Suchman, 1964; Scambler et al., 1981) have found that the majority of patients reporting to a doctor had already consulted extensively with lay colleagues and discussed the various symptoms which were subsequently presented to the doctor.

The concept of the lay referral system and lay interventions has produced a significant body of research into the role of social networks in the presentation of illness to a professional physician. One consequence of this research is that we should distinguish between the sick role and the patient role. In particular, Parsons's conception of sickness should be analysed as a contribution to the sociology of the patient role. Not all sick people are patients and not all patients are sick people. This distinction draws attention once more to a set of potential conflicts between the lay cultural analysis of sickness and the professional conceptualization of the patient role.

The distinction also points to the presence of a reservoir of undiagnosed illness in the community. Social surveys of the general population have persistently shown a number of serious conditions which are characteristically undiagnosed; these include high blood pressure, anaemia, bronchitis, obesity and diabetes (Tuckett, 1976:23 ff.). Whether or not these complaints reach the doctor's clinic will depend a great deal on the strength of the network of lay consultations and significant lay groups. Parsons's analysis of the patient role therefore tends to be a rather narrow slice of the total character of illness behaviour and help-seeking behaviour.

The second area of significant criticism of Parsons has been concerned with the character of conflict and disagreement in the doctor–patient relationship. It has been argued that Parsons's model assumes an ideal patient who brings real illness to the doctor, accepts the medical diagnosis without question and complies entirely with the doctor's recommendations; the model also assumes an ideal doctor who has a concern for the total patient, provides an effective diagnosis of the patient's problem with reference to the medical and social context of the patient, and finally is professionally committed to the rapid and effective healing of his client. A large body of sociological research has suggested that Parsons's ideal typical analysis of the doctor–patient relationship is not appropriate as an orientation to actual empirical doctor–patient interaction. For example, much research has been concerned to analyse the typification of patients as 'bad patients' who diverge from this ideal model (Murcott, 1981).

The sick role model suggests that the doctor–patient relationship is complementary and functional, whereas much medical sociology research has suggested that the relationship is very variable (Bloor and Horobin, 1975). There is a certain contradiction between the expectation that the ideal patient will be well informed and strongly motivated to seek medical help, and the expectation that the patient will submit to the expert knowledge and guidance of the doctor. That is, the patient is expected to be sufficiently informed to bring real rather than trivial symptoms to the doctor but sufficiently compliant to follow the doctor's advice without question or interference. The patient's expert character in deciding to consult the doctor terminates once the patient enters the clinic.

Because the patient is expected to be literally naive, there is considerable conflict, or at least potential conflict, in terms of power, knowledge and status between doctor and patient. Social differences in power and knowledge create a set of conflicting discourses between patient and doctor which in turn produce situations of low trust and minimal confidence. The potential range of conflict appears to be infinite, but one might suggest a continuum between a situation where the patient attempts to get 'better' before the doctor is adequately convinced that health has been restored (Roth, 1963) and a situation where the patient stays 'sick' where the doctor thinks a new drug or therapy may be desirable and appropriate (Sacks, 1976).

The third area of major criticism of the sick-role concept concerns the type of disease which may have an important bearing on the character of the patient/sick role. In general, Parsons's analysis of the sick role refers to acute rather than chronic illness, since Parsons's analysis of the role assumes that the patient will get better. Some diseases may be long term and the sick person is not necessarily excused from commitments and may be expected to cope with a long-term disability. For example, in the case of diabetes mellitus, there is no known cure. With early onset the patient will have to manage a sick role for life in an isolated social context, with increasing forms of disability including blindness. Another example of such long-term management where social responsibilities are not absolved would be epilepsy. Similarly, diseases like Parkinsonism render the patient incapable of maintaining long-term social commitments and, while the disease might enable legitimate withdrawal from social engagement, there is often little opportunity for release from the disease so that the patient could occupy normal social roles.

Parsons's conception of the sick role is also limited in the area of somewhat ambiguous forms of medical illness and deviance from normal patterns of behaviour. For example, pregnancy might eventually cause a woman to withdraw from full-time employment, but it is not entirely clear that Parsons's notion of the sick role would include pregnancy as a legitimate reason for withdrawal from the full range of expectations relating to social roles. Another example would be aging which produces disability and withdrawal from social roles, but it might be somewhat problematic to regard aging as a genuine sick role. If aging is regarded as a form of sickness, then retirement would be a form of transference of the individual to a permanent sick role. In short, there are a wide range of long-term illnesses from diabetes to dementia which force the individual to withdraw from social roles, but may not have the full legitimacy which patients usually expect from the sick role.

A fourth type of criticism of Parsons relates to the problem of the universalistic character of treatment of patients regardless of class, gender or status. Parsons's sick-role formulation assumed that doctors would orient to the patient on the basis of a universalistic norm irrespective of the particular characteristics of the patient. This assumption about universalism does not appear to be borne out in empirical research. One significant variation in the treatment of patients is explained by social class. Research on medical consultations in the UK, for example, shows that the length of consultations varies with social class so that patients in social class 1 had an average consultation of 6.1 minutes where members of social class 5 had a consultation length of 4.4 minutes (Buchan and Richardson, 1973). In a study of elderly patients, Cartwright and O'Brien (1976) found that middle-class patients' consultations lasted for 6.2 minutes whereas consultations for working-class patients lasted for 4.7 minutes.

The content of the consultations also varied according to social class so that middle-class patients would be more likely to receive an explanation of their condition than working-class patients. There are also important variations in terms of gender. For instance, MacIntyre and Oldman (1984) have described very different responses from the medical profession to their common complaint of migraine where these differences in response appear to be at least partly related to their gender, age and status. They suggest that female sufferers from migraine are more likely to be treated as neurotic females whereas middle-class migraine sufferers who are male are more likely to be regarded as persons exposed to extreme stress and tension from demanding occupational routines. Sociological studies in the USA have shown that there are also extreme variations in the treatment of persons defined as mentally ill according to class, status, gender and ethnicity (Hollingshead and Redlich, 1958). Variations in the treatment of patients by social status are not confined to the interview within the clinical situation. Sudnow (1967) has explored through an ethnographic study variations in medical responses to persons arriving at an emergency unit who are suspected of being dead on arrival. Sudnow was able to show how the medical response varied in terms of the presumed moral character of the patient. For example, patients who were deemed to be alcoholic did not receive the same treatment as those who were deemed to be sober. In short, there are wide variations in the treatment of patients by doctors according to the particularistic status of the patients, and therefore it is difficult to argue that in practice universalistic criteria apply.

Parsons has been criticized therefore on the grounds that his model of the sick role is an ideal typical construct which does not necessarily match the empirical variations in the treatment of patients. In addition to his neglect of the lay referral system, empirical research has shown extreme variation in the treatment of patients according to their status, class, age and gender. The implication of this research is that the doctor–patient relationship is characterized more typically by conflict and misunderstanding than by reciprocity and agreement. In addition to these criticisms, one might suggest that Parsons was writing about a medical setting in which a one-to-one, face-to-face interaction took place on the basis of a fee-for-service. Medical practice has subsequently become more bureaucratized and specialized by the development of large-scale medical settings, an extreme division of labour in the medical profession and by crucial technological changes. The patient and the doctor are now involved in medical settings where the doctor is part of a team and where there may not be a stable, long-term relationship between the doctor and the patient. That is, the whole professional setting of medicine has changed significantly since Parsons's analysis of the sick role. In addition, given a considerable amount of social criticism of the medical profession, there have emerged powerful consumer organizations which have changed the relationship between the doctor and the patient. These changes include the development of malpractice legislation and alternative medicine which have called into question the professional relationship between the doctor and the patient. In retrospect, the problem in this debate with Parsons centres ultimately on the character of communication which takes place between the patient and the doctor. In western society the doctor–patient relationship is defined by the fact that what is involved is unspecialized consumption of highly technical and specialized medical services. Attempts to improve the doctor–patient relationship therefore centre on the problem of improving medical consultations from the point of view of sharing ideas and communication of feeling.

The medical consultation
There is a large body of research on the problems of patient compliance and doctor–patient interaction which has had an applied perspective, namely to reduce the extent of doctor–patient miscommunication (Enelow and Swisher, 1979). This research suggests

that, not only do doctors and patients employ entirely different languages of disease, but often they have conflicting interests. While the patient may be seeking general reassurance, the doctor may be attempting to communicate specific technical information with respect to specific symptoms. This 'competence gap' is at least partly a consequence of the fact that the professional doctor has a social monopoly of expertise and knowledge which is the very basis of the professional claim to a privileged status in society. The doctor's authority in the consultation depends to a considerable extent on this monopoly of knowledge; we would expect at least initially that doctors would not be inclined to transform this prestige by sharing technical knowledge with the patient. On the other hand, it is clear that sharing of information where this brings about reassurance and understanding is an important part of the actual process of therapy. There is some empirical evidence that the sharing of information as an aspect of surgical treatment improves recovery rates and enhances the outcome of medical intervention (Skipper and Leonard, 1968). Sharing information with a patient is also important as the basis for achieving the patient's cooperation with the therapeutic process. In fact research suggests that approximately 50 percent of patients will not follow the doctor's advice and do not comply with the medical regimen. One estimate suggests that wasted drugs as a result of non-compliance may well cost in excess of £300m. per annum (Walton et al., 1980). Successful communication with the patient is an important part of the therapeutic process in so far as successful interaction may well restore the confidence and sense of wellbeing of the patient. Finally, it may well be the case that information is all that the doctor has to communicate to the patient.

There is a sociological argument therefore that the medical consultation should be regarded as a meeting of experts, since the patient is often well informed of his or her illness and may, over a long period of time, become technically competent in the analysis of their problems (Tuckett et al., 1985). For example, in the case of diabetes the patient has to become skilled over a long period of time in the diagnosis of certain symptoms and in the management of their condition. In the UK, Tuckett and his colleagues studied 1302 consultations conducted by 16 doctors; from this sample they selected 405 consultations for detailed study. They attempted to measure the success or failure of consultations in terms of the sharing of information with respect to diagnostic significance, treatment-action, preventive-action and implications. This research found that medical consultations were successful in situations where they simply confirmed the patient's existing view of the character of their illness. Since in most consultations which are part of a sequence of visits to the doctor, there will be little new or unexpected information communicated to the patient, we would expect a common sharing of information. However, where there were differences between the doctor's and the patient's views of the illness or where the patient's knowledge was inappropriate medically, then consultations with doctors tended to be unsuccessful in the sense that information was not successfully communicated, not remembered or not acted upon. Despite the so-called competence gap, the great majority of patients succeeded in remembering or making sense of their doctor's views. The patients who were least committed to what the doctor said were more likely to come from minority ethnic social groups, to be women bringing children to see the doctor or patients who were new to the doctor. Where the patient commenced the consultation with views which were already divergent, the doctor's information did little to change their views of their medical condition. The failure to communicate was also reinforced by the stereotype of the patient held by the doctor, namely that failures to communicate are to be blamed on the patient's ignorance. This particular study of doctor–patient interaction concluded that:

> we conceive of the consultation as a meeting between one person who has, by his training and experience, access to scarce and specialist knowledge and another person who has, by experience, immersion in his culture and past discussion, a set of ideas about what is happening to him. Both parties form models of what is wrong, what should be done, what are the consequences of the problem, its treatment and so on, based on their own reasoning and background knowledge. (Tuckett et al., 1985: 217)

The major practical proposal for resolving the competence gap has been to encourage doctors to treat seriously the lay knowledge of their patients and to listen more carefully to what is said and expressed by lay persons in the consultation. In addition, it has been argued that patients should be more systematically encouraged to present their views of their problems so that the consultation can be a genuine sharing of information by 'experts'.

These models of doctor–patient interaction are interesting and important from a practical point of view, but they lack a powerful sociological and theoretical framework by which these consultations could be seen in a more systematic framework. Since we could regard the competence gap and the failure of consultations as a form of distorted communication, it is appropriate to consider the doctor–patient relationship from the perspective of Habermas, whose analysis of rational discourse has been precisely concerned with those structural factors which inhibit successful, open communication between equals.

The aim of Habermas's philosophy has been to provide a critique of those elements of the social structure and culture which deny individual freedom and growth by imposing unnecessary forms of social control and coercion on rational individuals. In order to develop this critique Habermas has developed a theory of communication and cognitive interests in which he identifies three knowledge-constitutive interests, namely the technical, practical and emancipatory (Habermas, 1970, 1972, 1976, 1979, 1984). The empirical–analytical sciences are concerned with the technical cognitive interests, the historical–hermeneutic sciences are focused on a practical–social interest and the critical social sciences embrace an emancipatory cognitive interest as their object of analysis. These three cognitive interests are parallel to the three basic dimensions of social life, namely work, social interaction and power. A principal direction of Habermas's argument is that the cognitive interest of the empirical–analytical sciences is inadequate as a criterion of rationally valid knowledge and that these three interests are separate, autonomous and distinctive. In the context of this discussion of dialogue, Habermas's analysis of the emancipatory interest and the social conditions for realizing open, democratic dialogue is the most significant feature of his theory of communication.

For example, Habermas sought to criticize the limited emancipatory critique of Freudian psychoanalysis. Given his training in traditional medicine and neuropsychology, Freud had grounded his analysis of the 'talking cure' in psychoanalysis on a neurological model, namely a medical model of illness behaviour. Freud's attempt to use an energy model in a mechanical fashion to account for psychic behaviour was simply inadequate. The clinical results from psychoanalytic consultations were simply not comparable to observations in the controlled experiments of the natural sciences, because the special feature of therapy was not exact control, but the inter-subjective interaction between analyst and patient. The core of the psychoanalytic interview was language, not the behavioural events of an outpouring of energy within a mechanistic model. In order to recognize the emancipatory critique which was implicit in psychoanalysis, Habermas argued that critical theory should be a form of language analysis which exhibits and exposes the restraints and distortions which are present in human communication. In Habermas's model of communication, the production and development of true critical knowledge can only take place in situations of democratic dialogue and open communication. For example, the participants must be free to engage in unrestrained and unregulated debate which is in principle unlimited, since it is only under these social conditions that self-reflective critical and viable awareness and knowledge can emerge. The emancipatory interest attempts to expose and criticize the political circumstances which distort human communication and render knowledge unreliable and inaccurate. For example, torture is the most unacceptable condition for communication, since one could place no confidence in the reliability of the information extracted under conditions of political torture and harassment. We cannot therefore separate the sociological analysis of the conditions of communication from an enquiry into the truthfulness or otherwise of information and knowledge.

Habermas was particularly interested in the possibilities of psychoanalytic communication in traditional Freudian therapy. According to Habermas, the analyst, through a process of open dialogue, offered the conditions by which a patient could arrive at adequate self-knowledge through introspection and reflection. There are major structural inequalities between the doctor and patient in terms of education, knowledge, skill, social standing and prestige. Thus, the relationship between doctor and patient is closer to that of confessor and penitent than between members of an open discursive community (Hepworth and Turner, 1982). Habermas provides us with a utopian model by which these inequalities might be criticized but the solution to the doctor–patient relationship would require macro-sociological changes in the relation between professions and lay groups in order to bring about a more effective system of communication in the consultation. Re-education of doctor and patient would not be sufficient to transform the dialogic relationship.

Habermas's model is useful as a tool for analysing the relationship between professional groups and clients in terms of access to knowledge and the communication of information. It would be possible to use Habermas's approach to consider historically the evolving relationship within the role-set of the doctor–nurse–patient relationship. In the traditional Nightingale system the flow of information was from the doctor to the nurse to the patient in a single line of command where the nurse simply fulfilled the expectations of the doctor and in which the patient appeared as an object or target of their professional activity. In the professional relationship which has emerged as a consequence of the critique of this patriarchal model of health care, there is a more open relationship between the doctor, the patient and the nurse. However, it is not clear that the development of consumer groups, the professional development of nursing and the transformation of the hospital setting will produce an entirely open and democratic system of communication in health-care systems. In brief, the health-care role-set can be seen as a microcosm of the wider social structure; in so far as there has been a democratization of social relations in western industrial societies, then we might expect an opening and democratization of the sick role. These issues of professionalism and professional ethics are the subject of Chapters seven and eight.

We have seen that Parsons's analysis of the sick role has been subject to extensive and detailed criticism over more than three decades of sociological research. The concept of the sick role fails to provide a satisfactory analysis of patients experiencing long-term chronic illness. It fails to analyse adequately the conflicts and differences of interest between doctor and patient. The concept is inadequate in conceptualizing the processes which lead patients to seek medical help, namely it fails to analyse the lay referral system. It is also inappropriate because it fails to make a satisfactory distinction between a patient role and a sick role. As a consequence of these problems and criticisms, commentators on the original Parsonian formulation of the sick role have suggested that we need to abandon this legacy in medical sociology in order to forge a new paradigm and approach. For example, Levine and Kozloff (1978:339), after a judicious and lengthy investigation into the sick role concept, concluded that:

> we believe we now need to leave the Parsonian formulation in the background, to free ourselves of the limits of the paradigm and to learn much more about the social behaviour of the sick person. We believe more processional and longitudinal studies may be indicated to deepen our understanding and to discover new dimensions in the patterned life of the sick person.

While this observation on the legacy of Parsons is perfectly appropriate, there is nevertheless an important defence of the Parsonian interpretation of sickness which has often been neglected in medical sociology. Parsons lays the foundation for a broad comparative sociology of the sick role which would investigate the culture of sickness between various social systems. Although Parsons is often criticized for being abstract and general, in fact it is possible to argue that his theoretical work lays down a broad framework for concrete empirical investigation. The core of the original concept was that different cultures and social structures produce different roles and definitions of sickness; therefore it is possible to analyse social systems comparatively by an examination of the nature of sickness in those social systems. Parsons's concept of the sick role was not therefore a narrow and one-sided approach to a specific aspect of medical sociology; by contrast, it was an attempt to create a perspective which would lead to broad comparative studies of the availability of different forms of sickness behaviour in different social systems. In order to illustrate this defence of Parsons, I intend to examine a number of case studies as an illustration of the basic argument.

A defence of the sick role concept

Parsons had argued that the specific character of the sick role in American society was the product of a culture which gave special emphasis to individualism, achievement and activism. To be sick in American society was to be inactive and withdrawn from the competitive race of a society which gave an emphasis to moral individualism. Parsons had suggested that different social structures would produce different sick roles and he was particularly concerned to provide a contrast between sickness in state socialist societies and sickness in competitive capitalist society. As a defence of Parsons's legacy, it is interesting therefore to compare different social systems in terms of the presence or absence of this syndrome of individualism–activism–achievement values.

If the sick role is regarded as an exit from social relations for a temporary respite from social obligations, then we can argue that sickness and health are criteria of social membership and engagement. It is for this reason that Parsons argued that permanent incumbency of the sick role should be regarded as a form of social deviance. In fact the sick role as a form of social withdrawal is widespread in human cultures and clearly not peculiar to modern industrial societies. For example, in the Islamic Middle East illness behaviour can be a method for legitimating behaviour which deviates from conventional social expectations. In the Nile delta, the possessed male or female may display a variety of symptoms but the social manifestations have a single theme, namely the breaking of social customs (Morsy, 1978). A woman who is sick by possession may reject the offer of a marriage selected by her father, oppose her husband's sexual desires and decline to nurse another's child without social criticism since her deviance is explained by her illness. Medical labels in this context provide an acceptable label for deviant activity and also institutionalize this form of deviance. Thus it is interesting to note that:

> the very term 'uzr' (excuse) provides the illness with a social definition. It offers the ma'zur (excused) a temporary dispensation from the requirements of social canons. (Morsy, 1978:603)

Those afflicted with illness ('uzr') are able to maintain a marginal position in society while avoiding the ultimate punishments of social exclusion traditionally connected with serious forms of deviance. The illness of the excused is normally terminated by re-engagement in a variety of collective rituals which have a medical–social character.

Anthropological research points to the fact that all known societies have what we might call culturally patterned disorders which are social roles in which deviance is legitimated and indeed institutionalized as an available social pattern. Research from a variety of pre-modern societies indicates the widespread prevalence of these culturally patterned forms of disorder which we may simply regard as sick roles. Anthropological investigation of North American tribes shows that behaviour which we might want to call 'psychotic' is in fact institutionalized by ritual and custom (Barnouw, 1979; Bishop, 1975; Hay, 1971). In western society a common expression for deviant behaviour is the concept of the 'berserk' by which we attempt to describe abnormal deviant behaviour of a frenetic character. The word berserk is itself a corruption of a Norse word meaning 'bear's shirt'; in fact the word berserk therefore refers to institutionalized deviant behaviour. The berserk was somebody who occupied a special role in the tribe and was expected to put fear into tribal enemies. The behaviour of the berserk, far from being random and peculiar, was in fact culturally patterned and structured.

These illustrations from pre-modern conditions have two common features. First, sickness is related to marginality and exclusion from mundane activity, despite the fact that these exclusions are themselves ritualized and institutional. Second, the cure for such behaviour involves social rituals designed to reintegrate the individual in the social group and reaffirm conventional membership by the expurgation of offending sickness. We can argue that all human societies are organized in terms of rituals of exclusion and inclusion. In traditional Christianity, the primary rituals of inclusion were such sacraments as baptism, confirmation and marriage, while the rituals of exclusion included excommunication, ritual death and various forms of social exclusion. In this respect illness is a form of marginality and the primary mechanisms of therapy are social integration. From this perspective, the important feature of Parsons's analysis of the sick role in the American context is the emphasis on the individual and the individualization of deviance. While in this sick role the incumbent deviates from the values of achievement and engagement, the sick person does not deviate from the values of individualism. In part this is because western medicine itself emphasizes through modern theories of disease the individuality of sickness.

In secular western societies, there are few public rituals by which sickness and health can be demarcated through collective processes.

We have lost most of the major ritualized expressions of social membership and social engagement; our rituals are fragmented and secularized. The definition of social membership in contemporary industrial societies is signified by political conceptions of citizenship which in turn typically depend upon the possession of language and therefore a particular form of education (Gellner, 1983). The rituals of modern society are concerned with definitions of nationalism rather than with medico-social definitions of deviance and normality. It is characteristic of western societies that when we fall ill, we are isolated from our public activities and we may well be isolated from kin and relatives. Because we are sick, we are removed from public surveillance and inspection, retreating to the privacy of our beds and our private spaces. Alternatively, within the hospital setting we will again be institutionalized, isolated and often prevented from the enjoyments of regular interaction with our kin folk or friends. Illness under these circumstances is alienating and degrading; sickness involves removal and departure rather than reintegration and incorporation within social groups. In this respect, we can support Parsons's contention that in western societies the sick role is a form of social control which regulates the amount of sickness in society, making return to health and work personally and socially desirable.

This pattern of sickness and health presents a sharp contrast with the form of illness behaviour and therapy in contemporary Japan. While Japan and the USA are clearly industrial capitalist societies, they have significantly different cultural systems. Specifically, Japan does not have the individualistic culture which is typical of industrial western societies and therefore the patterns of illness behaviour in Japan do not exhibit individualistic values (Abercrombie et al., 1986).

In Japanese culture there is a more positive approach towards sickness, not simply as the absence of work but as positive vacation and recreation. The Japanese pamper their sick in a way which would be unusual in western societies. The Japanese approach is to emphasize 'ansai' (peace and quietness) as the principal form of therapy for all illness. Hospitalization is a form of vacation which is positively required for the restoration of health. This attitude towards illness and rest may in part explain why the average length of hospital stay for a patient in Japan is far longer than in any other industrial society. Whereas the average length of stay in the USA in the 1970s was 8.1 days and in England and Wales 13.1 days, the average length of stay in Japanese hospitals was 42.9 days. Furthermore, entry into hospital in Japan does not signal the end of close kinship relationships. In Japan, regular contact is maintained with the relatives through a ritualized system of visitation where the sharing of food is particularly important. The Japanese hospitalization resembles the treatment of the socially deviant in pre-modern society where illness often brings about an intensification rather than a diminution of social relations:

> through the crisis situation of hospitalization, the patient's entire social network becomes activated and reaches a new height of intensity, both positively and negatively. All the participants in the 'drama' are forced to re-examine their human relationships. During the hospitalization, every fibre of the patient's social network is tested. (Ohnuki-Tierney, 1984:210)

The integration of the kinship system, the patient and the hospital is symbolized by the fact that patients continue to wear their own clothing while in hospital and are not subject to the usual forms of bureaucracy so common in the western system. Entry into hospital in a western system is often accompanied by what have been called 'degradation ceremonies' (Garfinkel, 1956). The degradation has the effect of reinforcing the desirability of health, engagement with the social system and a return to individualistic autonomy and self reliance.

Conclusion
Although Parsons's concept of the sick role has been the subject of appropriate criticism, the empirical implications of Parsons's theory of sickness have yet to be fully explored. Especially in the framework of comparative sociology, the sick-role concept is a powerful instrument for the analysis of culture and social deviance. Parsons's notion that sickness is subject to social control provides a useful way into the analysis of culture in relation to illness behaviour. His discussion of sickness brought to the foreground the whole question of responsibility for sickness and the social response to illness behaviour. The notion of the sick role is a critical alternative to the medical model with its emphasis on objective causation of disease within a framework which denies the involvement of the individual and precludes a voluntaristic framework for the analysis of sickness as a form of social action. However, the medical model by ruling out responsibility absolves the patient from routine tasks and social employments. Because they are no longer responsible, they are no longer subject to moral criticism and legal punishment. In return for this denial of responsibility, the patient may well be subject to various forms of social degradation, however implicit such rituals may be. This question of responsibility and individual autonomy becomes paramount in the analysis of mental illness.

4
Madness and civilization

In this chapter I am concerned with three aspects of the sociology of insanity. In the first section, I examine the history of madness and the asylum through the perspective of Foucault (1971) who has provided a powerful framework for modern historical studies. In the second section, I examine the recent history of social policy towards the insane paying special attention to the debate about decarcer-ation (i.e. care in the community rather than in special institutions). In the final section, I turn to the contemporary analysis of the social and psychological causation of mental illness which I consider from the perspective of Parsons's concept of the sick role, and from the analysis of motives and excuses. Madness is a crucial topic for the sociology of rational action, the emergence of penal institutions and the sociological conceptualization of the relationship between power and knowledge in the formation of modern capitalism. This analysis of madness through the perspective of the sociology of knowledge is a further demonstration therefore that the funda-mental concepts of medicine (health, disease and sickness) cannot be understood without a historical and comparative perspective, since concepts such as madness, unreason and folly are effects of fundamental transformations of systems of discourse and the distri-bution of power.

The history of madness
Following Foucault, we can outline the history of madness in Euro-pean societies in terms of a number of significant events. These are the decline of leprosy and the closing of leprosaria at the end of the Middle Ages; the establishment of the General Hospital of Paris in 1656; the emergence of a moral treatment of the insane by William Tuke and Philippe Pinel; and finally the emergence of a rational architecture of the prison in the nineteenth century as the final solution to the management of insanity. In Foucault's analysis of madness, these transitional events in the emergence of insanity as a scientific category are determined by a number of important changes in the dominant conceptual apparatus of European thought which found their physical expression in the institutional changes which we associate with the growth of the asylum, the hospital and the prison (Cousins and Hussain, 1984).

Part of the intention of Foucault was to provide a systematic critique of what might be called the official history of insanity within the psychiatric profession. This official history of madness conceptualizes the problem of unreason in terms of a series of improvements in knowledge whereby a scientific analysis of insanity eventually emerged as the long-term consequence of the evolution of specific concepts of insanity. This unfolding of scientific knowledge also corresponded with the progressive development of the modern system of treatment which is seen as a liberation of the individual from pre-modern forms of constraint, ignorance and prejudice. In this official perspective, the prejudice and irrationality of the Middle Ages was eventually replaced by science which adopted an increasingly liberal and humane approach to the insane. From this perspective, the liberation of people from the constraints of ignorance is itself simply the history of enlightenment, reason and progress. Improvements in knowledge and understanding were associated with, and to some extent required, improvements in the political status of the insane and their incorporation within the concept of citizenship.

Political repression from the point of view of the official history is always hostile to criticism and therefore liberal forms of individual freedom are the institutional conditions for rational knowledge itself. The treatment of insanity is a prime example of this liberal interpretation of history as the history of freedom and rationality. Even the labels used to describe mental illness are thought to be illustrative of such changes. The notion of 'demonic possession' by evil spirits and the term 'madness' have as a result been gradually replaced by descriptively neutral terms and scientific theories expressed in the notion of mental illness which, it is argued by psychology, do not carry or imply any moral judgement on the behaviour of those labelled as mentally ill. These theoretical changes have gone hand in hand with more liberal forms of therapy.

It is pointed out that in the Middle Ages the insane were often whipped liked naughty children since madness was essentially a form of unreason. For example in 1533, a lunatic who often disturbed religious services, especially at the elevation of the Host, by lifting the skirts of praying women was seized and flogged until the lesson was driven home. While flogging was a common therapy for unreason, the insane were often incarcerated in small cells and by the fourteenth century most towns in Europe had a mad cell where families could request that lunatic relatives be subdued by forceful means. Thus the concept of the 'Toll Haus' was in common use in the middle of the fourteenth century alongside the concepts of the 'Tollkiste' (mad cell) in 1375 at Hamburg and the 'Tollkoben' (mad hut) at Erfurt in 1385. Against these punitive treatments of mad people as naughty, rebellious subjects, the official history of psychiatric treatment attempts to show that modern practices are humane and scientific.

In essence, Foucault's argument is that there is no unity to the concept of madness or insanity and that these concepts do not refer to any 'coherent' form of behaviour. These concepts do not trace the evolution of a unitary phenomenon; by contrast, it is the discourse of insanity within the medical profession itself which creates and constitutes a unity which we then call sane and insane behaviour. In short, scientific concepts are not neutral descriptions of patterns of behaviour, but on the contrary they produce through discursive activity the behaviour which they seek to describe. As a consequence it is impossible to separate out value judgements from social and scientific accounts of illness behaviour. Psychiatry from this perspective simply becomes part of an apparatus of regulation and control which disciplines persons who have been identified as in some sense problematic.

There is therefore a convergence between the critique of insanity by writers like Thomas Szasz and the followers of Foucault. For example, Szasz (1961, 1970 and 1978) argued that psychiatrists were agents of political control of deviant populations and that the concepts of schizophrenia were incoherent and masked the psychiatrists' political activities behind the screen of a bogus science. Szasz compared the treatment of lunatics in contemporary societies to the social response in the seventeenth century to witches who were labelled and ostracised as a deviant sub-group. In both the Soviet Union and the USA, psychiatry has been used to regulate political deviance and to diminish social rights through the subtle but pernicious growth of psychiatric therapy and coercive institutions.

Szasz (1970) argued that in practical terms, despite apparent changes in labels and improvements in therapeutic technique, the basic problem of madness in society had not changed fundamentally. To label somebody as 'insane' is not qualitatively different from labelling them a 'witch', 'heretic' or 'madman'. The labelling is an exercise of social control which restrains the offender and robs him or her of certain basic social rights. Therefore, the ancient mandate of physicians to treat their suffering patients with their consent and for their own benefit becomes problematic where individuals are treated without their own consent and to their detriment. The concepts of insanity and mental illness provide the justification and explanation for medical intervention without the consent of the patient. They provide the rationale for the sane members of society to deal with their insane fellows. The concept of insanity is thus a useful legal device for dealing with troublesome nuisances within the community. For Szasz, the notion of insanity is too frequently used as a convenient legal device for dealing with criminal offenders and, unlike other labels, insanity provides the basis for indefinitely removing the legal status of otherwise free and autonomous citizens. Throughout history notions of witchcraft, vagrancy, antisocial behaviour and irrational behaviour have provided the bases for indeterminate incarceration without due regard to legal processes (Busfield, 1986).

Although Foucault and Szasz adopt very different epistemological and theoretical positions, there is a certain convergence in their approach to the history of madness. For Foucault, to write about madness at all is to make a judgement, that is a judgement from the point of view of reason itself. It is to give reason a privileged position and to involve oneself in a relationship of power. When Foucault speaks of madness, he attempts to do so not from the standpoint of reason. Foucault characteristically provides no definition of madness as a term, because he refuses to perceive it as a constant or fixed reality. Madness as a concept remains both general and vague having a wide usage in the community where it is a non-medical term referring to forms of behaviour which are generally unacceptable (Sheridan, 1980).

Like Szasz, Foucault's view of madness was influenced by political events relating to madness as a social problem; in the French context, Foucault's views were shaped by the political and medical response to the madness of Artaud. Through the development of the theatre of cruelty, Artaud expressed his assault on the conventional values of society and the traditional conception of drama. By rejecting rational language, Artaud attempted to develop a new theatre of drama and expression using an assembly of sounds and preconceptual noises to convey emotion. Artaud, who believed that God was incompetent otherwise the world would be less bizarre, saw the body as the basis of emotion through which life is realized in its complexity and fullness. It was Artaud who developed the notion of a 'body without organs' as the way forward for human beings who wanted to realize their autonomy and perfection (Esslin, 1976). During his life he suffered physically and mentally from what he referred to as his 'mental erosion' and from the late 1930s he spent the remaining part of his life in four mental hospitals. Being subject to electro-convulsive therapy, Artaud became the great focal point for political and social criticism of the psychological establishment and its methods of therapy. It was Artaud who came eventually to influence, not only Foucault's conception of madness as a heroic struggle against society, but also writers like Laing, Deleuze and

Guattari. It was from the Artaud tradition that Foucault adopted and developed the conception of the madman as the hero struggling against the iron cage of rationality in its diverse forms which may be collectively called 'panopticism'.

Foucault starts his historical critique of the western response to insanity with the observation that by the end of the Middle Ages leprosy had ceased to be a major problem for the urban centres of western society. For many centuries, leprosy had defined the boundary of the human, leaving beyond leprosy a great waste land of terror. It is possible to argue that leprosy was one of the earliest forms of moral–religious definitions of the social, and therefore of human membership. We have already seen that physical health was closely associated with the notion of spiritual health and that saving the soul had a basis in the idea of salving the body. The term for leprosy was derived from 'lepra', that is scaly; it was employed to describe a wide range of skin diseases such as eczema, skin cancer and scrofula. Interestingly medieval science and religious thought made little distinction between leprosy and venereal disease. The result was that leprosy was regarded as a disease brought about by moral failure, especially adultery and promiscuity. It was further assumed that leprosy actually expanded sexual desire so that lepers were thought to be particularly debauched.

Leprosy first appeared in England during the seventh century. With its rapid spread, a variety of leprosaria or lazar houses were constructed as places of exclusion. By the thirteenth century, many traditional alms houses were converted into lazar houses. In addition to their institutional seclusion, the Church developed a number of ritual activities for the ritualized exclusion of lepers. For example, lepers were forbidden ordinary social relations with children and strangers, being forced to wear special clothing including the clapper and begging bowl. The Church developed a special ritual called the office at the seclusion of lepers where the leper was pronounced symbolically dead and excluded from social contacts (Brody, 1974).

While leprosy had been the scourge of the Middle Ages, it began to disappear as a major problem between 1450 and 1550. Foucault suggests that vagabonds, vagrants, common criminals and deranged minds were people who came eventually to replace the leper in the European social structure. The old rituals and structures by which lepers had been excluded were now directed towards a new category of deviant, namely that endless crowd of fools. A new institution emerged to cope with these madmen, namely the Ship of Fools. The archaic practices of seclusion and exclusion were replaced by the institution of embarkation. Madmen were now cast adrift on these boats which transported fools along the major canals and riverways of Europe. The symbolism of embarkation is interesting. The rocking of the waves resembled the madness of the human mind, while the rocking movement of the ship was thought to be a primitive therapy bringing relief to troubled minds. In European art and literature from the fifteenth century onwards, madness came to haunt the imagination of European creative literature, replacing death as the main symbol of anxiety and hopelessness.

This imaginative world of the voyage of folly came to an end with the classical production of madness with the growth of the hospital. Embarkation gave way to incarceration in what Foucault calls the great age of confinement. The madman no longer wanders free on the waste lands and moors of the human imagination like the Fool in Shakespeare's play *King Lear*, but rather has to be confined in the centre of social relations within a set of institutions which segregate unreason from reason. As the date for this age of the great confinement, Foucault takes 1656 with the decree that created in Paris the General Hospital. The General Hospital was important because it had in fact nothing to do with a medical concept, being instead a system of order based upon monarchical and bourgeois power. The hospital of the classical age was concerned with correction, punishment and management not with therapy or moral cure. In European society the hospital had one particular and common aim, namely as a response to the economic crisis of the seventeenth and eighteenth centuries, functioning as a form of discipline over the unemployed and the unemployable.

This age of confinement in which the unreasonable and the unemployable were excluded from normal social relations corresponded with a philosophical movement in the work of Descartes to exclude madness from the domain of philosophy (Brown, 1985). Descartes had noted that a rational person could suffer from illusions and be subject to mistakes, but such a person could not be mad. In order to develop a new methodology of rational enquiry for the establishment of a cognitive order, Descartes could admit the possibility of dreams and illusions but was forced to banish madness as a threat to thinking itself. The exclusion of madness in the philosophical works of Descartes corresponds to the institutional confinement of the unreasonable in the hospitals of France.

It is important to emphasize that Foucault notes that in this classical period of confinement the madman was not regarded as sick. The madman was not in need of a therapy but rather of a discipline which would manage the animality which threatened the madman from within and the social structure from without. The madman who enjoyed an animal strength was invulnerable to the dangers of disease. These institutions of internment sought not to cure or to sustain the mad population, but to bring about a discipline of the animality of the insane through a brutal form of punishment. The madman was someone crazed by the fury of the beast whose extraordinary strength had to be broken by the disciplines of correction and penal violence. Madness was connected with unbridled passion and the role of correction was to regulate these animal passions in order to restrain the inmates of these general hospitals. The chain and the whip were the instruments for dealing with persons possessed by animal passion.

In Foucault's re-analysis of the history of madness itself, the great turning point in the modern treatment of madness occurred with the foundation of the Retreat by William Tuke in 1729 at York as an institution for the care of the insane relatives and friends of Quakers (Godlee, 1985). Behind Tuke's moral treatment there lay a new concern for the contagious effects of mental institutions on the general population. In the middle of the eighteenth century, a new fear arose that the sane population would be gradually infected by prison fevers, scurvy and other diseases emerging from houses of internment. Society had to deal not only with the animal passions of the inmates, but with the contagious horrors that spread from these institutions. For example, in 1780 an epidemic spread throughout Paris and was attributed to an infection arising from the General Hospital. Institutions for the insane now had to be purified in order to prevent the spread of fermentations, impurities, vapours and impure air. There was, according to Foucault, a parallel form of thought that inmates required the purification of hygiene alongside the purification of morality. The notion that the mad had to be confined by chains gave way to the idea that madness required moral discipline on an individual basis plus an architectural environment which was conducive to hygiene.

In the moral restraint of the Retreat, Tuke pressed home the argument for individualized treatment where the guardians of the insane appealed to the sensibility of the unreasonable in an atmosphere that emphasized the importance of the family norms and moral guidance. Punishment and incarceration were in this regime to be replaced by education, gentle but firm control, encouragement and instruction. Tuke was highly critical of existing medical treatments of insanity and proposed instead warm baths and human kindness. As an alternative to punishment and incarceration, Tuke proposed classification, watchfulness, vigilance, kindness and cleanliness (Skultans, 1979). The Retreat at York, run under Quaker principles, was not essentially a medical institution but rather a system of humane values with the aim of moral reform.

A similar development was brought about by Pinel (1745–1826) in the *Treatise on Insanity* (1801) which offered a new explanation of mental illness and therapy. By unchaining the inmates of the Bicetre, Pinel became a founder of the modern asylum movement. In removing the mechanical constraints upon the insane, Pinel in a dramatic symbolic gesture opened up the modern era of reform. Pinel proposed that the indulgence of the insane which had characterized previous forms of confinement was not only misguided but detrimental to the insane. As an alternative, he argued for the advantages of continuous employment and occupation. It was labour which provided a form of discipline through regularity and method. To train the animality of the madman, it was necessary to impose a system of regularity of labour (Donnelly, 1983). As a result, Pinel traded upon the metaphor of disease and anarchy, suggesting that just as the politician manages the body politic, so the physician should concern himself with the regulation of the insane through a system of moral constraint and education.

While Tuke and Pinel are regarded as representative of a new humane medicine, Foucault suggests that the new systems of moral constraint were dictated less by humanitarian interests than by concepts of a new regime of authority. According to Foucault, Tuke replaced the old system of fear of physical constraint and enforced idleness by a new regime of personal conscience and hard work. Tuke generated a conception of the asylum where the importance of terror was replaced by the anxiety of individualized responsibility. Fear no longer regulated the individual and physical punishment was replaced by the anxieties of conscience. The asylum no longer punished the individual madman but it organized guilt in the interests of order. Tuke did not remove social control; rather he made social control more subtle, more indirect, more efficient and more moral by removing the exterior constraints of physical violence. According to Foucault, Pinel, while removing the physical chains upon the insane, nevertheless imposed an uncompromising system of psychiatric coercion upon lunatic inmates. While removing chains and assaults on mental patients he imposed upon them a new system of social coercion which did not remove the political constraints upon the insane. Both Tuke and Pinel brought about a moral treatment of insanity which was more efficient and economic than the old system of physical coercion.

While the houses of internment in the traditional system had concentrated on the attempt to make the insane productive and useful, the new moral prisons of the era of reform were focused more on the question of the moral transformation of inmates by new systems of discipline and architecture. In order to achieve a reform of inmates a system of dietary management was proposed to control the passions of inmates and this dietary management was associated with a new principle of solitary imprisonment and religious instruction. In this organization of moral management, the dungeon was to be replaced by the cell. The emphasis on moral reform, as we have seen, was brought about by a set of anxieties about gaol fever. The era of prison reform was dominated by the search for a form of architecture which would protect the general population from infectious diseases whilst also regulating the inmates in terms of a discourse of moral reformist individualism.

An emphasis was given to the role of ventilation as a system for the control of gaol fever but this conceptualization of ventilation was also closely allied with a notion of moral hygiene. There was a parallel between the spread of vice and the spread of contagious disease. The reform of prisons came eventually to combine a transformation of architecture, a re-analysis of moral constraint and a new theory of crime and penology. That is,

> security required enclosure; salubrity required exposure and fragment-ation; reformation required a compartmentalization. In a reformed prison all these needs had to be reconciled. (Evans, 1982:142–143)

Ventilation was seen to be a crucial feature in the medical struggle against filth and disease where a new emphasis was given to the scientific management of water supply and drainage. The reformation of prisoners by moral coercion required a system of standard uniforms, an organization of cells which emphasized solitary confinement, a new emphasis on regulation and passivity, combined with moral training and religious reform. Bentham's utilitarian philosophy provided the philosophical overview for this system of restraint and penal regulation. It was on the basis of this utilitarian philosophy that Foucault developed the idea of the panoptic system of regulation which in an architectural discourse resulted in a new philosophy of physical constraint for the prisoner which combined hygiene, solitary confinement and moral development. This system of architectural restraint eventually expanded from its English location to become the dominant paradigm for penal control in the colonies.

Throughout the nineteenth century in the UK there was an extensive expansion of asylums for the treatment of the insane and correspondingly a progressive increase in the number of lunatics in the population (Scull, 1979). The problems of lunacy were closely related to the problem of pauperism, since approximately three quarters of the insane came under the Poor Law Authorities and the increase in the lunatic population occurred primarily among the paupers, not among private patients. In England in 1744 the Vagrancy Act recognized that those suffering from mental disorders required treatment. By the beginning of the nineteenth century, there was increasing disquiet concerning the amount of pauper lunacy in the population. The campaign to improve the public management of insanity was directed by Christian evangelicals and Benthamite utilitarians. A number of select committees of the House of Commons in the early part of the nineteenth century enquired into the conditions of the lunatic population and the management of madhouses. The outcome of these political and religious movements was a steady increase in the number of asylums which were built in a mood of utilitarian optimism. Incarceration and restraint could cure unruly passions when these were properly managed under a system of panoptic control. Bentham's deontology had suggested that through public surveillance the lunatic could be cured. However, these psychological theories of utilitarianism were faced with the problem that the lunatic population increased with the increase of asylums. Successful cures were rare and there appeared to be no limit to the size of the insane population (Skultans, 1979; Scull, 1977; Donnelly, 1983). The highest recovery rate for admissions was 42 percent recorded in 1885 and the lowest was 37 percent in 1873. As Table 1 demonstrates, there was an increase in the number of asylums throughout the nineteenth century which corresponded to an increasing size of the insane population (Jones, 1965).

TABLE 1
County asylums in England and Wales

	Asylums	Patients	Average no. patients
1827	9	1046	116
1850	24	7140	297
1860	41	15845	386
1870	50	27109	542
1900	77	77004	961

Sources: Donnelly, 1983:164; Jones, 1965:357; Skultans, 1979:122.

It appeared to be the case that asylums had become increasingly a dumping ground for the great mass of physical and mental wrecks who formed the debris of nineteenth-century industrial capitalism. With the increasing cost of asylums and with mounting evidence that they were not effective in curing the mentally ill, social reformers began to push for alternative systems of treatment and began to argue the case for community care.

A similar history of asylum development took place in the USA in the nineteenth century. In the USA, attitudes towards the insane were influenced by religious reformists such as Dorothea Dicks (1802–1887) and by Social Darwinism which regarded insanity as hereditary and was committed to the notion of the survival of the fittest (Hofstadter, 1955). Primarily through the influence of reformers like Dicks, forty-eight public asylums were opened in the USA by 1861 (Mumford, 1983). The state hospitals became increasingly crowded and were utilized as large dumping grounds for the poor insane. The patients became socially isolated and cut off from relatives and other forms of social support. The result was that recovery rates were very low and patients became dependent upon the institutional support of these mental institutions. The growing importance and use of mental asylums was associated with the decline of the family as a caring unit, the increasing age of the population and the prevalence of individualistic norms which did not encourage the establishment of a social policy towards the insane. Research in the USA has shown a close correlation between senility and insanity (Grob, 1977). In New York State for example, 18 percent of all first admissions to mental asylums in 1920 were associated with senility and this had increased to 31 percent by 1940. The increasing trend in mental hospitalization was also associated with periods of economic downturn. During periods of recession, the role of poverty was important in the development and prevalence of mental illness (Mechanic, 1968).

Mental illness in modern society
In the industrial societies of Europe and the USA, mass warfare has played an important part in drawing attention to the plight of the insane. For example, in the USA between 1942 and 1945 1,875,000 of the 15,000,000 men examined for military service were rejected because of psychiatric disorders. A large proportion of men discharged from the armed forces left on grounds of neuropsychiatric disturbance (Felix, 1967). In the UK similarly, the policy of mass conscription into the army exposed high levels of physical and mental illness in the community and emphasized the need for a new policy (Marshall, 1985; Titmuss, 1963; Trowler, 1984). The consequence was a growing awareness of the scale and complexity of the problem of mental illness in the community. In the USA by 1955 there were approximately 560,000 mental patients in state and county long-term care hospitals with approximately 150,000 first-time inmates admitted each year and 60,000 former patients exhibiting recidivism. Of course, there is also the problem of untreated

mental disorder and general surveys of the population have suggested that approximately one-fifth to one-quarter of the American population has exhibited significant psychiatric symptoms and that less than one-fifth of the general population is actually free of such symptoms (Clausen, 1979).

Similar prevalence rates are found in other societies. For example, in Australia it was found that about $1^1/_2$ percent of the population have some serious mental illness problem and an additional 18–23 percent experience some significant psychological disorder. Almost 10 percent of all general practitioners' contacts in the mid 1970s were for mental disorders and in 1979 a survey suggested that 25 percent of all general-practitioner contacts were for psychological rather than physical illness. One in three of all patients presenting at an out-patient clinic for the first time was for a primary psychiatric disorder (Davies, 1966). Finally, one in every four beds in Australian hospitals was for a mental patient (Burrows, 1984).

While public attitudes towards the existence of mental illness have been changing, there has also been a significant shift in the treatment of the mentally ill. Before the 1960s, the mental patient was typically treated in a large, bureaucratic and hierarchical institution; there is now a significant tendency to treat the mentally ill in a community-care programme, an out-patient institution, a system of shelter care or in a general voluntary hospital (Mechanic, 1968; Mumford, 1983). The social causes behind this change of policy are complex. They include a wider interest in Freudian psychotherapy, especially among the middle class who came to reject the traditional 'warehouse approach' to the mentally disabled and disturbed. Secondly, there was a strong anti-psychiatry movement associated with the work of Szasz, Goffman and others which presented a critique of the asylum, drawing attention to the negative effects of long-term incarceration and the low rates of recovery. Thirdly, there were improvements in antipsychotic drugs which meant that patients could be treated outside the traditional asylum. In the UK, Cooper (1968) and Laing (1960) had an important impact on attitudes towards psychiatry and mental institutions in the growing radical critique of the medical model in relation to mental illness (Ingleby, 1980). In Italy, the approach to mental illness especially with respect to the use of mental hospitals was challenged by radical thinkers like Basaglia (1967) who developed the notion of the 'negative institution' as a description of psychiatric care (Basaglia, 1967; Scheper-Hughes and Lovell, 1986). There were, for a variety of ideological and economic reasons, strong pressures towards a policy of de-institutionalization and decarceration as procedures for the management of the mentally ill (Scull, 1977 and 1979).

The result has been that, while rates of first admission continue to rise, the number of people who are resident in mental hospitals has declined significantly in the majority of industrial western societies and the length of residence has also declined. For example, the resident population in state and county mental hospitals in the USA between 1950 and 1974 has declined by approximately 50 percent (Table 2).

TABLE 2
Resident population of state and county mental hospitals in the USA
1950–1974

Year	Resident population
1950	512,500
1954	554,000
1958	545,200
1962	515,600
1966	453,100
1970	339,000
1974	215,600

Source: Scull, 1977:68

Similarly in England and Wales between 1951 and 1970 the resident population in mental hospitals declined from 143,200 to 103,300 in 1970 (Table 3).

TABLE 3
Resident population of mental hospitals in England
and Wales, 1951–1970

Year	Resident population
1951	143,200
1954	148,100
1958	142,800
1962	133,800
1968	116,400
1970	103,300

Source: Scull, 1977:70

These significant reductions in the number of long-term resident mental patients have been brought about by a uniform policy of de-institutionalization which involves the provision of alternative forms of treatment within the community, the release of institutionalized patients who have been provided with adequate preparation for a change in their social status and the establishment of community support systems for these de-institutionalized patients. The problem with the process of de-institutionalization is, however, that decarceration is often sought in order to achieve economic benefits rather than to provide benefits for patients. In short, patients are being dumped on the wider community without adequate systems of support and preparation for their return to normal community relations. The consequence of this programme of de-institutionalization in societies like the USA, the UK and Australia has been the emergence of the so-called revolving door syndrome, where patients are shunted backwards and forwards between the institution and the community, since they cannot find an adequate location within the wider society. De-institutionalization without adequate community support is unlikely to be an adequate solution to the health problems of the mentally ill.

Patients who become institutionalized tend in any case to be characterized by the absence of strong ties within the wider community, family structure or work; they are typically vulnerable because of their age, their lack of economic resources and their poor educational background (Wing, 1967). De-institutionalization, far from being a humane and progressive measure, may well in fact be a cynical economic strategy for reducing health-costs under the ideological umbrella of anti-psychiatry. Modern psychiatry is caught in a dilemma where it is clear that long-term institutionalization of psychiatric patients produces dependency, but in the absence of adequate community facilities there is little alternative to these institutions. Adequate community care requires not just a new collection of clinical skills, but also a new range of managerial techniques involving multidisciplinary teams. In addition, these new systems of community care call into question the professional role of the psychiatrists who may be inclined to argue the case for conventional forms of therapy, since they may lose professional control over 'mental illness' within the community. The development of alternative systems of treatment is therefore closely related to the nature of the definition and explanation of mental illness. We may consequently turn to the sociological explanation of mental illness and the critique of the concept of insanity.

Labelling theory
In the sociology of mental health, the dominant paradigm for the explanation of mental illness has been labelling theory which is also referred to as 'social reaction theory' as originally formulated by Lemert (1951) and Becker (1963). Medical sociology came to adopt

a range of models which had been designed initially for the explanation of deviance, because medical sociology following Parsons had
approached sickness as a form of social deviance; this theoretical
interpenetration was perfectly appropriate. However, we should
perceive the labelling theory of deviance in the specific context of
post-war American society with its emphasis on impression management, social reputation, consumerism and the lifestyle of organization man. The success of Goffman's analysis of stigma (1964) may
be regarded as an effect of a society based upon the reputational
self. This post-war culture might be suitably summarized in the
sociological approach of Cooley (1902) who developed the theory of
the 'looking-glass self'. The direct implication of the symbolic interactionist perspective is that people become deviant or sick or
mentally ill when they cease to receive positive definitions of themselves from their primary social groups.

Labelling theory contains three central propositions. The first is
that deviant behaviour has no consistent unitary content or essence;
it is merely behaviour which is labelled as deviant by powerful,
influential or significant social groups which are important in
shaping public opinion. Secondly, people who are labelled as deviant suffer stigmatization which excludes them from normal interactions and thus converts their behaviour into a distinctive career of
deviance. Thirdly, behaviour which is stigmatized by social labelling
becomes amplified because alternative lifestyles and careers are no
longer available for the deviant. The paradox is that social intervention by agents of social control produces deviance and amplifies it.

The labelling perspective as applied to mental illness can be
clearly illustrated in the work of Scheff (1966). He argued that all
societies have labels for describing and designating major violations
of social norms; these designations involve concepts of sin, crime,
deviance and bad manners. In addition to these categories, there is
a sort of residue of definitions which refer to a diverse range of
violations for which the culture provides no specific or explicit label.
These vague and general violations of social norms are lumped
together for the convenience of society as a whole. Historically,
these vague and non-explicit social labels included witchcraft,
demon possession and, in contemporary society, the concept of
mental illness. Deviations from everyday, taken-for-granted norms
are identified as symptoms of mental illness and those persons
transgressing these norms are identified as social offenders who
become labelled as mentally ill; subsequently they are treated as
insane.

One important illustration of Scheff's argument would be the
experiment undertaken by Rosenhan (1973). In this study, nine

subjects (mostly professional people and academics) behaved as pseudo-patients by presenting themselves at the admission office of a hospital complaining of hearing voices. On entry they ceased to simulate any symptoms of abnormality and told the psychiatric staff that they felt well and did not need treatment. Eight of these subjects were diagnosed subsequently as schizophrenic and one as manic-depressive. They were not detected by the staff as pseudo-patients, although a few inmates challenged them as merely pretending to be insane. The length of hospitalization for this group was between one and seven weeks, with an average stay of nineteen days. During this experience, these pseudo-patients experienced the usual forms of stereotyping which are directed at the insane when staff talked over them, ignored their requests or treated them as incompetent and insane. These nine subjects received two thousand, one hundred tablets during their stay, although they managed to flush the majority of these down the toilet. While this study can be criticized on ethical grounds (Bulmer, 1982), the experiment showed that labelling is a powerful force in social relations and that, since asylums are insane places, people who enter them cannot be sane.

Labelling theory was an important critique of the medical model of mental illness as a disease with organic, biochemical aetiology. It drew attention to the fact that health and illness are social concepts which necessarily imply value judgements (Lewis, 1953). However, in recent years labelling theory has been subject to extensive criticism. For example, Morgan (1975) has pointed out that the concept of mental illness differs in one significant way from the concept of deviance. Deviant and criminal activities are initially regarded as motivated and wilful, being the activities of a rational agent with purpose and intention. In the case of infractions of legal norms, the individual offender is held to be responsible for their activities; this involves the notion that a criminal could have always behaved otherwise. However, the concept of insanity is entirely different, since it normally rules out the idea of responsibility. The mental illness label excuses the individual by transforming his deviant social activity into a specific disease. Morgan argues therefore, that the imputation of an illness label is most likely to occur when a deviant action cannot be intelligently understood or explained as the outcome of rational purposeful activity. The use of the label of insanity is thus most likely to occur as a label of last resort, when alternative definitions of behaviour have failed to account for this particular form of deviance.

Medical labels represent a peculiar form of the vocabulary of motives, namely they act as a system of excuse which rules out moral responsibility. The disease model of illness in the case of mental illness explains unacceptable social deviation in terms of a set of motives, which do not blame the victim on moral grounds, since the individual is not held responsible for their actions. As a sick role, mental illness is the final form of excuse in which the individual's behaviour is seen to be determined by causes over which they have no control. This label therefore permits the use of extensive forms of intervention in the personal autonomy of the individual, including chemotherapy and electro-convulsive therapy.

The conventional labelling approach to mental illness can also be criticized, because it does not distinguish between different forms of social deviance. That is, the theory is too general in failing to distinguish between different categories of mental illness. For example, in psychological theories the *Diagnostic Statistical Manual III* distinguishes between psychoses (such as a loss of contact with reality typically described as schizophrenia), neuroses (such as an exaggerated sense of reality illustrated by the range of phobias), behavioural disorders (such as various forms of antisocial behaviour which might be illustrated by alcoholism) and finally organic malfunctioning (such as brain damage or senile dementia). Labelling theory would not attempt to distinguish between these forms of mental disorder, but it seems reasonable to believe that at least some forms of malfunctioning might be caused by physical decline brought about by aging. Dementia may well be complicated by labelling and stereotyping, but it would be unreasonable to argue that dementia is necessarily caused by labelling. If we are prepared to accept the idea that there are different types of mental illness and that the DSM III classification is an appropriate characterization of types of illness, then labelling theory would be relevant to behavioural disorders as an explanation, but not to organic malfunctioning. The increase in mental illness in the advanced industrial societies is at least partly explicable in terms of the aging of the population and therefore labelling theory might not be relevant as an explanation of all forms of mental illness.

There are a number of other problems with labelling theory. For example, if you have the notion of amplification as an explanation of the growth of deviance, you logically require a notion of 'de-amplification', since the alternative is a model of exponential explosions of deviance (Ditton, 1979). One consequence of these criticisms is that the labelling theory of mental illness as deviance has ceased to be the dominant paradigm in medical sociology (Goldstein, 1979; Gove, 1970; Mangen, 1982).

In contemporary explanations of mental illness, we find theoretical frameworks which have the following characteristics. First, there is a far wider plurality of models for the explanation of mental illness and a greater interest in multicausal epidemiological models. For example, Mangen (1982) and Mechanic (1968) suggest that a variety of perspectives have sociological merit as explanatory schema and that it is premature, indeed inadequate, to suggest that a single causal model could be valuable in the explanation of a complex phenomenon like mental health. Secondly, and as a consequence, there is a greater awareness of the diversity and complexity of mental health conditions. Some forms of mental illness in contemporary society are a consequence of the aging of the population and some forms of mental disturbance will be associated with senility. By contrast, certain behaviour disorders like alcoholism and sexual perversion would require a very different perspective, namely a sociological approach rather than an organic medical one. Thirdly, there is a greater awareness of the social consequences of medical categories. For example, if one regards mental illness from the perspective of a disease model, then one absolves the sufferer from all responsibility for their mental condition. Within contemporary social theory especially in the area of social policy formation, there is an awareness that the disease model in the judicial process may prevent the successful prosecution of criminals or at least direct attention away from the victim. However, there is no real consensus over the nature of responsibility in criminal law and the conditions for diminished responsibility are widely disputed (Smith, 1986). In contemporary social theory, there appears to be a greater emphasis on victimology. There has been as a consequence a return to a range of traditional concerns with the nature of rational action, motivation and intention.

The life-events model
While there is increasing scepticism about the possibility of formulating a general theory of the character and prevalence of mental illness, one model which has drawn considerable support is the notion that mental illness might be explained epidemiologically within a framework which places particular emphasis on the notion of social stress. Adopting the perspective of Dewey, Cooley and Mead, the original framework for the analysis of stress or 'life change' in relation to mental and physical illness was developed by Meyer (Lief, 1948). Within the framework of the symbolic interactionist approach which followed from the social behaviourism of Mead, Meyer argued that when people become separated from their primary social community which provides supportive, positive symbols and notions of self worth, they are exposed increasingly to

social stress which produces a variety of disorders (Holmes and Masuda, 1974). In terms of the perspective developed in this book, it has been argued that mental and physical illness are related to the problem of the definition of social membership in terms of power and ritual, particularly rituals of inclusion and exclusion. The sick role is a form of deviation from the boundaries of normal society and we can define therapy sociologically as a set of practices designed to restore a certain form of normality.

Unlike labelling theory, however, the social-stress approach attempts to offer a causal model of the primary features of mental illness. Sometimes these models are combined with genetic inheritance assumptions in which it is the social context and stress which act as the setting and the trigger which release an episode of mental illness. The main difficulties with this model have been to provide an adequate definition of stress, to provide precise measurements of stress and to resolve the problem of the subjective and objective nature of stressful events. These approaches to the sociology of stress normally accept a version of the social readjustment rating scale (SRRS) which was developed by Holmes and Rahe (1967). In the SRRS model, it is not a single event in the life of an individual which brings about life stress, but a combination of events and circumstances which accumulate into a total stressful situation. The individual life events are rated on a scale of 1–100 and the accumulated stress in an individual's life can be quantified by the accumulation of stresses. These quantifications of stress have to be based upon the perceived degree of seriousness and the subjective evaluation of the level of undesirability.

This model is useful in explaining the greater psychiatric risk experienced by different social groups, classes and social strata. Differences in the rates of mental illness experienced by different social groups and classes are directly associated with the differential prevalence of stressful life events and the vulnerability factors which increase the likelihood of stress. We can argue therefore that the level of adversity, the presence of stressful events, social vulnerability and individual management of stress are important features of this life-events framework. The notions of social stress and vulnerability are combined with an emphasis on the significance of social support in the lives of individuals. Social support is defined as:

> support accessible to an individual through social ties to other individuals, groups, and the larger community. The general assumption is that social support is negatively related to illness. The greater the social support that an individual receives, in the form of closer relations with

family members, kin, friends, acquaintances, co-workers, and the larger
community, the less likely that the individual would experience illness.
(Lin et al., 1979:109)

These social supports act as a form of buffer against the threatening
life events which push the individual towards social, physical and
mental disorder.

The extent of an individual's social network is consequently
important in protecting the individual from external threat and
stress. The range of social relations available to an individual provides a mechanism whereby the burden of emotional stress can be
relieved and the objective sources of stress managed in a collective
fashion. This pull of social relations has been referred to as the fund
of sociability which is composed of intimacy, the network of common concerns, the ability to develop supportive social relations, the
confirmation of one's own prestige and the feeling of alliance with
others who provide a supportive base (Weiss, 1976). The dynamics
of inclusion and exclusion between social groups and the individual
may be an important feature in the development of a paranoid
personality (Lemert, 1962).

This general approach to stress, social esteem and mental illness
has proved useful in the study of social classes and mental illness
where it is evident that the higher the social class of a person the
greater the resources available for the control and management of
stressful circumstances. The model has also proved significant in the
analysis of gender and mental illness. For example, it has been
found that married women exhibit far higher rates of mental illness
than single, widowed or divorced women (Gove, 1972). An
explanation for this difference is that the married woman is often
confined within the restricted arena of the household where her
self-image and social prestige are diminished in relation to the
working woman. The housebound woman does not always have a
well structured social environment and the role expectations of the
unemployed woman are vague and contradictory. In a further
study, Gove and Tudor (1973) confirmed the argument that married, housebound women are more likely to experience mental
illness than unmarried women. In addition, married women are
more likely to have a problem of mental illness than married men.
However, the results of these enquiries were quite the reverse for
unmarried persons. Furthermore,

men were more likely than women to be mentally ill, for within each of
the unmarried statuses more studies found men to have the higher rates
of mental illness. (Gove and Tudor, 1973:828)

In short, marriage is more advantageous for men in minimizing stress than it is for women, so that suicide is far more prevalent for single than for married men. The results of sociological research (Gove and Geerken, 1977) show that the most exposed social role in modern society is that of the unemployed housewife who has the most vulnerable status from the point of view of mental illness. These findings are somewhat complicated by the fact that doctors and psychiatrists are more likely to regard women than men as prone to mental disorders. There may be an element of bias in the selection of women for the role of the mentally ill person (Clarke, 1983). Although there may well be a bias in the selection of women the social survey research on mental illness shows that undiagnosed mental disorder in unemployed housewives is far higher than for any other social group.

Research in Australia (Western, 1983), the UK (Graham, 1984) and the USA (Srole, 1975) indicates that women are twice as likely to suffer from depressive psychoses as men. The explanation of depression in women has been fully explored by Brown and his colleagues in a number of studies (Brown and Birley, 1968; Brown and Harris, 1978). Brown has produced a model for the explanation of depression as a process which combines economic, social and psychological factors. The research on depressed women in the UK has shown that low social class is important in providing a background social factor for depression in which working-class women have few social and economic resources to combat the stress in their lives. Secondly, there are a number of vulnerability factors which further threaten the working-class woman with a period of depression; in particular, unemployment and the presence of preschool children in the home will predispose the woman to stressful experiences. Thirdly, Brown considers a number of cognitive sets which are conducive to depression, namely hopelessness, grief and low self-esteem. Where these factors are all present, a woman is likely to experience depression unless there is a social buffer (such as a close friend) to minimize the impact of these structural and psychological forces. Where there is no buffer and a woman finds herself experiencing extreme social isolation, then depressive psychoses are likely to develop. While Brown draws upon the life-events model, his research was also shaped in a more general way by Durkheim's study (1951) on suicide which was first published in 1897, since one explanation for both depression and suicide is the absence of social integration in supportive groups which bring about a regulation of the individual but also contribute to their sense of self-esteem. A number of studies have attempted to follow Durkheim's original theoretical perspective by demonstrating that suicide rates vary directly with the presence of social isolation (Gibbs and Martin,

1964; Hassan, 1983). The sociology of suicide is, however, a topic which is still surrounded by controversy (Atkinson, 1978).

Conclusion

Following Foucault, we can argue that all human societies are characterized by a certain dynamic of exclusion which is defined by a certain set of practices and beliefs. These practices are the embodiments of social power as expressed through certain dominant discourses. The boundaries of society and reason are patrolled by social elites who enjoy the privileges of power and the authority of the symbols of knowledge. The precise character of these practices is variable and the definitions of social membership may take a religious, a moral, or a legal form. We have seen in this chapter that madness and unreasonableness have constituted a threat to the social stability of the inner core of the social group. From this perspective, madness has no essential or permanent characteristic, but is constituted by certain practices and discursive formations. Madness may well be defined by economic criteria such as pauperism and vagrancy; it may be as equally defined by medical–moral concepts, such as furiousness resulting from unbridled passions. In contemporary society, although apparently scientific concepts of insanity are increasingly dominant, these concepts still embody a moral and legal discourse. The research of Szasz has in particular drawn attention to the function of the label of insanity in circumnavigating the judicial process by robbing individuals of their political rights. This model of madness which we find in Foucault in fact bears a close resemblance to aspects of Durkheim's sociology of moral facts. Madness is a category which defines the common consciousness of the community and this common consciousness is further categorized and defined by ritual processes.

Insanity is not therefore simply a disease according to a medical model, but on the contrary a form of social behaviour which is regarded as problematic and undesirable. Labelling theory has drawn attention to the importance of stigmatization and exclusion in the effective deployment of medical labels. However, madness is not regarded as wilful and the attribution of the label is one of last resort. Mental illness in this respect is a peculiar form of the sick role, since the individual is now held to be incapable of significantly helping themselves back into a normal community. Insanity is a sick role which removes and subordinates any notion of moral responsibility and voluntariness. Within the vocabulary of excuses for untoward behaviour, mental illness legitimizes extreme forms of social deviance, but often at the cost of personal freedom. We have also seen that in the recent treatment of mental illness, there has been a distinctive movement towards de-institutionalization which suggests that the best method of treatment is to reintegrate the isolated and stigmatized person back into the community. Within a period of economic recession, these new methods of treatment may well be ineffectual without adequate support and community backing for the mentally disturbed.

Attitudes towards mental illness and therapy are necessarily shaped and influenced by the prevailing political climate. In particular, attitudes towards insanity will depend a great deal on whether the state and the medical establishment are regarded as agents of social control, regulating deviance under the ideology of psychiatric help, or whether the state is seen to be the great protector of vulnerable and isolated individuals in a social system where the traditional supports of the family and the community are in many industrial societies in a stage of rapid decline and collapse. The dynamics of social inclusion and exclusion will be at least partly determined by the political culture of a community.

Madness is also an important feature of the total relationships between men and women, where women are the producers of men, who define the boundaries between culture and nature. The history of madness is closely connected with the changing power relationships between the sexes, since the political culture of a community will depend in part on the authority of husbands over wives as the parallel of the power of kings over their people. Medical sociology therefore has to consider the whole question of patriarchal authority in relationship to the prevalence of madness and physical diseases.

5
Women's complaints: patriarchy and illness

Introduction

From the perspective of historical sociology, the construction of categories of disease and deviance appears to be closely related to the problem of the definition of social membership. We can argue that the social struggle over deviance and disease is a political conflict over the distribution of power. These boundaries of society, both cultural and physical, are managed and policed by certain elite groups within the community whose management of knowledge and power gives them a controlling surveillance over the construction and distribution of resources. We can quite legitimately treat health and illness as resources, alongside power, wealth and prestige. Since to be healthy is to be saved, to be sick and deviant is to depart from the central cultural apparatus of society or to deviate from its routine practices. Disease is simultaneously the cause of certain forms of alienation from normal patterns of life and in some circumstances its consequence. In previous chapters the importance of symbol and metaphor in disease categories has been emphasized. For example, leprosy in medieval society was regarded as the effect of sexual promiscuity; the social response to leprosy was exclusion through the use of certain religious rituals which separated the patterns of social interaction between the leper and the normal community. This approach to the historical problem of disease can also be illustrated by reference to the categories of madness, epilepsy and venereal disease.

If we approach disease as a cultural definition of social exclusion, then it follows that disease and illness have no essential core which defines them continuously over time. Foucault in particular has drawn attention to the importance of discontinuities in the discourse on disease as opposed to the conventional perception of disease categories having consistent and continuous histories. Under some circumstances, disease is defined in terms of a collection of undifferentiated categories which in a modern society we would recognize as legal, religious or moral frameworks. In Christian Europe, disease was perceived within the framework of a moral–theological perspective and the therapy for disease was within a Christian framework. The manner in which disease is conceptualized will be an effect of the prevailing cultural system and the power structure associated with dominant discourses. The way in which we are sick is culturally defined. However, if disease has one important thematic unity, it is that disease represents a form of social deviance and the enduring merit of Parsons's concept of the sick role was precisely to identify sickness as deviance from the expectations of normal social intercourse.

We can imagine pre-modern human societies as precarious social systems which were caught between the threat of epidemic disease and food shortages, where a balance of population was an essential prerequisite for survival. However, these pestilential invasions were in the medieval imagination simultaneously physical and metaphorical. The dominant metaphor of social, political and medical disturbance has been that of the body and its equilibrium. The threat of an epidemic for the social body was conceptualized within the framework of disturbances to the body politic; there was a close parallel between the notion of conflict within the human body from a medical perspective and the larger political vision of authority, legitimacy and power for the society as a whole. Unschuld (1985) has shown how in China political disruptions of the imperial structure resulted in medical systems and concepts which emphasized personal responsibility for social stability. Within Chinese society, the idea of disease as an invasion was embodied in the use of spears and sharp instruments to frighten away magical or demonic invasions of Chinese society. It was the use of these spears which gave rise eventually to the use of acupuncture as a form of individual medical therapy. Since under conditions of Oriental despotism China developed a centralized political system for the control of grain supplies, the human body came to be conceptualized as a large irrigation system where the flow of goods (through the blood stream) could be stimulated by the technique of acupuncture.

In historical terms, religious systems have therefore played an important part in the definition, construction and management of human disease and deviance. Through a variety of rituals of inclusion and exclusion, religious systems have provided the practices by which individual members can be ejected from the community and re-incorporated back into society through a system of retribution and forgiveness. In classical Rome, the notion of 'prodigia' was important in understanding the contract between the gods and human society ('Pax Deorum'). These prodigia were signs which pointed to the disruption of the pact as Roman society was visited by unnatural and natural disasters. The authorities through their priests responded by appropriate measures ('remedia') to restore the social balance.

Within these religious systems, the restoration of the individual to society was brought about by an intensification of social interaction and exchange. While these therapeutic systems were dominant in pre-modern societies, it is possible to discover examples within contemporary cultures which have the same social dynamic, trading upon the same range of metaphors. Therapeutic communities and religious cults concerned with personal stability continue to be important even in contemporary secular societies. In a study of spiritualist groups in contemporary Britain, Skultans (1974:44) concluded:

> spiritualism can therefore be seen as a ritual of reconciliation. The supportive and therapeutic nature of the groups is underlined by the fact that there is little, if any, interaction between the members of a spiritualist group outside the group.

In order to claim that religious groups have a therapeutic function especially for marginal groups and for powerless individuals, we do not have to adopt entirely a functionalist view of religion. While religion may address itself to certain problems of sickness and disease, there is also a sense in which religion generates certain problems of a medical character through the mechanism of guilt. By establishing a normative structure, religion often forces the individual into a position of necessary deviance given the high expectation of conformity to norms. There is in the sociology of religion considerable evidence that religion leads to compulsive behaviour and, in extreme circumstances, we can identify 'the obsessive–compulsive scrupulosity syndrome' (Corcoran, 1957). This syndrome gives an obsessive significance to cleanliness, order, detailed control and adherence to discipline. The syndrome is in particular concerned with the management of bodily order.

In attempting to provide this sociological perspective on the historical and cultural problem of disease and deviance, I have given a special prominence to the symbolic parallel between the body and society. The body is prominent in medical discourse not for the obvious reason that we can conceptualize disease as a malfunction of the physical organism, but because the body hovers ambiguously between the world of nature and the world of moral facts. Our bodies are simultaneously the natural environment in which we, as moral agents, operate, but it is also the case that my moral condition depends upon my management of the body as a personal responsibility. However, the implicit division between the mind and the body in this metaphor is itself culturally specific, since from a philosophical point of view one can argue that the concept of embodiment more adequately expresses the conjunction of being and consciousness in human life (Levin, 1985; Turner, 1984).

This interpretation of body in relation to society depends to a considerable extent on the anthropological theories of Douglas. Human cultures can be conceptualized in terms of dichotomy between purity and danger, in which the secretions of the body are held to be morally and religiously threatening to the stability of the social community and the natural environment (Douglas, 1970, 1973). For Douglas, the social functions of symbols are closely related to the moral management of human bodies and their reproduction:

> the human body is common to us all. Only our social condition varies. The symbols based on the human body are used to express different social experience. (Douglas 1970:vii)

The training of children in the management of their bodies is the crucial process by which they are brought into the wider social structure. Although culture can be mobilized to regulate our physical existence, the body (its functions and its secretions) constantly threatens the social order by irregularity and resistance to symbolic management (Koepping, 1985). One problem with disease is that it threatens the moral management of our bodies by robbing us of voluntary control and organization. As a result, we need the social support of a medical regimen and therapeutic intervention.

Women's bodies — between nature and culture

Throughout human history women's bodies have been treated as especially threatening to the moral and social stability of society (Suleiman, 1986). In particular, female sexuality has been the target of religious and magical practices which have been mobilized to restrain women and to provide a surveillance of female reproductive capacity. Magical systems, mythology and shamanism were typically preoccupied with the problems of taboo and pollution surrounding the female menstrual cycle. For example, the Polar Eskimos relied upon their shamans to regulate the dangerous forces of nature, the dead and women. The deviant behaviour of one member of the tribal community could by breaking a powerful taboo threaten the hunting activity of the whole group. The correct control of menstrual blood was a significant feature of this moral regulation. A woman who during menstruation broke one of the norms or prescriptions of the group would dangerously undermine the hunting activity of the men. If hunting proved to be unsuccessful, the group would collect together and, through a seance, bring about a confession of sins committed by the deviant woman. Shamanism was thus an important institution for the regulation of women and the maintenance of social order (Eliade, 1964; Lewis, 1971).

Of course the regulation of female sexuality was not an issue peculiar to primitive religious systems. The literature on witchcraft and demonology in European societies has drawn attention to the special relationship between witchcraft crazes and the status of women in traditional societies (Thomas, 1971; Trevor-Roper, 1967). From the fourteenth century, the Church began to make a more significant difference between magic and witchcraft, regarding the latter as essentially a contract between witches and Satan who provided the witch with magical strength. Within this Catholic framework, witchcraft was regarded as a false or inferior religion and various inquisitions or campaigns were mounted against these sects of witches in Europe. Before 1700, approximately 200,000 people had been executed in continental Europe as a consequence of witchcraft crazes. Various theories were developed in this period by which witches could be identified and subdued. The campaign against witches and heretics produced a rich crop of suspects and victims, and the consequence was to expose a vast undercurrent of subterranean oppositional religion throughout Europe (Le Roy Ladurie, 1980).

Women were closely associated with witchcraft, because it was argued that they were particularly susceptible to the sexual advances of the devil. This relationship between women and witchcraft was reinforced rather than diminished by the Protestant Reformation which had the consequence of exposing women more significantly and extensively to witchcraft accusations. To some extent because of its individualism, Protestantism removed much of the protective screen of magical practice which had created the wall to surround the medieval lay person from evil and witchcraft. In their review of the evidence Ehrenreich and English (1972:26) conclude that three central accusations developed during the history of witchcraft in northern Europe:

> First, witches are accused of every conceivable sexual crime against men. Quite simply, they are accused of female sexuality. Second, they are accused of being organized. Third, they are accused of having magical powers affecting health — of harming, but also of healing. They were often charged specifically with possessing medical and obstetrical skills.

Women were seen to be irrational, emotional and lacking in self-restraint; they were especially vulnerable to satanic temptation. This social view of female irrationality was often supported by an ideological appeal to the story of Adam and Eve in Genesis. This negative view of women was reinforced by the publication of James Stuart's *Daemonologie* in 1597. In this treatise, Stuart attempted to prove the reality of witches and he clearly felt especially skilled in identifying and detecting witches (Davies, 1959). This publication gave a royal and religious legitimation for the common view that women were the social basis of witchcraft and the carriers of demonic forces. Between 1563 and 1727, somewhere between 70 and 90 percent of witchcraft suspects throughout Europe were female (McLachlan and Swales, 1980).

It has been argued that the history of witchcraft and the suppression of female witches should be seen as part of the history of the exclusion of women from medical practice (Ehrenreich and English, 1973). The attack on women as witches was primarily a critique of their sexuality, but also an attempt to prevent 'wise women' from practising herbal and folk medicine at the village level. As medicine became more distinctively a profession backed by the authority of a technical language and a university education, so medical activity became the preserve of men. The result was that the status of female midwives and wise women became increasingly ambiguous and threatening from the point of view of the male monopoly of health giving. The witchcraft craze did not remove the common woman healer, but it did have the consequence of labelling women healers as suspect. The witchcraft craze therefore provided the perfect excuse for male medical practitioners to exclude women from the competitive struggle for clients throughout Europe (Ben-Yehuda, 1980).

Physicians and midwives
Although women had dominated the delivery of children throughout traditional societies, they were particularly unsuccessful in achieving a professional structure for midwifery and closing their ranks to competition. For example, in 1616 the midwives of London petitioned James I for a charter to create a society for the development of midwifery and the incorporation of midwives (Donnison, 1977). The aim of incorporation was to regulate the practice of midwives and to enhance their skills by a more formal level of education. Although the petition of the midwives was received with some interest by the king, the petition was opposed by the Royal College of Physicians who presented a number of counter proposals which blocked the professionalization of midwives. There was a further petition by the midwives in 1633 but this was also rejected. As a result of these failures in the seventeenth century, the male control of midwifery through the eighteenth century became increasingly obvious in English medical practice. The professional strategy of male practitioners was to confine the midwife to the role of a mere attendant at the birth and to encourage midwives to leave

all 'abnormal births' to the intervention of men equipped with the new instruments of medicine, especially forceps (Mitchell and Oakley, 1976).

The history of midwifery has become something of a theoretical battleground in the history of medicine where there is a clear competition between feminist and other forms of explanation. Shorter (1983) provides a valuable distinction between rural and urban midwives, seeing the former as largely ignorant and uneducated. By contrast, the urban midwife before 1750 was probably better equipped than the male doctor to provide a competent service to women in terms of the knowledge available in the period. The traditional midwife was clearly unable to handle major obstetric problems and would be compelled to call in the services of a trained doctor. However, it is also the case that the majority of deliveries did not require any significant medical intervention. Feminist historical criticism has been valuable in drawing sociological attention to the sexual division of labour within medical practice, where by the end of the nineteenth century the male medical practitioners had been successful in imposing a professional control over female midwifery and in preventing the emergence of a competitive professional group dominated by women. Within a broader perspective, we can see the development of male management of midwifery as part of the medicalization of motherhood (Oakley, 1984).

Women, sexuality and hysteria
These illustrations have been used to reinforce the notion that women's bodies and female sexuality have been seen as threatening to the moral and social fabric of human societies. Social anxiety about sexuality was directed against women and this anxiety has been expressed historically through a variety of medical categories which pinpoint and articulate the subordination of women to patriarchal authority. The history of hysteria is probably the most dramatic and dynamic example of patriarchal medicine; it most clearly expresses the subordination of women, the notion of sexuality as dangerous and the necessity to regulate women in the interests of social order.

Foucault (1979) took female hysteria as a very pertinent and prominent example of the discourse of sexuality and the distribution of power in the nineteenth century. Foucault has argued that the eighteenth and nineteenth centuries experienced a major medicalization of the female body which was conceptualized in terms of the social responsibility which women had for the wellbeing of their children, the continuity of the family and the preservation of society. The hysterical woman rather like the nineteenth-century masturbatory child and sexual pervert was a product of the all-pervasive ideology of sex which came to cultural predominance in the nineteenth century. For Foucault, the discourse of sexuality produced the hysterical woman as the object of a detailed medical discourse and a medical practice. The concept of the hysterical woman, the analysis of female melancholy and the social functions of 'vapours', were clearly an important feature of nineteenth-century medical culture, especially in the French analytical tradition of Charcot and Freud. The traditional rest-cure for women in nineteenth-century medical practice was also indicative of the prevailing view of women as frail creatures in need of protection and surveillance (Bassuk, 1986). However, the history of hysteria is clearly longer and more complicated than Foucault's emphasis on hysteria in nineteenth-century society would suggest (Turner, 1985c).

The term 'hysteria' is derived from the Greek word 'hystera' or uterus (womb). Hysteria was viewed as having ultimate physiological roots in the malfunctioning of the womb and hence hysteria was regarded as a condition peculiar and unique to women. The behavioural manifestations (weeping, screaming, the rigidity of the arched body, fainting, moodiness and tantrums) were consequently located in the physiological constitution of the female anatomy. One treatment for hysteria in the mid-nineteenth century was hysterectomy (the surgical removal of the womb) and this treatment was obviously proof of the fact that from a medical point of view the psychological phenomena of hysterical conversion were thought to have a specific physical causal basis. However, the very notion of hysteria carries with it a certain moral, evaluative and judgemental impact about women as a whole and about their role in society. Women were culturally considered to be the weaker sex, given to constitutionally structured fits of weeping, fainting and uncontrollable laughter. This tendency to hysterical behaviour was particularly common among young single women, old widows, divorced women or women who abstained from marriage and normal sexuality in order to pursue careers in education or other professions. In short, it was the absence of normal sexual activity designed to bring about reproduction which was associated in medical discourse with the prominence of hysteria.

The implication of this medical model was that women could only lead healthy lives in so far as they were sexually connected to a man in a lawful marriage which had the aim of reproduction. Sexual relations outside marriage were associated with another sexual disorder, namely nymphomania. The medical theory of the hysterical woman supported the status inequalities between men and women, supported the medical analysis of the social and psychological values of pregnancy inside marriage, and finally acted as an argument against further education for women on health grounds. A protracted period of education would delay the necessary functions of reproduction and satisfaction inside marriage and therefore professional women were particularly exposed to the damaging implications of delayed pregnancy.

The development of a discourse of sexual deviance in the nineteenth century as the product of a new medical ideology was held by Foucault to be intimately bound up with the cultural specialization of men and women in terms of power, status and knowledge. Against Foucault's position, it is possible to argue that hysteria is one of the oldest known medical conditions in human society and therefore the idea of the 'hysterization' of women in the nineteenth century is problematic. Furthermore hysteria has been universally regarded as a specifically female disorder. Therefore, the continuity of hysteria as a designation creates problems for Foucault's emphasis on historical discontinuity; by contrast, the long history of hysteria as a medical category and the idea that women's social behaviour is peculiarly determined by anatomy provide evidence for the continuity of patriarchal power, irrespective of other major changes in social and economic relations.

The early history of hysteria can be located in classical or ancient Egyptian society since an early papyrus (1900 BC) provides an account of hysterical behaviour in women brought about by the presence of a wandering womb; this condition was thought to be the product of the dryness of the womb resulting from the lack of pregnancy. As the womb dried out, it became lighter and floated about the body causing various disturbances. When this floating womb touched the brain, it sparked off an episode of hysterical crisis. In the Egyptian medical tradition, this crisis was treated by using sweet smelling herbs in a process of fumigation to entice the womb back into its normal position. The herbs used in this therapy were symbolic of masculinity and male power, and therefore the attraction of the womb back to its normal functioning was achieved by the sexual symbolism of these herbs. The social implications of this practice was that pregnancy was normal, desirable and indeed a necessary medical condition for women in order to preserve their sanity.

Within the environment of Greek medicine, hysteria had a similar set of implications and symbolic meanings. It was in Greek medicine, in the form of the Hippocratic writings which came eventually to dominate western medieval medicine, that hysteria came to have a close association with the malfunctioning of the reproductive organs

of women. Within Platonic philosophy, the womb was conceptualized as an animal which longed to generate children. When this
organ remained barren it became distressed and disturbed, straying
about the body and causing problems of respiration and tranquility.
These disturbances continued until the womb was satisfied by its
reproductive function.

The legacy of Greek and Egyptian medicine was maintained by
Galen of Pergamon who developed a variation on this theme,
namely that hysteria was caused by the degeneration of female
seminal secretions. In Galenic medicine, successful reproduction
was brought about by the union of male and female semen.
Abstinence from reproduction in women whether through choice,
through widowhood or through other circumstances meant that
these seminal secretions were retained within the womb bringing
about putrefaction, contamination and finally hysteria. The medical
solution to this problem was again thought to involve the satisfac-
tions of sexual intercourse. An interesting feature of Galen's theory
was that he thought it was possible for male hysteria to take place.
Men who abstained from sexual intercourse also suffered from
seminal putrefaction resulting in hysterical outbursts. This aspect of
Galen's theory was in the long term abandoned in the medieval
period and it was eventually taken for granted that only women by
definition could experience hysterical disturbances. Since men had
no hystera (womb), there could be no such thing as male hysterical
conversion.

The debate about female hysteria was conducted in a medical
setting where detailed knowledge of the human anatomy was
obscure and rudimentary until the Renaissance when, in certain
Italian universities, post-mortem dissections of bodies were carried
out. The cross-sectional drawings of Leonardo da Vinci (1452–1519)
are indications of a growing knowledge of anatomy. The understanding of reproduction owes a great deal to the work of Gabriele
Fallopio (1520–1574). The result of these investigations was to
demonstrate that there was no seminal flow in women during sexual
intercourse and that hysteria was not the product of a floating womb
nor of seminal retention. Despite these discoveries, it was still
assumed that hysteria was caused by certain abnormalities in the
sexual life of women. There was a definite trend in medical theory
to suggest that women in fact had relatively little contribution to
make to the reproduction of men, serving simply as a vessel for
human reproduction; that is, it was assumed that the female was
simply the vessel which received the creative male seed (Hewson,
1975).

While the medical profession and the universities adhered to some version of Galenic medicine in which hysteria had a natural cause (for example the retention of putrefying seed), the clergy regarded hysteria as a form of possession by evil spirits. Hysterics were persons on whom a magical spell had been cast, blinding and paralysing them and making them impotent in their marriage relationships. As we have seen, witches were thought to be persons particularly subject to the influence of the devil through sexual passions and their strange hysterical behaviour was the product of these wicked alliances. The majority of witches were women and the explanation for this fact was given in *The Malleus Maleficarum* (The Hammer of the Witches) in 1495 which argued that women were a necessary evil and an inescapable calamity, being subject and susceptible to temptation.

Social changes in attitudes towards hysterical women were associated with the eventual disappearance of witchcraft and witch crazes by the late seventeenth century and the collapse of witchcraft as a legal offence. Changes in attitudes may have also been related to improvements in the knowledge of anatomy and the development of experimental medicine after Harvey's discovery of the circulation of the blood. While the idea of sexual disturbance as the cause of hysteria was never entirely abandoned, it was also assumed that the brain and its functions were crucial in understanding hysteria. Jorden (1578–1632) in *A Discourse of a Disease Called the Suffocation of the Mother* in 1603 and Burton's *The Anatomy of Melancholy* in 1621 suggested that idleness amongst wealthy women was the cause of emotional disturbance and the cure for these disturbances was to be located in renewed domestic activity, marriage and pregnancy. Although there was not a major shift in social attitudes, it was recognized that hysteria was connected, not simply with female physiology, but with the social and emotional life of women in the context of the family and marriage.

Although significant developments in the classification and treatment of nervous disorders took place in the late eighteenth century and early nineteenth century, the real medical breakthrough in the analysis of hysteria was associated with Charcot (1825–1892) who suggested that at least some aspects of hysteria were forms of learnt behaviour or mimicry; he furthermore argued that men can have hysterical attacks. Charcot experimented with hypnosis as a diagnostic device to understand the psychological trauma which lay behind hysterical convulsions (Ellenberger, 1970). However, it was Freud who under the influence of Charcot realized eventually that the therapeutic importance of hypnosis was that it provided an outlet for the tensions of the hysterical person through a talking therapy which enabled a cathartic effect to take place. Eventually

Freud and Breuer (1974) came to suggest that hysterics are persons who suffer mainly from bad reminiscences. Freud became particularly interested in the role of traumatic events in childhood, their repression in memories and their eventual release through the cathartic influence of psychotherapy and the talking cure, whereby resistance to the buried event could be released through psychoanalytical investigation.

One cause of the decline of hysterical behaviour in the twentieth century may be the lack of social support and social interest in the behaviour of fainting and thrashing women since this behaviour is regarded as socially inappropriate (Veith, 1965). Thus in the nineteenth century it was fashionable for young women in the middle class to express the problems of their social relations through an indeterminable illness involving hysterical conversion. This type of behaviour was less tolerated in sophisticated circles by the end of the nineteenth century and fainting was no longer regarded as an appropriate form of female behaviour in public. The expression of hysterical problems can be regarded therefore as some confirmation of Parsons's notion of the sick role, that is the idea that hysteria became a form of legitimate deviance from the expected norms of sexuality. The sociological and historical analysis of hysterical behaviour therefore suggests significantly that a variety of illnesses in European society were closely connected with the dominant conceptual framework of normal sexuality. In short, the history of medical categories of female complaints is a product of the wider analysis of western sexuality.

The history of western sexuality

The analysis of female sexuality has to address itself to the relationship between nature and culture on the one hand, and the relationship between the production of property and the reproduction of persons on the other. The difficulty with female subordination through patriarchy is that the sexual division of labour and the political subordination of women do not appear to correspond neatly with any mode of production. That is, women are subordinated in slavery, in feudalism and in the early stages of capitalism. One explanation of this cultural division between the sexes is that traditionally men create enduring cultural symbols while women simply reproduce the perishable bodies of men (Ortner, 1974). The social roles of women within the private space of domestic reproduction come therefore to be seen as socially inferior to the productive performance of men within the public domain. Whereas women are allocated and trained into a psychological structure of emotions which sharply distinguishes them from the neutral rationality of the public sphere, men are socialized into a lifestyle emphasizing the importance of reason and restraint. This cultural dichotomy between cognitive reason and emotional desire is closely related to the dichotomy between private and public space so that women occupy the world of private emotion and affection, whereas men are allocated to social roles emphasizing reason, instrumentality and public responsibility. This type of explanation is important in understanding the division between nature and culture but the argument has a number of significant problems.

In traditional societies, patriarchy characteristically involved the exercise of power by adult males over women, children, relatives and other dependent persons. While the heads of households dominated women, it was also the case that fathers dominated their sons. Since male identity is understood in terms of sexual and social power, power over women and political organization, patriarchy forced single males into a role of dependency and quasi-female status. The result of this social determination of power is that young men often acquired a feminine personality. In some traditional societies therefore young men suffer psychosomatic illnesses which are the parallel of female complaints (Crapanzano, 1973).

The argument about patriarchy has also been criticized for its generality in that the subordination of women seems to be present across very different societies regardless of their culture and social structure. Finally, the conventional argument about the division between nature/culture within the framework of a patriarchal theory of female subordination has to address the problem of the maintenance and continuity of attitudes towards women in changing circumstances. For example, the notion of 'nature' is not continuous in social formations and attitudes towards women clearly have changed and cannot be regarded as continuous.

Women, property and the household
The analysis of female subordination can be made coherent when it is combined with an analysis of the role of property in human societies, especially when we take into account the important historical continuity of arguments about primogeniture, private property, population regulation and political power. All human societies have to find some relationship between the reproduction of persons and the management of property which will produce stability in social and political relations. In European societies historically, there has been a strong pressure for population restraint in order to secure a continuity of property, and these requirements have been achieved through a religious doctrine of restraint combined with certain legal relations for property

inheritance through the first-born male. Given the rather critical relationship between productive land and the population in early European societies, north-western European communities developed a distinctive set of institutional arrangements for the regulation of their population growth in relation to the availability of arable land. Population growth was limited by the widespread practices of late marriage, contraception inside marriage, celibacy, high rates of widowhood and female infanticide (Andorka, 1978). One consequence of this marriage pattern was to produce a large pool of unmarried men and women within the land-owning class who, because they could not have access to inheritable wealth, were not in a position to form marriages or households of their own. The resulting pool of uncommitted youth provided a highly unstable social group in the very structure of medieval societies.

The character of these social, familial and legal relations begins to provide the framework within which we can understand the particular development of love and sexuality in western societies and finally the pattern which developed with respect to the definition of women's complaints. For the land-owning aristocracy, the primary aim (indeed the only aim) of wedlock was the production of a male heir who would ultimately inherit the total property of the household. Since life expectancy and childbirth were particularly uncertain and unstable, women had to be highly fertile and therefore continuously pregnant during their marriage with the aim of securing the title to aristocratic land. In a period of considerable interpersonal violence, the longevity of aristocratic males was always uncertain. The women of the household had to produce a male heir, but importantly this heir had to be a legitimate offspring of the head of the household, otherwise significant disputes would emerge with respect to legitimate titles to property. Heads of households were especially anxious that the women they took into their households as wives were not already pregnant. Without a guarantee of virginity there was always the possibility that the first-born male would not in fact be the legitimate heir. The consequence of these social and economic pressures was that a profound emphasis was given to the virginity and chastity of the woman, and upon the virility and strength of the male. Similarly, daughters had to be morally correct and sexually pure in order to become desirable and indeed marketable mates within the aristocratic marriage market. The sexual behaviour of younger sons and daughters was of less concern to parents and therefore younger sons acquired a reputation for immorality and sexual deviance. While an emphasis was given to the moral character of the woman at the point of marriage, the marriage relationship was not historically characterized by affection or

emotion, since the wife was not intended to be the domestic com-
panion or equal of the head of the household. The male figures
within the household would be more likely to achieve affection,
emotion and sociability from other male members of the household
or from persons outside it. The sole aim of the sexual relationship
between husband and wife was the production of children and
eroticism or sexuality had no part to play within this relationship.

The marriage system of early Europe was based upon private,
dissoluble marriage contracts between men and women which were
secured by their parents. The marriage service was consequently a
domestic, private and secular ceremony in which the Church had
relatively little influence (Ariès and Bejin, 1985). From the twelfth
century, two distinct models of marriage began to emerge in European Christendom (Duby, 1978). The lay system maintained the
traditional form of marriage as a secular private union which could
be dissolved were the woman to prove barren or unfaithful. Alongside this older model, there developed an ecclesiastical system of
marriage which had largely the opposite set of characteristics. The
ecclesiastical model established a set of principles whereby the
marriage bond became a sacramental union, performed through a
public ritual and which established a pact which could not be dissolved prior to death. The Church reinforced the principles of chastity
and loyalty, precluding all extramarital unions and laying the foundations for a rigid set of norms regarding appropriate sexual
behaviour. Since the Church regarded marriage as a necessary evil
against fornication, the Church argued that married couples should
not enjoy their sexual relationship, but regard it merely as a system
of reproduction. The Church also established a rigid set of conventions regarding sexual positions, homosexuality, perversions and
various forms of deviance. Women came to be seen increasingly as a
major threat to the stability of these social relations of marriage,
since the Church regarded the woman as the weaker partner. It was
assumed that the woman would be more susceptible to temptation
and deviance. The Church therefore provided a powerful ideology
for controlling women through such institutions as the confession
(Hepworth and Turner, 1982).

These patriarchal households were further defined and redefined
by the Protestant revolutions of the seventeenth century when there
emerged a distinctive doctrine of patriarchal powers which linked
together the secular authority of the king and the male heads of
households. Writers like Filmer attempted to criticize the social
contract theories of the time by arguing that the authority of kings,
bishops and fathers was based upon divine authority. His book
Patriarcha: A Defense of the Natural Power of Kings against the

Unnatural Liberty of the People was published posthumously in 1682. Filmer offered a defence of royal absolutism, but simultaneously established the authority of fathers over their households on the model of God's authority over His people. For Filmer, familial authority was natural and divinely sanctioned; it provided a clear basis for the authority of kings. This view of patriarchy conflicted profoundly with the growing individualism of political philosophers like Locke who attacked Filmerism in his *Two Treatises of Government*.

These bourgeois conceptions of the relationship between man and woman signal the emergence of a different type of society. There is a sense in which the union of aristocratic groups through marriage produced merely the household, whereas the union of men and women under the social conditions of early bourgeois capitalism produced the family as an entirely new social unit somewhat separate from the surrounding kinship structure. Within the bourgeois family, there was an emerging emphasis upon affection, companionship and intimacy. One can detect this new emphasis in the writings of Milton who argued the case for divorce on the basis of a conception of companionate marriage. This notion of emotional union took some centuries to develop, flourishing finally in the latter half of the nineteenth century with the increasing importance of a romantic attachment (Shorter, 1977). As the notion of romantic attachment became more widely acceptable in society, there was correspondingly an increase in divorce and the social acceptability of the dissoluble marriage.

If we argue that patriarchy was the dominant system of sexual authority in Europe from the twelfth to the nineteenth century, then we require a new concept to describe the development of sexual inequality with the decline of the nuclear family, the stable household and the social acceptance of divergent patterns of marital and sexual unions. One alternative description of this new system of competition and conflict between the sexes might be the concept of 'patrism' (Turner, 1984). A patriarchal relationship is one in which the male head of household dominates the members of the house whether these are male, female, adult or juvenile. This patriarchal structure is legitimized by legal, political and religious norms which give the adult male a virtual monopoly over the subordinate groups within the traditional household. In such a system, the wife ceases to be a legal personality on marriage, and divorce is typically proscribed as a system for the dissolution of marriage. By patrism, I refer to a culture which is based upon prejudicial beliefs and practices of men towards women, but this system lacks a clear backing in law or religion. Men and women remain unequal in the market place, but this is not fully sanctioned by an overarching system of patriarchal values. Patristic conflicts between the sexes take place in a society where the household is no longer necessarily based on the nuclear family and where a variety of sexual unions begin to evolve. Patrism also characterizes societies in which, for example, homosexuality has become far more acceptable as a form of sexual activity. With the growing influence of feminism as an analysis of society and as a social movement, we can also suggest that a defensive form of patrism evolves and the relationship between the sexes becomes overtly more conflictual and acrimonious.

The transformation of patriarchy does not therefore necessarily bring about an equality of men and women, although it may result in an increase in equality of opportunity. The development of patrism does not guarantee an equality of outcome between the sexes, but rather describes a social and political set of circumstances which are volatile, undefined and insecure. The point of this argument is to suggest that the character of women's complaints will change with the transition from patriarchy to patrism. Under patriarchy as we have seen, the problems which beset women were closely related to the whole dynamic of production and reproduction under patriarchal circumstances; that is, women were characterized as unreliable and dangerous. Therefore, witchcraft, hysteria and melancholy were medical categories for the regulation and control of subordinate women. Under patrism, women are more likely to experience what I shall call 'representational problems of the self' in a society where image is more closely associated with the notion of the self and wellbeing.

Regulating populations and bodies

The thrust of the argument in this book is that it is impossible to develop a medical sociology without a sociology of the body. Furthermore, the thesis is that the sociology of the body would involve an analysis of the dynamics of populations, and the dynamic of the singular body and the self. Following Foucault (1977), it can be argued that human societies are faced by a problem of order which involves the reproduction of populations and their regulation in space and time, but it also involves the restraint of singular bodies and their representation in time and space. In a previous publication (Turner, 1984), I have suggested that this Hobbesian problem of order can be expressed diagrammatically as shown in Figure 3.

Because the government of the body is in fact the management of sexuality, the issue of regulation is in practice the regulation of the sexuality of women by a system of either patriarchal or patristic powers. The reproduction of human populations and the restraint of

FIGURE 3

	Populations	Bodies	
Time Patriarchy	Reproduction Onanism	Restraint Hysteria	Internal
Space Patrism	Regulation Agoraphobia	Representation Anorexia	External

singual bodies require at the institutional level a system of patriarchal households for the control of fertility and at the level of the
human individual a culture of asceticism for the regulation or
delaying of sexual gratification in the interests of familial control.

As we have seen, the reproduction of populations can be conceptualized within a classical Malthusian framework. Malthus in *An
Essay on the Principle of Population* in 1798 had claimed that any
political efforts to improve the standard of living of the poorest
section of the labouring classes above the level of mere subsistence
would be self defeating, because the consequence would be an
increase in population. In Malthus's thesis, human society is dominated by two universal requirements (to eat and to satisfy sexuality)
which he regards as fixed laws of the natural world. Unfortunately,
these two urges are contradictory since reproductive capacity will
always outweigh the capacity to produce food. The consequence is
that human societies require certain preventive checks on population. These preventive checks may be either negative (prostitution,
homosexuality and abortion) or positive (a variety of moral means
for the restraint of desire such as delayed marriage). Where human
societies did not apply one or both of these checks, then human
populations would be controlled by the natural means of starvation
and epidemic.

Within the framework of this Malthusian problem of populations
it is not surprising that medical discourse became particularly concerned with the health problems relating to homosexuality, delayed
marriage, melancholy and masturbation. In the great epoch of
patriarchal power, medical discourse was necessarily focused upon
the social and moral consequences of a patriarchal system of household formation in which women were regarded as particularly
dangerous to social stability. In the discourse of political economy,
Malthus provided two arguments against sexual vice. In the first, he

suggested that moral deviance (such as homosexuality, abortion and masturbation) was simply against Christian teaching. However, he recognized that this might not be entirely compelling as an argument; he therefore offered a second proposition which took the form of ethical utilitarianism, namely that we would be happier inside marriage if we arrived at that state with our sexual energies undiluted by prior activities. Asceticism before marriage was conceptualized in economic terms as a form of moral and sexual accumulation. Once this accumulated wealth of sexuality had come to maturity, it could be consumed inside marriage through productive activity resulting in children.

Given this medical and economic framework in which sexuality was conceptualized along the lines of the labour theory of value, masturbation became the target of severe moral criticisms in the second half of the eighteenth century (Shorter, 1977). Before the eighteenth century, medical and religious attitudes towards juvenile masturbation were relatively relaxed, but in the eighteenth century the problem of onanism became acute within the medical theories of the period. One indication of this more rigid set of attitudes was the anonymous publication of *Onania or The Heinous Sin of Self-Pollution* in 1710 which became a popular text for parents and medical authorities. The author of this text suggested that a great number of disorders resulted from this wicked practice. In 1758, Dr S. Tissot published a medical treatise on masturbation in which he argued that it produced dire consequences and was largely incurable. Similar medical texts appeared in France and Germany in the middle of the eighteenth century and in Germany infibulation was recommended as a medical cure for the problem.

In her study of English madness, Skultans (1979:70) has suggested that the medical debate about onanism was in fact a minor discussion within the more general medical concern for seminal loss. The nineteenth century generated an entirely new diagnostic label called 'spermatorrhoea' which was held to be a form of involuntary disease similar to 'nocturnal pollutions'. In the 1850s physicians showed increasing anxiety about the medical consequences of this problem in young men. Involuntary seminal loss and masturbation had similar consequences, such as baldness, stammering, blindness, skin diseases, insomnia and finally madness.

Several explanations have been put forward for the growth of these new diagnostic categories (Engelhardt, 1974). For example, male children from middle-class families were spending more time away from the home as a consequence of the growth of public boarding schools. Parents experienced a loss of control over the moral development of their children. Within these new public schools, it was feared that children would become influenced by the questionable moral values of their peers and school teachers. This change in childhood training was related to a social change in urban culture, but it also had an association with a new emphasis in Protestant communities on the fundamental value and significance of socialization of children (Grylls, 1978).

For Foucault (1979), the increasing medical concern for seminal loss in the nineteenth century was part of the medicalization of society which came under the surveillance of medical institutions and professional groups acting as the moral guardians of the community. It has also been suggested (Stone, 1979) that delayed marriage in ambitious middle-class families meant that men and women were spending a longer part of their sexually mature years without a legitimate outlet for their sexual requirements. There was as a result a general religious and medical anxiety about the attractions of masturbation or prostitution for impressionable young people.

Within a longer cultural perspective, unproductive sexuality had always been regarded as deviant within the orthodox traditions of Christianity and Judaism. Masturbation from a theological point of view has the same implications as coitus interruptus. These forms of sexual deviance suggested that sexual relations could be enjoyed without the responsibilities of reproduction. The Church argued against the growth of contraception on exactly the same set of principles. However in Britain, Protestantism had brought with it a greater emphasis on the idea of total sin of a personal character; puritanism also contributed to the growing concern for childhood training and the responsibilities of parenthood. In the eighteenth and nineteenth centuries, the growing importance of individualism brought with it a critique of patriarchal authority of an arbitrary character. Patriarchal authority was not entirely consistent with the puritan notion of individual responsibility. While the medical category of masturbatory insanity may have been a defensive reaction of parental authority against the growth of autonomy amongst children, especially in the public school system, there was also a parallel between the notions of wasted semen and under-utilized capital. The problem with self-pollution was that it was secret and individual; it was a particularly deviant form of the very individualism which characterized society as a whole.

Corresponding to the social problem of the regulation of populations, there is the individual restraint of sexuality and desire in the interests of public order. This problem of the relationship between individual sexuality and social regulation has preoccupied western philosophy in the shape of the conflict between desire and reason. In social theory, it has been particularly prominent in the theories of

Weber, Freud and Marcuse. Although the restraint of sexual desire has been regarded as a problem general to society, it is important to note that female sexual desire is characteristically seen to be the most dangerous form of passion, when this is not adequately regulated. In short, the problem of restraint is a problem of patriarchal power over women's bodies and we have discussed this issue in the history of hysteria.

Female sexuality was conceptualized in a system which was contradictory, or at least paradoxical. For example, once inside marriage, women were thought to be sexually frigid and underdeveloped; because the married woman was naturally not interested in a continuing sexual relationship, there was an implicit excuse for married men to resort to the company of prostitutes. The passionate woman outside marriage suddenly became the frigid mother within wedlock, while the husband was released to find his sexual enjoyments outside the household, thereby creating a double standard of sexual morality. Within the confines of the private domestic sphere, the married woman with the burden of children was likely to become increasingly depressed, requiring close medical supervision and intervention.

Medical ideology constitutes women as psychologically and socially vulnerable and therefore in need of close medical (that is male) surveillance, advice and guidance (Ehrenreich and English, 1978). Since in the medical literature both menstruation and pregnancy are regarded as 'medical problems', there is a basic logic to the medical view that women are, as it were, natural patients. This view of women as sick is one dimension of the contradictory medical view of women's sexuality. Women have to be simultaneously 'damned whores' and 'God's police' (Summers, 1975). From the male medical point of view, women both reproduce men within the moral confines of the family and function as a moral policeforce, but their very sexuality means that they are equally prone to whoredom. Sexual deviance in men was regarded as deviant, but within a patriarchal social framework this could be tolerated. However, sexual deviance in women was particularly threatening to the social fabric; it was for this reason that an endless debate has surrounded the whole problem of illegitimate births and the social standing of women (Gill, 1977).

We have seen how the theory of hysteria and the increasing interest in the hysterical paroxysm perfectly expressed this male medical view of women as patients. Hysteria in women resulted from the fact that they were more emotional than men but, because of marriage and the desire of parenthood, they were forced to restrain their emotionality and sexuality; this repression or restraint of feeling found its expression in the hysterical syndrome. This situation was complicated by the growth of delayed marriage for middle-class women who were entering teaching and nursing as middle-class professions in the late nineteenth century. It was assumed that this 'superfluous' pool of women would produce a new wave of hysterical outbursts. It is interesting that, while doctors were concerned with the problem of female hysteria, the growing diagnostic use of the notion of hypochondriasis as an explanation of male emotional distress did not carry with it the pejorative and negative meanings which surrounded hysteria as a label. If hysteria was a dominant psychiatric label in the last decades of the nineteenth century, there is evidence that hysteria as an 'acceptable' sick role declined significantly in the first decades of the twentieth century (Smith-Rosenberg and Rosenberg, 1973). This decline in the prevalence of hysteria may be partly explained as the outcome of a transition in western culture from a predominantly patriarchal to a patristic system.

As a consequence of mass warfare in the twentieth century, women returned to the labour force in increasing numbers, replacing men within the labour force and gaining important industrial and political skills as a consequence. In the USA and Europe, legislation provided wider grounds for divorce and changes in the judicial procedure made divorce more readily accessible to the working class. Changes in education also meant that women enjoyed greater opportunities for social mobility. The political system was also changed by wider definitions of voting rights to include women as genuine political citizens. The spread of contraceptive practices from the 1880s created a situation in which women were more able to control their fertility; more importantly, cheap forms of contraception broke the relationship between sexual enjoyment and reproduction. There were also important changes in the nature of the household and its relation to property. The family was no longer a major feature of investment sources for capital accumulation, since the banks and other investment institutions were expanded to meet the demand for both long- and short-term investment. The significance of 'family capitalism' gradually diminished with the development of industrial capitalist societies towards a system in which the state and large institutions became increasingly central to the management of investment, wages and production. In short, the ancient connection between property, inheritance, regulated sexuality and religion began to disappear. In contemporary society, the nuclear family in societies like the USA, the UK and Australia represents approximately one-quarter of all households. The consequence of these changes was that important aspects of the institutional structure of patriarchy crumbled and the conflict between men and women assumed a more distinctively market character. The competitive struggle between the sexes is now more overt and more conflictual. If witchcraft, demonic possession, melancholy and hysteria were the diseases of a society based on patriarchy, then neuroses and phobias are the complaints of women under conditions which I have described as patristic. Agoraphobia and anorexia may be taken as two powerful illustrations of this argument that patrism produces a new range of disease entities within medical discourse.

We have seen that diseases of restraint associated with delayed marriage and seminal loss were diseases of scarcity, that is the inability to create and maintain new households in the absence of personal property. By contrast, we might regard anorexia as a disorder of abundance, since it appears to be particularly prevalent in affluent families where there is a narcissistic problem of consumption. Anorexia in part expresses a certain social contradiction between mass consumption and the norm of thinness through the practices of restraint and dietary management. We might also suggest that hysteria and onanism were, so to speak, diseases of time, especially delayed time. The problem of seminal loss expressed the notion of delay where sexual gratification was deferred. By contrast, anorexia and the phobias are diseases of space; they express the problem of the self in a representational space within a society which is image conscious. They are diseases of individual presentation and social reputation. Agoraphobia perfectly symbolizes this problem of the relationship between space and illness, since it is literally the fear of the market place. These forms of disease while having different metaphors are nevertheless all problems of dependency, especially the dependency of women and the powerless on the property-owning heads of households.

With urbanization and the growth of the metropolis, there is in western society an increasing sense of confinement, overcrowding and urban disruption. Urban space has two rather separate problems. The first is the problem of overcrowding and demographic pressure, which is associated with nineteenth-century infectious diseases and other epidemics. The second relates to the alleged anonymity of urban life, producing through the stimulation of nerves, an entirely new mental attitude, which Simmel saw in the blasé personality (Sennett, 1969). Overcrowding and anonymity were thought to be particularly dangerous for the sensitive middle-class women of the late nineteenth century. Women were seen to be susceptible to the social dangers of a false self-estimation; the theatre was thought to encourage women to decorate themselves in a series of reputational competitions which were dangerous both for their morals and for their health. In the city, with the emergence of a romantic conception of marriage, a new series of sexual excitements were prevalent; these gave rise to dangerous alliances involving infatuation, insults, abductions and personal degradation. These sexual crises within the anonymous city became the primary topic of the nineteenth-century novel in both France and Britain. The adventures of Madame Bovary in Flaubert's novel of 1856 anticipated the genre of the romantic novel by exploring the problems of the educated woman in the urban environment where sexual temptations were increased because of the very anonymity of this individualized environment. If public space had become dangerous, then the woman who stayed happily at home far away from the dangers and temptations of the market place displayed her moral standing while also proclaiming the economic status of the household. Women who appeared on the congested streets of the metropolis were either women who were forced of necessity to work, because their husbands could not provide for them, or they were morally suspect women going about unlawful activities (de Swann, 1981).

It was at the point when the conditions which made the urban street life safer for women (lighting, a professional police force and the decline of public violence) had been extended by the end of the nineteenth century, that the anxiety of husbands about their mobile wives appears to have increased. It was in this situation that the first medical description of agoraphobia emerged in 1871; the syndrome has not changed significantly since that period, being defined rather simply as an anxiety about leaving the safety of the home, visiting public places and travelling alone in crowded spaces. From a Freudian perspective, the fears of the agoraphobic are focused upon the possibilities of sexual seduction and the associated guilt of discovery. Agoraphobia expresses the possibility of sexual seductions with strangers in a cultural context which was still somewhat repressive in sexual terms. The agoraphobia of married women was in this sense metaphorically expressive of the anxieties of husbands regarding their capacity to control the domestic sphere and the economic arrangements of the household in a situation where their wives were potentially more independent in economic and status terms. To some extent, there may be a degree of collusion between husband and wife as to the symbolic importance of this new illness. The woman had the compensation of moral praise in exchange for staying at home, while the husband had his status and economic power reinforced by the apparent incapacity of his wife. The anxieties and fears of both partners concerning the character of the market place were then successfully translated into a medical condition via the intervention of medical professionals who legitimated the power relationships of the bourgeois household. Agoraphobia expressed the problem therefore that there was an incompatibility between the impersonality of the market place and the moral standing of the members within it (Sennett, 1974).

Female complaints can be regarded as a psychosomatic expression of certain emotional problems which are built into the division of the social world by a public arena of authority and a private world of emotion and sensibility. While agoraphobia as a diagnostic label purports to describe a psychological disorder, it was expressive of Victorian morality in which the good woman was a woman within a household. However, these diagnostic categories can be regarded as retrospective and defensive, since the agoraphobic label emerged in a period when middle-class women were already beginning to leave the home as workers and professional employees.

The first clinical descriptions of anorexia nervosa in modern medicine occurred in France and England in the 1860s. Gull in a lecture at Oxford in 1868 provided an account of the characteristics of anorexia which were elaborated by further research in the 1870s. In France, the work of Charcot in the 1880s indicated that anorexia was one aspect of the hysterical syndrome, a theme elaborated by Freud and Breuer in the 1890s in the famous analysis of Fraulein Anna O. Like hysteria, anorexia is almost wholly a disorder of young women (Palmer, 1980; Kalucy et al., 1977). The onset of anorexia appears to be at the age of fifteen and the majority of cases are clinically identified prior to the age of twenty-five; the illness appears to be concentrated in the period between puberty and menopause. There is some evidence that the diagnostic label has become increasingly popular among medical professionals, suggesting an increased prevalence of the illness (Crisp et al., 1976).

Much of the critical literature on the illness has been motivated by feminist theory which treats the disorder as a consequence of women's position in society which is shaped by the sexual division of labour and patriarchal power (Caskey, 1986). Women are seen to be caught in a contradictory set of expectations concerning their beauty, their social value and their moral character (Chernin, 1981).

The condition itself is complex medically and the symptoms of the disorder are diverse and varied including amenorrhoea, lanugo, bradycardia, bulimia and vomiting. Because of the presence of weight loss and disturbed menstruation as part of the syndrome of the anorexic, some writers have suggested a broader category for this type of disease, namely 'dietary chaos syndrome' (Palmer, 1979). However, other authors prefer to emphasize the psychological criteria of diagnosis, drawing attention to the fear of fatness and the pursuit of thinness as important features of the disorder (Bruch, 1978). In social psychological terms, anorexia represents a control paradox (Lawrence, 1979) which can also be seen in religious terms as a form of asceticism in which there is a struggle to achieve a spirituality through the management of the flesh.

The disorder also has important symbols relating to the contradictory character of sexuality in young women. From autobiographical accounts, there is some indication that excessive slimming is connected in puberty with a rejection of adult sexuality through the suppression of menstruation. Over-obedience to parental regulation in order to achieve moral purity is part of the management drive to control emotions in a period of their lives when these women are beginning to form their first mature alliances with men. Furthermore, since consumer norms place a great emphasis on slimness, there are strong social pressures towards controlling obesity (Orbach, 1978). While conforming to the norm of slimness, the anorexic also suppresses her sexuality by the suppression of menstruation. It is culturally interesting to note therefore that ballerinas, who in many respects encapsulate the modern notion of sexual attractiveness, are particularly susceptible to anorexic symptoms (Druss and Silverman, 1979). These contradictions are nicely encapsulated in the title of Bruch's book *The Golden Cage* (1978) by which metaphor she sought to describe the middle-class, over protected, inward-looking, expressively charged family caught in the pressures for consumerism and social achievement. Within this type of family, we can see anorexia as a form of adolescent rebellion against parental control where the young woman seeks to assert her individuality against the powerful conventions represented by her mother and her typically absent father. Within these families there is a contradictory relationship between the stress on individual achievement and competition which requires a high degree of personal independence with respect to the outer world, and the emphasis on obedience, subordination and compliance which the 'good girl' owes to her mother. The regulation of diet and the control of body size represent immediate areas within which the young woman can express government and authority. Faced with the possibility of a disastrous failure at school, the young woman may choose the sick role of anorexia as a perfect solution to her sexual, social and moral dilemmas.

Although we can see anorexia as in part the struggle of young women against the parental authority of the mother, in more general terms anorexia in the twentieth century, like hysteria in the nineteenth century, is expressive of the political limitations on women within a society characterized by inequality between the sexes. In such a culture, medical discourse provides the moral instruction of women into social roles which are deemed suitable to their contradictory social status. The shape of a woman is particularly significant in this cultural contradiction. The obese woman is a woman who is out of control because the unrestrained body is indicative of moral laxity. To control women's bodies is to control their personalities and this act of authority over the body is symbolic of a general political process which attempts to regulate the competitive nature of male–female relations under a system of patristic control.

However, as the social status of women begins to approximate that of men in terms of their citizenship rights (especially in employment, education and welfare), then we may expect the disease categories of men and women to become increasingly parallel. An improvement in the social status of women should bring about a transformation of their health status. There is some evidence of such a trend in both mental and physical disorders. In terms of mental health, evidence from the USA suggests that the traditional disparity between men and women has been reduced in the post-war period (Mumford, 1983). In areas of deviance traditionally associated with men, there has also been an increasing involvement of women in deviance and criminality. Throughout the industrial western world, higher rates of alcoholism amongst women have been regularly reported in recent years. In some areas of Britain, female admissions for alcoholism are almost as high as male admissions. In Germany, there has been a dramatic increase from 8 percent in 1966 to 30 percent in 1969. Over the last 10 years, the number of female alcoholics in Stockholm has doubled. Alcohol problems appear to increase with women seeking greater social equality through employment and competition. Some sociological perspectives regard this as a situation in which women are deviating from the conventional female role and adopting masculine social characteristics. An alternative perspective is that, precisely because women are subordinated, they tend to emulate the behaviour of the dominant group (Sargent, 1979).

Conclusion: medical constructions of women as patients
Although there may be aspects of health and disease where men and women appear to approximate, there are nevertheless major differences between men and women in modern industrial societies in terms of both mortality and morbidity rates. Health surveys from the USA have been recently summarized by Verbrugge (1985). Women's social activities are restricted for health reasons about 25

percent more than for men; women spend approximately 40 percent more days in bed per year as a consequence of illness on average than is the case for men. In the age group 17–44 women have twice as many visits to the doctor and hospital stays as do men. Women obtain substantially more prescription medicines per annum than men in all age groups, but this is particularly important in the young reproductive ages of 19–34. In addition, women's use of medically prescribed drugs is approximately 50 percent higher than men's use of drugs. In summary, men are more likely to suffer from threatening diseases and from diseases which cause more permanent forms of disability and early death. By contrast, women are more frequently sick although their illnesses are typically short-term and minor. These differences persist even when problems relating specifically to reproduction are removed from the statistical calculations of male/female differences. Thus

> men and women essentially suffer the same *types* of problems; what distinguishes the sexes is the *frequency* of those problems and the *pace* of death. (Verbrugge, 1985:163)

These differences in health-reporting behaviour may be accounted for in a variety of ways. For example, it may well be that women are more willing to express and report their symptoms to others. This willingness to report may be in turn the result of a greater acceptance of sickness amongst women as a complaint which can be verbalised. In addition, women may recall their health problems in a more precise and exact manner than men. Women may be more interested through socialization in health matters and therefore more knowledgeable of basic health issues as a consequence of mothering their children. There may also be a difference in the 'vocabulary of illness' available to men and women. The vocabularies of complaint may be more developed with respect to the sick role for women within a culture which expects women to verbalise their health problems. There is also the widely held view that doctors are trained into a medical culture which emphasizes and highlights the health problems of women, thereby constituting women as patients. In contemporary medicine, women's disorders are characteristically conceived to be psychogenic in character relating to women's neurotic behaviour and associated with the hazardous character of reproduction. There may be a vicious circle connecting the fact that women report their symptoms more frequently and more readily than men and the fact that male medical practitioners have been trained to expect women to so describe and discuss their symptoms. The expectation and the behaviour are thus mutually reinforcing. However, a less charitable conclusion would be derived from Ehrenreich and English (1972) who have argued that the medical ideology of female frailty simultaneously solved two issues, namely the disqualification of women as practitioners and their qualification as patients. In practice, these various explanations and perspectives converge on one issue: medical disorders are associated with low social status and the absence of power where medical doctrines, because they reflect dominant values, tend to express and reinforce existing hierarchies of social control. The professional development of medicine has been quite closely associated with a patriarchal and/or patristic culture where the sexuality of women has been a crucial issue in the definition of their problems, both moral and medical.

6
Aging, dying and death

Introduction
Aging is an important topic in medical sociology for at least two major reasons. Firstly, the nature and prevalence of modern disease are closely connected with the aging of modern populations. Secondly, the aging of the populations of industrial societies has a very significant social impact on the economic performance of modern capitalism because of the growth of so-called dependent populations following retirement. In modern industrial societies, there has been a significant decline in infectious diseases (especially whooping cough, measles, diphtheria and scarlet fever) since the Second World War. These changes are partly explained by the introduction of anti-microbe drugs between 1941 and 1951 (McDermott, 1980; Mumford, 1983). The decline of the infant mortality rate and general improvements in life-expectancy have contributed to the aging of the population and this in turn has resulted in a new range of diseases. The principal causes of death are now diseases of the circulatory system, malignant neoplasms and diseases of the respiratory system. The economic dependency of the elderly has become an issue of considerable political importance with the introduction of compulsory retirement in a wide range of occupations. By 1980, in Britain 88 percent of the male population over the age of 65 was retired and therefore formally defined as dependent. Approximately nine-tenths of all elderly people are dependent on some form of state benefit for all or a part of their household income. Because the percentage of the elderly retired within the community is steadily increasing, there are considerable economic problems associated with an aging population in capitalist societies (Walker, 1982).

By the 1970s the problem of aging for the economic development of the advanced capitalist societies had become obvious through national surveys and census material (Russell, 1981). From Table 4 we can see that the European capitalist societies had at least 13 percent of their population over the age of 65 while the white-settler capitalist societies such as Australia, New Zealand and Canada had at least 8 percent of their population in the retirement age group. In the case of societies like France, we can see that the population over 65 represented almost 25 per cent of the population between the age range 20–64 years. By the 1980s these trends had continued. For example, in Great Britain the number of the elderly (that is, women over 60 and men over 65) had increased from 2.9 million in 1911 to 9.8 million by 1981 (Phillipson, 1982). If we make a further distinction between the retired and the very old, then by the end of this century the very old (that is, those over 75 years of age) will represent almost 45 per cent of all elderly people in Britain (Abrams, 1979). In Australia similar trends are discernible. Various government publications in 1982 (*Projections of the Populations of Australia, States and Territories 1984–2021*) reported that those aged 0–4 years would decline from 24 percent of the population in 1984 to 20 percent of the population in 2021. For those aged 65 years and over there will be an increase from 10.1 percent in 1984 to between 14.6 and 15.6 per cent by 2021. This will bring about an increase in the dependent population, a proportionately smaller tax-paying community, smaller domestic markets and a correspondingly larger group of people on welfare benefits. In the USA, projections for the aged population suggest that those over 65 years of age will increase from just under 10 percent in 1970 to over 12 percent by the year 2000 (Cockerham, 1982). As we will see, the elderly, because they are the targets of considerable social stigmatization and stereotyping, are often seen as helpless dependents. In reality those between the ages of 65 and 75 lead lives which are relatively auto-

TABLE 4
Population age structures

Country	Date	\multicolumn{4}{c}{Percentage in age group}	65+ as a % of 20–64
		0–19	20–64	65+	Total	
Australia	1971	37.5	54.2	8.3	100	15.4
Japan	1970	32.6	60.3	7.1	100	11.7
Canada	1971	39.4	52.5	8.1	100	15.4
New Zealand	1971	40.9	50.6	8.5	100	16.8
Italy	1971	31.6	57.7	10.7	100	18.5
USA	1970	37.9	52.2	9.9	100	18.9
Netherlands	1971	35.5	54.2	10.3	100	18.9
Denmark	1969	31.2	56.7	12.1	100	21.3
UK	1971	30.8	56.1	13.1	100	23.4
Germany (West)	1971	29.7	56.9	13.4	100	23.6
Sweden	1971	27.6	58.5	13.9	100	23.8
France	1968	32.2	54.4	13.4	100	24.7

Source: Jones, 1979: 83; Russell, 1981: 26.

nomous and not dependent on extensive welfare support. Nevertheless, industrial societies will increasingly face a situation where a large section of their population is retired because of legislation controlling the years of employment, and therefore the economies of the western world will be impeded and retarded by the absence of a youthful working population. Some societies, such as Australia and Argentina, may be able to modify their demographic structure by increasing their dependence upon overseas migration, but this solution is unlikely to be significant for the European societies.

The demographic transition
The aging of western industrial populations is conventionally explained by the demographic transition which brought about a shift from a situation where European societies experienced high birth rates and high death rates to a contemporary context in which they have low birth rates and low death rates. Demographic transition theory argues that human societies pass through a situation of stable populations (balancing high and fluctuating death rates with high birth rates) to a context of stability where both death and birth rates are relatively low. We have seen in earlier chapters that the absence of growth in traditional European societies was brought about by a variety of institutional conditions, especially late marriage, celibacy and the use of religious institutions for the 'surplus population' of young men and women from land-owning classes. As a general rule, in traditional European societies, a man could not marry until a niche appeared in the social structure to permit the formation of a new household (Laslett, 1972).

During the eighteenth century there was a considerable growth in the European population. Although there is a great controversy surrounding the causes of population increase, in the UK the explanation for the acceleration of the population is that the death rate declined sharply. This was brought about by improvements in agricultural production and distribution, changes in sanitation and the water supply, improvements in the system for the distribution of food, an expansion of medical services and the absence of serious plagues and epidemics. The population of the UK expanded from 10,501,000 in 1801 to 46,605,000 in 1941 (Royal Commission on Population, Report, 1949). The debate about the causes of population growth in the UK is complex (Wrigley, 1966; Wrigley, 1969; Wrigley and Schofield, 1982). However, the primary cause of population change was a sharp decline in the infant mortality rate which was a sensitive indicator of improvements in the social environment in the UK. In addition to a decline in the infant mortality rate, there may have also been an increase in fertility after 1800 as a consequence of a decline in the average age of marriage (Andorka, 1978).

The growth of the British population does not appear to have depended in any significant measure on an improvement in the quality of medical practice or upon major medical changes. The improvement in the food supply appears to have been a particularly crucial feature. This was brought about by various improvements in the organization of work in agriculture as a consequence of the concentration of land following further enclosures between 1760 and 1820. There was also an extension of land under cultivation and an improvement in techniques. These included crop rotation, the conservation of soil, improvements in seed production, changes in winter feeding, the introduction of new farming implements and the development of new crops (especially clover and the potato). Improvements in distribution were brought about by the development of canals. The increase in fertility may have been related to industrialization and urbanization. There was an increase in the demand for labour during this period and, by providing an independent source of income for young people, the expansion of employment created a situation where there was no longer a significant need to delay marriage among the working class.

The demographic transition theory suggests that we can conceptualize the growth of populations in terms of the S-curve. In the middle of the demographic transition, populations grow at a very high rate but there are pressures and changes which slow this rate of growth to produce a plateau of relative stability. For example, in the second half of the nineteenth century in the UK, the population increase showed a considerable decline. One explanation for this is the relatively high rate of emigration from the UK to the colonies, but this is relatively unimportant in relation to the significant fall in the rate of natural increase. One explanation for the decline in the natural rate of production is that there was, especially in the middle class, a decline in reproductive capacity (Davies, 1982), but this remains a highly controversial viewpoint. There is far more evidence for the alternative view that the decline in population growth was brought about by voluntary family limitation through the use of new forms of contraception. With the invention of the vulcanization of rubber in 1843, it was possible to develop a reliable, cheap and easily obtainable contraceptive device. There was also a change in attitudes towards contraception following the expansion of birth-control propaganda in the UK after the famous trial of Bradlaugh and Besant in 1877. In the American context, Dr Knowlton's *Fruits of Philosophy* had advocated the use of various forms of birth control among young couples in 1834 (Banks and Banks, 1964).

More significant in terms of cultural changes was the increasing importance of the child within the family. The debate about breast-feeding in the nineteenth century is indicative of a greater concern for the physical and mental wellbeing of children in European societies (Shorter, 1977). There was a new emphasis on domesticity and the importance of family life which came eventually to redirect medical attention towards the health of the child and the mother (Donzelot, 1979). In the British context, it became clear with the greater survival of children following the decline of the infant mortality rate that the economic wellbeing of the family would depend increasingly on contraception and the limitation on the size of the family (Banks, 1969).

The tendency to control the size of the family began in the middle and upper classes, but by the end of the century there was also a decline in the size of working-class families. This decline was probably brought about more by coitus interruptus and abstinence than by the use of condoms. However, between 1860 and 1900 the average size of the completed family in England and Wales had declined from 6.16 to 3.20 children. By 1952 this had fallen further to 2.21 children (Fletcher, 1962). In short, in contemporary Britain the fertility rate is relatively low by world standards but the infantile mortality rate is also low. In the UK, life-expectancy at birth for men has increased from 40 years in 1841 to 68 years in 1961. The average life-expectancy for males in most modern societies is around 70 years of age. In the USA life-expectancy for those born in 1981 is 74.1 years. The consequence of a low rate of reproduction and increasing life-expectancy is an aging population with a distinctive shift in the age structure towards an elderly population.

Although demographic transition theory has proved to be a useful descriptive tool, it has also been the subject of considerable criticism and re-evaluation (Kumar, 1978; Wrong, 1966). Wrong has argued that we should distinguish a number of demographic transitions, since the population growth of European societies may be quite distinctive and unlike the population histories of other continents. The demographic transitions of Latin America, Central Africa and Europe were quite separate and specific. The optimistic feature of the original demographic transition theory was that population and industrialization would achieve an equilibrium, permitting a steady growth in the prosperity of a society. However, in most contemporary developing countries, the rate of population growth is not associated with economic development and one feature of the current population explosion is an increasingly oppressive form of poverty for many societies.

Although economic underdevelopment cannot be wholly

explained by the population explosion, unlimited population development has been directly associated with malnutrition, economic decline and grinding poverty in a number of societies. In the absence of economic growth, the developing societies of the Third World have become increasingly dependent on international aid and foreign assistance. In the Third World, population growth has been brought about, at least in part, by the rapid adoption of modern technical methods in advanced medicine. There has been little sign of a reduction in the birth rate in Latin America and Asia, partly because the historic Malthusian limits on the population have not come into play because of the presence of modern medicine and economic support. The critical problem then is that the growth of population in the Third World is not associated with a corresponding industrialization. It is difficult to achieve successful programmes for family planning because the traditional peasant family depends upon its own labour sources for its future existence. In the absence of an adequate form of collective welfare, heads of households will seek to reproduce themselves through their male offspring as a form of insurance for the future. In response to this crisis some societies (India, China and Singapore) have adopted stringent policies for population regulation often involving compulsory limitations on female fertility (Davis, 1976; Keyfitz, 1982).

Theories of aging

Although social gerontology is a relatively new sub-discipline within the social sciences, it is possible to identify a number of significant and competing theories of aging in the literature. The first is disengagement theory which is associated with the functionalist analysis of social systems. In this approach to aging, it is argued that there is a natural process of withdrawal of the aging from society. As the elderly disengage from society, society disengages from the aging population by a mutual process of declining reciprocity and commitment. This process of social disengagement is inevitable and beneficial, since successful aging requires a gradual adjustment to a decline in involvement with social roles and institutions (Cumming and Henry, 1961; Cumming, 1963).

As Cockerham observes (1982:278) the disengagement theory of aging is the obverse of the theory of social stratification (Davis and Moore, 1945). The functionalist theory of stratification suggests that in order for important and responsible posts in society to be filled by the most competent persons, it is important to have a system of stratified prestige to induce individuals to sacrifice their time through a process of education to acquire the skills to fill these positions. Disengagement theory suggests that the elderly need some motivation to relinquish their posts in society in order to create spaces for a new generation to achieve a social standing through education and achievement. Stratification theory and disengagement theory thereby conceptualize society as an escalator moving through the age structure whereby incoming members find niches in the social ladder made vacant by the retirement of the elderly. Disengagement theory argues that the benefit of retirement for the elderly is that they can shed the expectations and responsibilities of adult life in order to engage in personally rewarding activities which had been made impossible during the long years of full employment and social engagement.

This theory of aging has been criticized on a number of grounds. First, it is clear from an examination of the political systems of advanced industrial societies that the political elite is in fact dominated by a gerontocracy and that the elderly, in so far as they have power, do not easily or voluntarily relinquish their authority and prestige. By contrast, it can be argued that disengagement is brought about by a loss of power in an exchange relationship with society (Dowd, 1975, 1980). Furthermore, disengagement in retirement, far from offering an opportunity for personal consumption and leisure, is in fact a period of increasing impoverishment, especially in economic terms. In 1977 in the USA, it was reported by the Federal Government that 14 percent of the population over 65 were classified as poor; this compared with a 7 percent poverty rate for those 45 to 50 years of age. There are also important differences between elderly males and females so that in general the male elderly population enjoys a far higher level of economic support (Johnson and Williamson, 1980). In the British case, it has been noted that the process of retirement results in an average decline in disposal income of approximately 50 percent (Walker, 1982). In Australia, surveys have shown that the elderly represent a significant proportion of the population below the poverty line. It has been estimated that as many as 15 percent of the elderly in Australia live in poverty (Ford, 1979). The threat of increasing poverty in old age may be at least one reason why some elderly people would prefer to continue in employment and thereby remain engaged with society (Atchley, 1977). In summary, there is relatively little social evidence to support the notion that social disengagement leads to a normal adjusted life for the elderly (Palmore, 1981).

As an alternative to the disengagement theory a number of authors (Havighurst, 1963; Blau, 1973; Palmore, 1968) have suggested that there is no significant decline in activity for the great majority of normal elderly. They also argue that the levels of engagement and disengagement will be closely related to past experiences and socio-economic status. Finally, they argue that successful aging will require a substantial level of social activity rather than less activity. Palmore (1968, 1981) in a longitudinal study in America discovered that disengagement is more likely to be brought about by illness than any other cause. Activity theory therefore comes to conclusions which are more or less the opposite of disengagement theory, namely it argues that personal wellbeing and satisfaction are a function of continuing activity rather than withdrawal (Longino and Kart, 1982).

One problem with activity theory is that it attempts to establish a norm of involvement and activity which may reflect the activist values of middle-class white Americans rather than offering a realistic goal for the elderly. For some groups of the elderly who lack resources including health, these ideals of continuous activity may be entirely inappropriate and reinforce the depression and isolation which is the experience of many. Other research has shown that there is considerable cultural variation in the elderly population, especially according to ethnic background. Therefore a general theory of activity may be inappropriate to describe these various sub-cultures within the elderly.

Alternatives to both disengagement and activity theories have suggested that what is required is a more complex theoretical approach which would take into account variations in the experience of aging according to such variables as social class, ethnicity and gender (Cockerham, 1982; Neugarten, 1964). Gender is a crucial issue in the analysis of aging since women experience far higher rates of poverty in retirement than is the case for men; the female single elderly experience these processes of impoverishment more acutely than any other group. It is also important to distinguish between late maturity (55 to 75 years of age) and old age (over 75) since much chronic illness is confined to those who might be described as deeply aged. In the USA the great majority of the elderly (approximately 70 per cent) described their health as either good or excellent (Kart, 1981). Another variation is that, while rates of labour-force participation declined significantly with aging, in the USA and Australia it is still the case that approximately 10 percent of the elderly population are still employed; this contrasts with approximately 25 percent of the elderly in Japan who continue to work. In short, any theory of aging will have to take into account important social variations within the population of the elderly. While this observation is clearly valid, we should also note that the aging experience is typically accompanied by various forms of social stigmatization and victimization associated with the notion of elderly dependency.

Aging and dependency

Age categories are as much sociological and cultural criteria for the differentiation of populations as they are biological or psychological. What counts as a child or an old person will be the product of particular cultural traditions which define age groups in terms of their social functions and responsibilities rather than in terms of their chronological aging. We lack an adequate sociology of aging and generations (Eisenstadt, 1956). In recent years there have however been a number of exceptionally sophisticated contributions from historical sociology and social history, especially with respect to the analysis of childhood (Laslett, 1972). The historical development of the child for example can be seen as a rather late development in western culture where through a process of differentiation, the child emerged as a separate and unique social role, and childhood came to be regarded as a specific and separate age group with its own cultural requirements and psychological dimensions (Aries, 1962). Unlike medieval societies, contemporary western communities tend to identify a number of transitional age groups between infancy and adulthood. Having created childhood as a special category, we now have the notion of adolescence as a transitional stage which is shot through with social and personal ambiguity. The result is that youthfulness is associated with physical and psychological disorders.

Social attitudes towards the aged have been equally historically specific and culturally variable. In his influential collection of lectures, Fischer (1978) identified four significant periods in the American attitude towards the elderly. In the early American period of colonization (1607–1820), Fischer describes America as a gerontocratia because the predominant attitude towards the elderly was one of veneration whereas attitudes towards the youthful population were summarized by the notion of condescension. In Puritan America, values towards the elderly were dominated by biblical norms in which age and wisdom were connected together. In the period of revolution (1770–1820) there was a significant transition in American attitudes. The revolutionary values which spread from Europe were far more supportive of youth and change. A new set of words came into American culture which denigrated the elderly; for example 'old gaffer' by 1820 had become a word of pejorative significance. Also by 1830 'fogy' had become a term of abuse for old men. In the third phase (1800–1970), there was an increasing emphasis on the virtues and values of youth as against the elderly. Age was no longer associated with morality and wisdom but increasingly with greed and lasciviousness. Youthfulness became the emblem of hope and development; in the political arena there were strong youth movements such as Young America in the 1830s, Mazzini's Young Italy Movement, and finally the movement of so-called Young Turks. Gerontocracy was now associated with reaction and tradition whereby youthfulness came to the fore as the purification and reformation of corrupt political systems. In the final phase, with the development of retirement villages and special programmes associated with the new sciences of gerontology, old age is now seen to be a social problem requiring political change and welfare intervention. These social and cultural changes in the USA and Europe are the historical background to the current debate concerning dependency and the stigmatization of the elderly.

We may define the dependency ratio as the ratio between those who are not actively employed in work (those under the age of sixteen and those over the age of sixty-five) and the working population. This definition of dependency had its origins in the policy research of Rowntree (1871–1954) in the UK who defined poverty in relation to the life cycle of family need. This notion of economic dependency is defined arbitrarily by the age of retirement in any given society. Since retirement has an important function in expanding the labour demand for young people, there will be in a period of recession strong pressures from the trade unions to reduce the age of retirement in order to lower the rate of youth unemployment. In this political circumstance, there will be continuing interest in the dependency ratio. Dependency may also be defined in psychological and physical terms, simply designating that group of the population which requires considerable welfare support in order to maintain themselves. Physical disability is clearly an important measure of dependency in this sense. In association with these two conditions, there is also financial dependency since the retired elderly typically depend extensively on state benefits. The notion that the aged are dependent tends to reinforce the negative stereotype of the elderly as parasitic upon society as a whole. As we have seen, American survey data suggest that the elderly see physicians more frequently and use hospitals more frequently than any other age group, but over 80 percent of the elderly do not use a hospital in a given year, 13 percent report no consultations with doctors in the same period and furthermore the presence of a disease does not necessarily lead to medical demands by the elderly (Estes, 1979). Many other stereotypes concerning the elderly such as their loneliness or loss of memory have been shown to be inaccurate (Palmore, 1968, 1981). However, there is also evidence that the elderly suffer a sharp decline in their income on retirement and that they are stigmatized somewhat like other minority groups within the population.

Capitalism and old age

The plight of the elderly in contemporary industrial capitalism has led some writers to defend the importance of a Marxist analysis of the elderly in relation to the economic and political requirements of capitalist society. Since in capitalism age like sickness is in practice defined by the absence of gainful employment, there is an important sense in which old age is socially constructed. Specifically, retirement at the age of sixty-five arbitrarily defines a person as no longer productive and therefore for all practical purposes old. Since retirement is itself the outcome of a long struggle between labour and capital, we should expect that retirement patterns are closely associated with the particular economic and political requirements of a capitalist economic system. Early retirement brings about a restriction of the labour supply, enables young people to enter the workforce, controls the level of unemployment and reduces the cost of labour by introducing young workers to paid employment. Some writers have argued that the development of retirement has to be seen as part of a wider capitalist strategy for the restructuring of the labour force with the removal of certain segments from the labour supply in order to assist the further accumulation of capital. In his influential book Phillipson (1982:155) has argued that:

> the old are sacrificed in the corporation's drive for order and efficiency: speed-ups on the line, work-measurement techniques, etc., sealing the fate of the ageing worker.

The elderly worker is abandoned rather than retired because he or she can no longer function efficiently in the production of an economic surplus. Furthermore in a period of severe economic recession, provision for the elderly is seriously curtailed, bringing about a further deterioration of the social and economic position of the elderly.

There are a number of difficulties with the argument that the peculiar problems of the aged are effects of the economic requirements of a capitalist mode of production. First, the stigmatization of the elderly and their socially marginal position are features not peculiar to capitalism but to human society as such, at least through long periods of human history (de Beauvoir, 1972). Secondly, we should not underestimate or ignore the capacity of the elderly for political mobilization and reform (Fox, 1981; Stearns, 1977). Thirdly, there is evidence that in state socialist societies attitudes towards the old are not especially different in terms of stereotyping than attitudes in capitalist societies (Willcocks, 1983). Fourthly, while a significant extension of state-regulated institutions and systems of care for the elderly would most likely improve their material and social circumstances, the spread of gerontological institutions would also represent a massive extension of the systems of social control and regulation over the lives of individuals. While there is clearly a role for educational programmes for retirement, an extension of community-care facilities and for specific developments in gerontological practice (Taylor and Gilmore, 1982), these developments could also be regarded as an increasing medicalization of the aged as a specific and separate target group within the community. The unintended effect of these gerontological practices could be an increase in the objective and subjective elements of dependency by the poor.

An alternative approach is to consider the problem of dependency and stigma from the perspective of reciprocity. All social relations are characterized by endless forms of exchange, which create and require the norm of reciprocity. Unequal patterns of exchange create dependency through reciprocity. We can regard all forms of social service as systems of exchange (Pinker, 1971) because the norm of reciprocity is based upon the notion that there is no such thing as a free lunch, dependency is only acceptable where it is a contribution for previous contributions or where it is in anticipation of a future contribution.

The absence of reciprocity (for example, in the case of extreme poverty and disability) has important moral implications for the social and personal standing of the dependent person. People who are socially dependent are breaking the norm of reciprocity and therefore dependency is typically stigmatized, especially through the provision of social services to the unemployed and the poor. It is for this reason that begging has been typically a criminal act because it is a gross and public breach of the idea of reciprocity. In common speech a variety of descriptions are used to describe this parasitic relationship with the general community (such as scrounging, chiselling and bludging). Spicker (1984) argues that it is this lack of reciprocity in exchange which is the fundamental explanation of the stigma which is associated with the recipients of social welfare. It is the absence of reciprocity and moral standing which explains the stigma surrounding the real or perceived dependency of the aged rather than the economic requirements of production.

We could further develop Spicker's argument by comparing social attitudes towards youth and the aged. In medieval societies, the concept of 'youth' did not refer necessarily to a specific age group, but rather to any group of males who lacked social responsibility as a consequence of their social marginality, their lack of access to land and wealth, and therefore their single status. These groups of youth in medieval society were held to be irresponsible, parasitic and therefore dangerous, being socially disruptive elements within the broader social structure (Rossiand, 1985). In contemporary societies, young people especially unmarried young males are held to be, or thought to be socially disruptive, deviant and politically threatening. They are a threat to tradition and stability. Because the teenager and the elderly share a number of common social characteristics (such as the absence of work and social responsibilities) they are often described in the same pejorative and stigmatizing fashion. For example, we often refer to the elderly as childish and irresponsible; indeed we may refer to them as having returned to a second childhood. We can theorize the stigma of the aged and the youthful by reference to their real or imagined disengagement from the community, that is their lack of reciprocity. We might express this diagrammatically, as in Figure 4.

FIGURE 4
The reciprocity–maturation curve

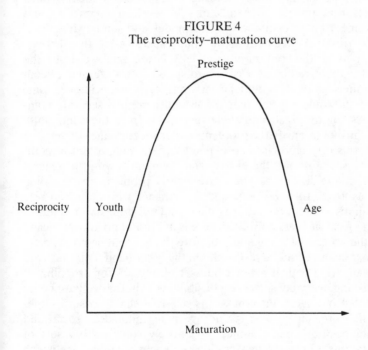

As people mature they typically acquire new responsibilities and occupy new social roles; for example, they may become married and have children alongside fulfilling permanent employment. As their reciprocity and integration with society increases so their personal prestige and esteem within the community increases (somewhat in line with disengagement theory). As people become elderly, they either through design or compulsion are forced out of traditional social roles involving full-time responsibility and commitment. As they withdraw from the social roles, their reciprocity and integration with society declines and they once more lose a certain amount of social prestige. It is for this reason that the social labels for the adolescent and the aged are similar, in pointing to a certain lack of engagement and reciprocity. Young people are typically held to be irresponsible precisely because of their lack of involvement in the community through the family, employment or voluntary associations. In the same measure, the aged are similarly held to be in a sense irresponsible because of their dependency on the community (whether that dependency is real or perceived).

In this model I have attempted to explain the victimization and stigmatization of the elderly in terms of an exchange theory which suggests that prestige depends on the level of reciprocity and involvement in the community. This model is to some extent compatible with disengagement theory, but it also suggests that increasing activity or the continuity of activity in the aged would be the basis for them retaining a certain degree of prestige and esteem within the society. This model clearly has social policy implications, because it would suggest that the establishment of separate communities for the aged and their separation from the community would further intensify the problems of dependency and stigma.

In terms of reciprocity and dependency, it is important to compare the social role of the elderly and their status with the general theory of the sick role. There are clearly problems in regarding aging as a sick role. For example, compliance with the social role and submission to a medical regime would not bring about a termination of the sickness episode. There is at present no known escape from the process of aging and therefore there would be no expectation that health could be restored. On the other hand, entry into old age does bring with it a bona fide set of excuses for dropping or diminishing everyday social responsibilities. Alternatively we could argue that old age is in terms of its sick-role characteristics somewhat like pregnancy; that is, old age is an ambiguous social and cultural position, being subject to entirely contradictory sets of expectations. Given the new emphasis on activism in old age which is expressed by the activity theory, it may well be increasingly difficult to sink into a comfortable and inactive maturity. Since the values of youth, individualism and activism are prevalent in all aspects of western culture, old age has not escaped this paradigm of youthfulness. One feature of this activist framework is the emphasis on sexuality in old age as a normal and indeed desirable activity.

This raises a further intriguing question as to whether aging should be in fact treated as a disease. One reason why aging is not conventionally regarded as a disease by the medical profession is that it is regarded as an entirely natural process. Since aging cannot be terminated and since it is so far a universal experience of humanity, there do not appear to be grounds for medical intervention. The medical view would be somewhat like disengagement theory written in biological terms, that is, the purpose of aging is to provide spaces within the species for new members. However, what the medical profession regards as natural and unnatural is in itself highly problematic. For example, in the nineteenth century, homosexuality was regarded as unnatural and therefore it was perfectly appropriate to consider medical intervention to remove or control homosexuality. When considered from a disease model perspective, there are very strong reasons for regarding aging as a disease. It can be argued:

> aging possesses a definitive group of clinical manifestations or symptoms; a clear-cut etiology of structural changes at both the macroscopic and microscopic levels; a significant measure of impairment, discomfort, and suffering; and, if we are willing to grant the same tolerance to current theories of aging as we grant theories in other domains of medicine, an explicit set of precipitating factors. Aging has all the relevant markings of a disease process. (Caplan, 1981:734)

There are a number of arguments against regarding aging as a disease. First, since aging cannot be terminated, there is little point in doctors regarding it as a disease. Secondly, to regard aging as a disease might intensify the stigmatization of the aging. Finally, to recognize age as a disease would increase the economic burden on a community as a whole. However, while these are perfectly reasonable arguments, the consequence of not regarding aging as a disease is to diminish its social importance and possibly to prevent the development of geriatric medicine. That is, there may be negative consequences of regarding aging as a natural process, namely that we do not invest a significant amount of social effort or resources into the care of the aged or into medicine designed to ameliorate the physical consequences of aging. It is certainly the case that geriatric medicine had a late and rather uncertain start within the medical curriculum (Stearns, 1977).

Aging and dying

There is a sense in which we can regard dying as the final process of aging. Sociologists occasionally suggest that we can distinguish three forms of dying, namely psychological, sociological and biological dying. As we grow old we are gradually marginalized within the community and begin to lose a number of personal contacts, which takes the form of a personal or psychological contraction (dying) from social relations. Through the process of dying our social contacts are gradually diminished and we find ourselves socially isolated. Finally, this process is terminated by a biological death which brings to a conclusion the long history of our personal disengagement. We can therefore regard dying like aging as a gradual attrition of social relations combined with increasing dependency often on institutions which are somewhat anonymous and bureaucratic.

The sociological and psychological treatment of dying as a form of human behaviour has in recent years been considerably influenced by a number of important studies in this area especially those by Kubler-Ross (1970), Hinton (1967) and Feifel (1959). These studies have suggested that dying has as it were a normal trajectory involving distinctive stages (such as denial, anger, depression and finally acceptance) by which the patient eventually successfully terminates their social relations.

By seeing dying as a form of status passage (Glaser and Strauss, 1965), we draw attention to the important idea that dying is a social process which is guided by expectations of appropriate behaviour. These expectations delimit a range of 'dying trajectories' (Glaser and Strauss, 1968) which define various forms of normal and abnormal dying. These expectations are particularly concerned with the degree to which a person is convinced that the patient will in fact die and with the appropriate duration of dying. Because of the emotional and social tensions surrounding dying and death, the aim of the hospital setting is to establish a regular and routine pattern of death for large numbers of patients (Sudnow, 1967; Wright, 1981). By establishing a social organization of dying, these norms and practices give shape to the institutionalized dying process, thereby avoiding contingent and disruptive events which would threaten, not only the organization of the hospital or hospice, but of the social environment and management of the dying person.

While these settings and expectations may have removed some of the uncertainty and anxiety which surround dying and death, the problem of dying remains acute, at least in existential terms, because the process of dying is essentially a lonely one (Elias, 1985). According to this argument, while we share a number of common features with animals, human beings are unique in knowing that they will and must die. Since this reality must ultimately be faced alone, some element of alienation and isolation is probably unavoidable. Loneliness may take many forms, but its essence lies in the fact that it involves a situation where we are increasingly without significance for others. The trajectory of individual disengagement is consequently a process of increasing isolation and loneliness. However, in order to understand the character of this dying in isolation, it is important to consider the historical and cultural response to death as a social fact in western societies over a number of centuries.

Western attitudes to death
The historical and social approach to the analysis of death in recent years has been dominated by the seminal work of the historian Ariès (1974); his analysis of death and dying has, however been criticized for its implicit romanticism (Elias, 1985). In his work on western attitudes towards the problem of death and the dying, Ariès detected an important change in attitudes and practices with the gradual individualization and secularization of European cultures. In pre-modern times, death was primarily a public event, that is an event situated within a densely structured kinship system. It was natural because of its regularity and persistence; it was often forewarned in the sense that it was expected, and finally death was not individualized or primarily personal. This public character of death was further underlined by the fact that burial was anonymous, public, collective and ecclesiastical. The Church acted as a collective guardian of bones in the charnel house where the dead lay in rest waiting the final judgement and the resurrection of bodies. One's own death was part of a general religious plan which was historical and teleological. Whereas the majority of people died traditionally within their own domestic space surrounded by their kin folk and neighbours, in contemporary society death is institutionalized and impersonal, because it takes place within the hospital setting. In the USA approximately 80 percent of the population die in hospital (both public and private); in the UK approximately 57 percent of the population die in a hospital or similar setting (Cartwright et al., 1973). This hygienic death within the isolated space of a side-ward in the modern hospital contrasts strongly with the public death of medieval times. One significant feature of this change is the secularization of western societies in which death is no longer clothed with the certitude of faith (Turner, 1983). The other significant change is the individualization of death and burial in contemporary societies in the West. The growth of individualized tombs with their own architecture and location is a clear indication of this individualism in contemporary cultures.

Another important change is the gradual rationalization of death and burial in contemporary societies. The dead become the objects of an increasingly differentiated and professionalized service, especially in the USA with the prevalence of embalming. Whereas death and burial in pre-modern societies were surrounded by a dense system of public rituals, marking out the distinctive phases of dying, death and mourning, in contemporary industrial societies these funeral rights have largely disappeared, apart from the rural fringe of some European communities (Valle, 1955). It has been suggested that the absence of a significant culture of mourning and a system of funereal rites has made the whole process of bereavement and grief in contemporary society highly problematic, uncertain and unsatisfactory (Parkes, 1972).

Conclusion

In pre-modern societies, both the aged and the dead had important social functions. The elderly were the repositories of tradition, lore and wisdom. Because of their mastery of social custom and ritual, the aged had an important political and normative function within the community. They also, because of the system of property distribution through the family, continued to have important economic roles in the social structure. We could also suggest that there was no significant break between the living and the dead, since in many societies the ancestors played an important role in the community, at least in a symbolic and religious sense. In China, the health of the community was to some extent dependent upon the continuing service provided to the dead. In general, prior to the rise of capitalism, there were functional relationships between the ancestors, the living and social continuity (Finucane, 1982; Goody, 1962).

The growing importance of the nuclear family in the eighteenth and nineteenth centuries meant that the small family unit became isolated and separated from a wider kinship structure. It is important not to exaggerate the social and cultural dominance of the extended family in previous societies. The two-generational family has been the dominant structure of the household for many centuries, because it was unusual for grandparents to survive, given the low life-expectancy of people in pre-modern societies. The isolation of the aged in contemporary society has been brought about by the dislocation of the nuclear family from the community and the wider kinship system; the aged do not have a major function within the family or in the community. Where families experience major geographical and social mobility, it is also the case that the aged often become separated from a wider system of kinship. In addition to these changes in the structure of the household and kinship systems, there have been developments in the forms of knowledge which are important in society, rendering the wisdom and lore of the elderly often socially redundant. Where societies are dominated by scientific knowledge through the process of intellectualization and rationalization, the authority of tradition is constantly undermined and challenged; the knowledge of the elderly thereby becomes merely archaic (Shils, 1981).

Although these social processes are to some extent global, the problem of the elderly in societies which place an emphasis on youthfulness, activism and individualism becomes especially acute. In American society there is therefore a serious social problem for the elderly, especially where there is little public provision for the old in a medical system which is dominated by market principles. It is not surprising therefore that the activity theory of aging should have been developed in the American context where there is a cultural emphasis on action and youth. It is also not surprising that it is in the American context that the political mobilization of the elderly has perhaps gone furthest with the formation of the Gray Panthers.

We have seen that a number of radical sociologists have suggested that it is capitalism which makes the dilemma of the elderly a specific and acute issue in contemporary capitalist societies. It is clearly the case that in a period of economic recession the social support for the elderly is an early target of government cuts. However, the relationship between the social problem of age and the capitalist economy is not direct or uniform across societies. For example, the social position of the elderly in Japan is quite unique, partly because of the specific historical development of capitalism in Japan and partly because of its cultural and religious system. In Japan, the authority of the kinship system and the family has not been undermined to the same extent that we have seen in the USA and the UK. In Japan, the family system has made a remarkable adjustment to industrialization and as a result the values of the familialism are relatively prominent, giving a continuing significance to the norm of duty towards the family. It can also be argued that individualism is far less prominent in Japan than in European and American capitalism (Vogel, 1967). Finally, within the Japanese economy, personal loyalty to the company over a lifetime is normally rewarded by social benefits in retirement.

Although there are important variations between societies, the elderly are faced with a number of common difficulties in societies where the importance of the family has declined. There is less emphasis on traditional knowledge. Where there is compulsory retirement current levels of life expectancy will mean that many old people experience a significant proportion of their life in isolation. This problem is especially acute for women who, because of their greater longevity, may experience a considerable period of personal isolation through widowhood. The result is, as we have seen, a major period of dependency where the elderly will be forced to rely on the state in the absence of a kinship system. This dependency on welfare is one component of the stigmatization of inactive elderly social groups who are seen to be parasitic upon the community. In a society where self respect depends a great deal on one's economic contribution to the social system, the elderly will appear to be in practice a deviant social group. In particular, the retired elderly deviate from the predominant social norm of work, individualism and activism. It is in this respect that aging can be regarded as a form of the sick role, at least in the sense that to age is to deviate.

III
SOCIAL ORGANIZATION OF MEDICAL POWER

7
Professions, knowledge and power

Introduction

The analysis of the role of professions in society is well established as a topic in sociology. For sociologists writing in the tradition of Durkheim, the liberal professions represented the institutionalization of altruistic values, since the professions were, within the social division of labour, officially committed to various forms of personal service and community welfare; their social role was meant to embody a disinterested commitment to community values. In a similar fashion, it is possible to detect in Weber's analysis of the calling in religion, science and politics the articulation of the notion that the professional is a person motivated neither by personal interests nor simply by the desire for economic rewards. In a secular society Weber suggested that an ethic of absolute ends had become increasingly impossible, but a commitment to the ethic of responsibility was a suitable motivation for a person with a vocation. Within the classical sociological tradition, Mannheim had argued that the intellectual in modern society was a person above sectional interests and the free-floating character of intellectual work was its main guarantee to objectivity in a world of relativistic knowledge. Within this sociological framework, the profession of medicine would appear to be *par excellence* a calling to the service of others in the absence of a direct and specific material reward. As we will see, Parsons was a significant representative of this particular tradition of sociology which puts an emphasis on the ethical character of the profession, its service to the person and its basis in technical knowledge.

This tradition was challenged by writers like Hughes (1958) who criticized the conventional approach for assuming and adopting the ideal image offered by the profession itself. He emphasized by contrast the material and symbolic benefits which derive from an occupational monopoly based upon a licence to practice. In medical sociology this perspective on the professions as occupations based upon a form of social closure was developed by Freidson (1970) who placed particular stress on the role of power in the medical division of labour and noted that the monopolistic power of the medical profession was such that it could subordinate adjacent and related occupations, keeping them permanently in the status of quasi-professions or paramedical groups. Marxist writers have subsequently adopted these perspectives on power to argue that professional dominance is of special importance to capitalism and that professional bodies under state protection have a peculiar contribution to make to the economic and political functioning of a capitalist system. Professional groups, alongside other members of the new middle class, contribute to the legitimization of production under capitalist conditions by contributing to the management and surveillance of the working class. The professional therefore contributes directly to the creation of a disciplined and subservient working class (Carchedi, 1977). The professions exercise control on behalf of the capitalist class under the auspices of the state; this form of regulation constitutes medical dominance (Willis, 1983).

This Marxist analysis of the professions denies the normative function of the professions and questions its ethical character, by emphasizing the role of power and market control over the legitimizing function of knowledge. To this Marxist framework, there has in recent years been added a feminist critique of the medical profession as a privileged occupational group exercising patriarchal authority and control over subordinate social groups, especially over women. The doctor reinforces and articulates patriarchal values by regulating the sexuality of women and supporting implicitly the structure of the family on behalf of existing social arrangements which are dominated by male control and privilege. As we have seen in previous chapters, the medical profession and medical knowledge constitute women as patients while also subordinating those occupations which are dominated by women and rendering these paramedical groups into subordinate associations. The apparently neutral advice of the doctor towards his patients and their illnesses is in fact a form of subtle but real patriarchal management (Ehrenreich and English, 1972, 1976, 1978).

There is no necessary contradiction between feminist and Marxist theories. Feminist theory argues that women cheapen the costs of labour by their domestic work in the traditional household; then we can see how in principle patriarchy in the household is functionally important for the continuity of capitalist relations (Kuhn and Wolpe, 1978). Within the division of labour in medical services, women continue to function as subordinate labour and this feature of female employment in medicine is forcefully illustrated by the case of nursing and midwifery. Feminist theory therefore argues that the division of labour which is characteristic of the conventional household is now reproduced at the place of work where once more women reduce the costs of labour in the hospital and clinical setting (Game and Pringle, 1983).

Sociological theory appears to develop through the contradiction of paradigms, whereby traditional frameworks are constantly rejected in favour of paradigmatic revolutions. As a consequence of these revolutionary theoretical transformations and the branching of knowledge, sociology as a discipline often appears to lack any form of theoretical continuity (Wagner, 1984). By constantly rejecting its theoretical past, sociology has an unstable and fragmented evolution. We have seen for example how in medical sociology constant shifts of paradigm result in the ejection and rejection of previous studies which, within their own framework, were both important and adequate. The sociological analysis of the professions is no exception. Therefore in this chapter I shall attempt a theoretical synthesis of previous positions in order to develop a more stable and comprehensive approach to professions and professionalization. Having considered the various theoretical traditions, I propose an approach to the professions which attempts to combine knowledge, power and ethics as necessary dimensions of professionalism; this perspective is then considered with special reference to nurses and hospital pharmacists. The nursing profession is particularly important within the whole framework of the debate about gender and patriarchy. Pharmacy by contrast provides an important case study for the debate over de-skilling and proletarianization (Abercrombie and Urry, 1983), given the revolution in pharmacological knowledge.

Frameworks for the analysis of professions

The sociological analysis of the professions has, especially within the British context, been developed in an interesting and important fashion by Johnson (1972, 1977, 1982). In this introductory account of the nature of the professions, I shall start with an overview of Johnson's position. We can argue that two themes were dominant in the traditional sociology of the professions. First, there was a view that professions act as a stabilizing force in capitalist society, since they counterpose the dominant ethos and organization of capitalism, in which the profit motive is paramount. This position was most clearly articulated by Parsons (1939). Within Parsonian sociology, the pattern variables were used to describe the profession as a vocation based upon universalism, disinterested service and affective neutrality. Secondly, there was an alternative tradition which argued that the professions are largely dominated by the monopolistic interests and bureaucratic forces of contemporary capitalism; the profession therefore does not escape from the dominant logic of industrial capitalist society. This view was associated with Weber's concept of social closure and in the American context with the work of Veblen and Wright Mills. For example, Veblen's *The Higher Learning in America* (1957), which was first published in 1918, was a sustained critique of the pretentions of professional academics, since Veblen argued that the university was entirely dominated by the business ethic of American capitalism. Academics, far from rising above the ethos of self-interest, were deeply implicated in the whole structural relationship between knowledge and production.

In attempting to reconcile these two contradictory perspectives in the sociology of professions, sociologists developed the notion of professionalization. Whether or not a professional group displayed the attributes of social altruism, professional competence, social responsibility and service to the client would depend on the degree to which that group was fully professionalized. As a result, it was possible for sociologists to regard departures from the ideal of professionalism as consequences of the absence of professionalization as a process of occupational change. For example, the presence of a business orientation towards the client would be taken as evidence of unsuccessful and incomplete professionalization.

In turn the professionalization approach in sociology can be broken down into two different and separate theoretical perspectives. Professionalization can be seen in terms of an accumulation of attributes; whether an occupation is a profession will thereby depend upon the satisfaction and achievement of a number of traits, including theoretical knowledge as the basis of skill, the development of specialized training and education, the testing of the competence of members by formal examinations, the development of a professional organization, the emergence of a professional code, and finally the development of an altruistic service (Millerson, 1964). The second approach suggests that professionalization is functionally significant for social order, because it involves the specialization of knowledge and skill which is then directed towards maintaining the social system. Functionalism therefore explains the privileged position of the professions on the grounds that they provide services which are socially valued (Ben-David, 1963–1964). This approach to the professions was one component within the broader development of a functionalist theory of social stratification (Tumin, 1970).

Both of these approaches to the nature of professionalization can be criticized. Firstly, the definitions of the content of these professional roles are based upon the official literature and ideology of the professions as developed by elites within those professional groups. In short, the sociological perspective simply reflects the dominant view of the profession itself. Secondly, these approaches ignore the role of power and the privilege enjoyed by professional bodies which enable them to manipulate and control their clients and markets. The profession from this perspective is an occupation which by licence has a monopolistic privilege over its particular practices. Thirdly, the attempt to define the traits of the profession involves a unilinear view of occupational histories in which there is an end-state to which the profession is directed. These unilinear or evolutionary theories of professionalism neglect the specific and contingent historical contexts within which professions develop in different societies. There may be, because of national variations for example, no particular historical trajectory for professions. Johnson (1982) has drawn attention to the fact that the development of professions within the British Commonwealth was largely determined by the special imperial relationship between the UK and the old colonies. In this particular instance, to utilize the English professional experience as a model for global professional development is inadequate.

As an alternative to these perspectives, it can be argued that professionalization should be regarded as a strategy of occupational control. This strategy of occupational control structures the relationship between experts, patrons and clients. We should start therefore by considering the professions within the social division of labour and how their position creates a relationship of social and economic dependence between the professional and the client. The specialization of knowledge and the delivery of a service by the professional on the basis of skill and expertise are accompanied by the absence of specialized consumption by the client.

The relationship between the patient and the client can be discussed in terms of an indeterminacy/technicality ratio (Jamous and Peloille, 1970). The specialized knowledge of the professional creates the basis for prestige and social distance between the expert and the client, since the client by definition is excluded from the esoteric knowledge of the professional association. The basis of professional knowledge is cognitive rationality whereby the privileged status of the profession is grounded in a scientific discipline. However, this special and systematic body of knowledge also provides the basis for external intervention and social control of the profession itself. Where this knowledge can be codified and developed by computer systems, the profession becomes vulnerable to the rationalization of knowledge. Where the knowledge of the profession is grounded in a natural science, this knowledge can become the basis of routine practices. The consequence of this form of knowledge is the possible fragmentation of the profession and its external control by bureaucratic means. It is for this reason that Jamous and Peloille argue that professions need a barrier to protect themselves from such routinization and this barrier is constituted by the indetermination of knowledge; the knowledge of the profession has to have a distinctive mystique which suggests that there is a certain professional attitude and competence which cannot be reduced merely to systematic and routinized knowledge. We might suggest that professions have to have a hermeneutic basis; that is, there has to be the development of interpretation which provides the barrier against external regularization through the routinization of its base in knowledge.

Johnson argues that the greater the indeterminacy within the professional relationship, the greater the social distance between the client and the professional, and hence the greater the helplessness of the client in relation to the expert. While the acquisition of this interpretive knowledge provides the basis for selection and therefore closure of the occupation, it is also the basis for the power relationship between the professional association and its clientele. The consequence is that we may argue that professionalism is a special type of occupational control within the market place rather than merely a list of attributes which define some fixed essence of a particular occupation. This viewpoint directs us towards the dynamic development of professions in relation to the state and their clientele, without committing us to some evolutionary scheme for the analysis of professional ethics. It also suggests that, while occupations may become professionalized through the development of monopolistic relations to the market place, professions can also be undermined and de-professionalized through the threat of fragmentation and external regulation.

In general, it is possible to identify three different systems by which the client–professional relationship has been structured. First, there is collegiate control whereby the producer defines the needs of the consumer and the fashion by which these needs will be satisfied. In collegiate control, the profession controls itself through a corporate system of regulation and surveillance. Law and medicine would be classic illustrations of this system of collegiate control especially in the UK in the nineteenth-century. The second form of client–professional relationship is that of patronage in which it is the consumer who defines his or her own needs and determines the nature of their satisfaction. There are two forms of patronage. Oligarchic patronage would be illustrated by the medieval court which employed artists directly to provide services to the court. The second is corporate patronage in which an occupation will be regulated by a large enterprise which provides services internally. For example, accountancy is an occupation which is often housed inside a corporate enterprise, and its skills and functions are directly controlled by the corporation itself. Thirdly, there is the structure of mediation in which a third party (typically the state) intervenes between producers and consumers of professional services to regulate and control occupational practices and consumer satisfaction. In advanced capitalism, the state increasingly has a role in the control and management of professions, through for example the welfare state system whereby social workers are controlled through a system of mediation.

These three structures therefore define different forms of the client–expert relationship, but they also indicate certain processes within this relationship which may involve changes in the nature of professionalism either in the direction of greater control and prestige, or in the direction of de-skilling and fragmentation. In order to consider these processes we need to return to the question of indeterminacy/technicality and specifically to the debate over the so-called proletarianization of the professions.

Professionalization versus de-skilling
Although a number of sociologists have commented on the fact that the learned professions have provided a model by which all occupations might eventually claim professional status (Wilensky, 1963), other sociologists writing about the professions have suggested that in contemporary society there is a definite and widespread process of de-professionalization or proletarianization (Haug, 1973; Oppenheimer, 1973). There are at least three processes by which de-professionalization might take place. First, there is the growth of bureaucracy where professionals working in bureaucratic settings often find their professional autonomy undermined by the hierarchical structure of rules and authority. Since the modern hospital is a large and bureaucratic organization, professional groups working inside hospitals often find their scope for freedom, autonomy and initiative limited by this hierarchical formation. Secondly, the very process of socialization and development of knowledge may bring about a fragmentation of a profession into quite distinctive and separate groupings. Thirdly, there is the pressure from new professionals and para-professionals to take over and encroach upon the domain of the most prestigious and established professions within the medical field.

The contradiction between professionalism and bureaucracy is of special significance in this debate (Hall, 1968). Oppenheimer (1973:213) has defined proletarianization as a process involving: (1) an extensive division of labour in which the worker performs a limited number of tasks; (2) the conditions of work, the nature of the workplace and the character of the work process are set and determined by a higher authority rather than by the worker; (3) the wage is the primary source of income and this is determined by the market place rather than by individual negotiation; and (4) the worker, in order to protect him or herself from the transformation of their work, has to form some association or union to bargain collectively for improvements. The development of a bureaucratic organizational system produces proletarian conditions of work and, in so far as professionals operate under these conditions, they will be progressively proletarianized. Because medical professionals increasingly operate within bureaucratic settings, we may expect a decline in the status of such occupations and the undermining of their professionalism.

This view of professions is opposite to the perspective presented by Bell in his analysis of the 'post-industrial society' (1974). Bell has emphasized the increasing importance of technical knowledge for controlling and managing social and political affairs in industrial society. Indeed, this knowledge-based society has replaced a previous social system grounded in the ownership of property. The explosion of knowledge and the increasing importance of planning are seen by post-industrial theorists as a foundation upon which professionalization in the future will be based. The expansion of professional norms and activities is further associated with the development of a service economy and the expansion of the tertiary sector. The demands of such an economy are significant in the development of a new middle-class, white-collar employment and professionalism.

We thus have two entirely contradictory views of the nature of professionalism and its future. The importance of the indeterminacy/technicality ratio is that it provides a theoretical solution to the dilemma posed by these contradictory perspectives. All professions will be characterized by a certain duality, that is by an opposition between technical and routine knowledge, and the ideology or mystique of interpretation. As a result we can conceptualize professions as occupations subject to contradictory forces which simultaneously push them towards proletarianism and professionalism.

Professions, like other occupations, are subject to certain external forces which fragment and subordinate their activities to the interests of capital which requires labour-saving and de-skilling processes. At the same time the professions are involved in the surveillance and control of labour, which is part of their social distance and authority in relation to society. To take the illustration of accountancy, the accountant's professional relationship is typically characterized by corporate patronage. Because accountancy has a direct relationship to capitalist processes, accountancy lacks the element of indeterminacy which is essential to the professional relationship. The accountant is housed within the accountancy firm or within the larger corporation, and does not control their work situation. The accountant is de-skilled by the technical complexity of the labour process in capitalism. However, it is also true that accountants have become significant in the management of financial institutions, investment and the management of the money market. We can see therefore that accountancy is split by this duality. By contrast, it can be shown within this framework that

> the professionalism of medicine – those institutions sustaining its auto-
> nomy – is directly related to its monopolization of 'official' definitions of
> illness and health. The doctor's certificate defines and legitimates the
> withdrawal of labour. Credentialism, involving monopolistic practices
> and occupational closure, fulfils ideological functions in relation to capi-
> tal and reflects the extent to which medicine in its role of surveillance and
> the reproduction of labour power is able to draw upon powerful ideo-
> logical symbols in the creation of indetermination. (Johnson, 1977:106)

Although this is a powerful statement of the role of medicine as a profession, it also appears to be the case that within medicine itself there is a fragmentation of the occupation into specialists who control the medical profession and those general practitioners whose income and status has shown a marked decline in recent years.

Criticisms and alternatives
Although Johnson's (1977) approach to the position of the professions within the class structure represents a theoretically important development in the literature on professions, his approach is not entirely successful. As Abercrombie and Urry (1983:77) have argued, his explanation of the functions of control and surveillance has to be considerably extended in order to incorporate the notions of certification and reproduction of labour-power in the case of the medical profession. In addition, the concept of indetermination is probably not appropriate as a description of the character of professional knowledge and the idea of interpretation is more suitable. While Johnson has attempted to provide a theory of professionalization based upon a Marxist analysis of class, a satisfactory explanation of professionalization as an occupational strategy will come

eventually to depend upon both Weberian and Marxist perspectives. Following Larson (1980) we can argue that the status and power of professions depends upon their ability to maintain a market situation and access to appropriate clients. This market strategy and the process of social closure will in turn depend significantly, in a society based upon knowledge, on university education as the basis for credentialism. In Larson's argument, professionalization is seen as a process by which the producers of services have attempted to constitute and manage a market for their expertise; this collective attempt to maintain status requires state backing for the establishment of a monopoly of knowledge and skill. The process of professionalization itself has an effect on the distribution of wealth and status thereby contributing to social inequality, especially between labour and capital. The maintenance of this privilege requires the continuing exercise of dominance over allied and competing occupations. This process is especially evident in the case of occupations providing health services in relation to the medical profession (Freidson, 1970; Parry and Parry, 1976; Willis, 1983).

The professionalization process as a strategy of occupational monopoly will therefore have three important dimensions. The first will be the production and maintenance of a body of esoteric knowledge which requires considerable interpretation in its application. In order to sustain this body of knowledge, an occupation will require a formal educational basis and systematic entry requirements; these in turn will require a university system of education. Secondly, a profession will attempt to maintain and cultivate an extensive clientele for its services and this will involve various exclusionary practices whereby competing occupations are subordinated or removed from the market place. This access to clients may well require legislation and therefore we can see the importance of the state in maintaining professional monopolies. Thirdly, a professional group will seek to maintain certain privileges at the point of work and the delivery of a service, namely to maintain autonomy over the delivery of skills and the relationship with the client. Professions will resist the de-skilling which is involved in managerial strategies at the work place which fragment and routinize the work relationship between expert and client.

Following Lockwood (1958), the professional strategy will require an occupation to secure its position in terms of its class, market and status circumstances. In class terms, a profession will be forced to secure its means of reproduction through the educational system in such a way as to reproduce the systematic inequalities between social classes which are to some extent manifest in the inequalities between expert and client. Secondly, a profession will be forced into market conflicts where it will struggle against competing occupations in terms of maintaining its privileged access to knowledge and to educational systems. Finally, in terms of status relations, a profession will seek, in terms of job autonomy and control over services, to ensure the continuing ignorance of its clients and thereby their need for a professional service.

In the health field, medical dominance is a necessary feature of the professional power and superiority of the medical practitioner in relation to other occupations. We may define medical dominance as a set of strategies requiring control over the work situation, the institutional features of occupational autonomy within the wider medical division of labour, and finally occupational sovereignty over related occupational groups. This medical dominance further involves a privileged location within the general class structure of society.

It is possible to identify three modes of domination with respect to allied occupations, namely subordination, limitation and exclusion (Turner, 1985b; Willis, 1983). Subordination describes a situation in which the character and activities of an occupation are delegated by doctors with the result that there is little scope for independence, autonomy and self-regulation. Occupational subordination to medical dominance characterizes both nursing and midwifery. By contrast, occupational limitation is illustrated by dentistry, optometry and pharmacy. These occupational limitations involve various forms of containment to a specific part of the body (as in dentistry) or to a specific therapeutic method (as in pharmacy). These forms of limitation and restriction follow from the fact that medical dominance is typically exercised by physicians playing an important part in the official registration boards of such occupations. Registration Acts specify the professional competence of such groups within a narrow occupational territory, while also confirming the control of the medical profession over such terrain. The final form of medical dominance is the case of exclusion whereby alternative and competing medical practices are denied legitimation through registration. In contemporary societies for example, the clergy have been generally excluded from psychiatric practice and psychological counselling by the predominance of the medical profession. The occupational conflict between the medical profession and chiropractic is another example of the employment of exclusionary strategies (Parkin, 1979) by the medical profession to protect its monopolistic control over the medical division of labour and their provision of various forms of health care. The marginality of the chiropractor is at least in part an effect of subordination to the medical profession (Wardwell, 1979).

Paramedicals and occupational strategy

We have seen that professionalization is now regarded as an occupational strategy in which social groups attempt to control their place
within the market. However, these market strategies also depend
upon the acquisition of an esoteric body of knowledge via the
university system under the general regulation of the state. Occupations can enhance their social status and power by the exercise of
control in the market place in order to secure greater occupational
autonomy; it is however also the case that occupations may become
de-skilled and de-professionalized by changes in the market,
developments in forms of knowledge and the availability of a clientele. De-skilling may well occur when conventional skills and expertise are replaced by new technology, especially by the use of
computers (Braverman, 1974; Littler, 1982; Penn, 1983). The capacity to withstand the processes of de-skilling will be to some extent
a consequence of the cohesion of a professional group, its level of
state support and its location within the hierarchy of professional
skills. We can illustrate some of these processes by considering a
number of paramedical professional groups.

Dentistry provides a useful illustration of the role of knowledge
and power in the development of professional status. In the British
case, the Dentists Act of 1878 was inadequate as the platform for
professionalization, since it did not give the qualified practitioner a
secure, monopolistic and exclusive control over the provision of
dental services. Unregistered and unqualified dentistry was a peren-
nial feature of the occupation into the twentieth century. For
example, many chemists practised dentistry as a secondary and
supplementary activity. Professional pressure to improve the dental
health of the British population was the result of war-time conditions, especially the Boer and First World Wars which showed the
poor dental health of recruits. Dentistry was also developed as a
consequence of various attempts to improve the health of children
following the 1907 Education Act. The result of public and professional pressure was that dentistry became a closed profession in
1921; entry into the profession was then regulated by schools under
the control of the General Medical Council (Davis, 1980). The
professionalization of dentistry in the UK was associated with a
growing public awareness of health needs, a demand for an
improved service and a situation where state backing was available.
During this period, dentists made important claims regarding the
benefit of dental health for the general wellbeing of their patients.
These claims were supported by reference to the theory of focal
sepsis, especially to oral sepsis. The dental profession argued that
good teeth led to good health; therefore the profession had a critical

role to play in promoting and maintaining the general wellbeing of the public. Subsequent research has demonstrated that the theory of oral sepsis was false and that professional claims made for a very interventionist dentistry were not justified; this rejection of the theory however took place after dentistry had achieved the goal of raised professional status (Dussault and Sheiham, 1982).

In the American context, the professionalization of dentistry may be dated from 1839 when the first dental school (the Baltimore College of Dental Surgeons) was established. This school was established precisely because the medical profession had excluded dental subjects from the curriculum (Young and Cohen, 1979). The professional status of dentistry is partly protected from the competitive presence of untrained groups by a system of dual control over admission to the profession, that is, through the professional accreditation system and the state licensing bodies. These accreditation boards are composed of dentists. Dentistry has attempted to improve its professional image and status by associating itself with the medical curriculum and by providing an educational basis which emphasizes the knowledge base of the activity. While dentistry enjoys a relative independence within the medical division of labour, dentistry is limited in terms of its scope for practice, and in the American context dentists tend to occupy a subordinate and vulnerable status in relation to the general practitioners because of the system of referrals.

The social tension between the ophthalmic opticians and the medical profession in certain respects parallels the history of dentistry as a profession. In the British case, opticians acquired a degree of autonomy and occupational control through the Royal Charter of 1629 which was granted to the Worshipful Company of Spectacle Makers. A number of scientific advances in the nineteenth century (the invention of the ophthalmoscope and ophthalmometer) established the technical knowledge base necessary for the development of ophthalmology. In the early decades of this century, ophthalmic opticians emerged as a special group within the paramedical division of labour because there was a growing market for spectacles and a shortage of professional ophthalmologists. In the years leading up to the establishment of the National Health Scheme in the UK, a growing market was expanding and eventually the British Medical Association sought to exercise greater medical control over the activities of the ophthalmic opticians. This professional struggle was couched in terms of the professional norms and values, the scientific status of the service and the profit motive which dominated the supply of spectacles. Medical control in the Opticians Act (1958) was established by restricting the optician to sight testing and guaranteeing that opticians always referred a suspected eye disease to a qualified doctor. State recognition of grades of work and confirmation of this division of labour had the consequence of recognizing an occupational ceiling and creating medical control of opticians (Larkin, 1981). While the professional rivalry between opticians and doctors was mainly economic, the arguments of opticians to have a valid expertise were based on important developments in the physical sciences in optics. The market position of opticians was grounded in a knowledge base as well as in a capacity to organize professionally and to provide a standardized service.

The work and market situation of pharmacy
The historical relationship between physicians and apothecaries was competitive and conflictual, because there was a significant overlap in both skill and service (Barrett, 1905; Poynter, 1965). In Britain, the apothecaries had separated from the grocers in 1617 and by the end of the eighteenth century they had abandoned their historical role as druggists. Pharmacy came eventually to be regulated by the Pharmaceutical Society which was formed in 1841. The pharmacists sought recognition as a professional group, which would provide them with an official monopoly over the compounding and dispensing of drugs. The professionalization of pharmacy has been limited by the petty bourgeois image of retail pharmacy and the inadequate apprenticeship system of training. In the twentieth century the traditional role of the pharmacist as a compounder of medicines has been rapidly undermined by the development of an international pharmaceutical industry. As a consequence of these economic and technical changes, the pharmacist has been described as a person who is over trained for what they actually do and under utilized in terms of what they know (Eaton and Webb, 1979). However, the growing complexity of drug therapy, the growth of public concern about iatrogenic disorders, and the recognition that the public needs drug education and counselling has created new social roles for the pharmacist, especially in the area of hospital pharmacy. The occupational opportunities which are created by these educational functions demand new types of university training and development for pharmacy. This development in pharmacy within the hospital suggests that there is an important transformation in the technicality/ indetermination ratio, because the clinical pharmacist is no longer merely supplying a drug, but providing professional services in relation to drug therapeutics.

Pharmacy has not received extensive enquiry from the social sciences and the history of pharmacy has also been somewhat neglected (Berman, 1966). There is, however, a general agreement that pharmacy is underdeveloped as a professional group and that it is limited by the medical authority of the doctor who delegates to the pharmacist within the medical division of labour. Pharmacy has consequently been described in the sociological literature as incomplete, marginal and limited (Wardwell, 1979).

The structural causes of this incomplete professionalization appear to be relatively clear. First, the occupation is divided into two principal sectors, namely private business and medical service. Since pharmacy training may result in a career in retail pharmacy, it has been suggested that pharmacists have not developed an ethical code of altruistic, disinterested service. For retail pharmacists, the profit motive is clearly an important feature of their work. Students undertaking training in pharmacy tend to have attitudes and aspirations which are not strictly compatible with a professional orientation of service to the client. In the USA, the majority of pharmacy students want to run their own business and their social background is primarily from small business and white-collar occupations. The presence of these business aspirations indicates that the majority of pharmacists would not have a clear sense of vocation to develop the profession as an autonomous and independent system of medical care. Second, there has been a significant process of de-skilling, since the pharmaceutical industry produces drugs which were formerly prepared by the pharmacist. Furthermore, chemists sell a number of commodities and do not specialize as retail outlets for drugs. Pharmacists have not organized themselves through an association to resist this de-skilling with the development of packaged drugs by the pharmaceutical industry. Thirdly, the pharmacy occupation is fragmented both horizontally and vertically. There are various types of retail pharmacists, in addition to hospital pharmacists, administrators and industrial chemists. One outcome of this fragmentation is that it makes professional action of a collective nature to protect and promote the interests of the occupation extremely difficult to sustain. Organizational fragmentation also means that it is difficult to develop a professional code of service and an occupational ideology which would unite pharmacists into a common body. Finally, although the hospital pharmacist is not involved in business activity, within the hospital setting the pharmacist is ultimately controlled or at least limited by the medical dominance of the medical profession.

Turning to the question of knowledge, one problem with pharmacy is that its knowledge base may be too precise and systematic to allow for a sufficiently wide range of interpretation. Pharmacology has been too susceptible to systematic development. Pharmaceutical knowledge is based on exact sciences and has been developed by widely accepted procedures of experimentation. Pharmacy leaves little scope for hermeneutics. Pharmacy has not so far developed a clear counselling role with respect to the patient without the mediation of other professional groups such as physicians. The paradox is that pharmacology may be overdeveloped as a science of drugs but underdeveloped as an interpretive skill with respect to patient wellbeing.

The expanding role of the hospital and clinical pharmacist has been made possible by the gaps left by physicians, inadequate drug counselling and drug information. This gap in the hospital service has provided an opportunity for the pharmacist to gain access directly to the patient. It has been suggested that

> pharmacists eager to extend their activities in hospital in a clinical direction have moved into those areas where medical practitioners have previously tended to take 'short cuts' or have neglected entirely, for example patient counselling, monitoring of drug side effects and the provision of drug information services. The assumption of these tasks, with the cooperation of the medical profession, may result in pharmacists doing more 'dirty work' for medical practitioners for relatively few gains. (Eaton and Webb, 1979:85)

The encroachment of the hospital pharmacist into the area of counselling and education has been controlled by the medical practice as a form of delegation.

Patriarchy and professionalism in the history of nursing

Sociological interest in the social role of the nurse was first expressed through occupational sociology under the influence of Hughes. Thus the initial approach to the problems of nursing in society was developed within a Chicago School perspective and came via Hughes to be dominated by an ethnographic methodology. It should be noted that, at least in America, nurses have had their own professional journal (*American Journal of Nursing*) which, from the beginning of the century, provided a substantial discussion of the occupational problems of the nurse. Hughes (1951) contributed a short note on the nurse's work but his principal contribution to the sociology of nursing was the study called *Twenty Thousand Nurses Tell Their Story* (Hughes, Hughes and Deutscher, 1958). This ethnographic approach to nursing gave special emphasis to role conflicts and work problems.

Following the work done by Hughes and his colleagues (1961) the main emphasis in these studies of the nursing role was professional socialization, the conflict between idealized perspectives of work and actual practice, the decline of idealism in nursing and finally the contradiction between bureaucratic and professional orientations to work (Corwin, 1961a, 1961b; Davis and Olesen, 1963; Hall, 1968). These early studies gave rise eventually to a more systematic and elaborate sociology-of-occupations approach to nursing; much of this work was collected in special editions of occupational sociology (Davis, 1966; MacLean, 1974).

Although this work fell within a conventional stream of occupational sociology, these studies converged on the central issue in nursing, namely its predominantly female character. In their study of the occupational status of nurses, Devereux and Weiner (1950) noted that, in the period 1860–1930 which covered the emergence of nursing as a distinctive secular occupation for unmarried women,

> the role and status of persons engaged in nursing is still determined by the close initial nexus between women and the bedside care of the sick. (Devereux and Weiner, 1950:628)

They drew attention to the historical, cultural and psychological resemblance between children and the sick, observing that the English language does not differentiate between the nursing of babies and the nursing of the sick. There was in addition the religious view of women as spiritually equipped to bear the pains of drudgery on behalf of the helpless and the dependent. In their view there was also a historical connection between service and nursing so that within the conventional household, the housemaid also operated as a bedside nurse. Finally, they argued that the connection between masculinity and leadership meant that nursing was conceived in a servile and subordinate perspective whereas the physician was seen to be responsible and dominant. The patriarchal structure of the nursing situation was thus identified in occupational sociology relatively early when sociologists drew a somewhat obvious parallel between mothering and nursing (Schulman, 1958, 1972).

The focus on the female character of nursing in a patriarchal culture has been the dominant issue in the social history of nursing which has been focused around the debate over the contribution of Florence Nightingale. Within social history the ambiguity of Nightingale's contribution to nursing has dominated the analysis of nursing as an emergent profession. The contradictory features of Nightingale's character were emphasized by the classical study of her life (Strachey, 1918 and a later study by Woodham-Smith, 1950). More recent historical commentaries on Nightingale have pointed out that, while she did much to establish the moral character of the nurse, her social attitudes towards the subordinate status of nursing in the delivery of health care were much in line with existing authoritarian values in the Victorian family (Holton, 1984;

Turner, 1981). By separating nursing from the religious orders, Nightingale created an occupational niche for socially mobile, middle-class women seeking gainful employment outside the household (Abel-Smith, 1960). By contrast, her attitude towards the registration of nurses did much to damage and delay the evolution of a fully fledged professional perspective within nursing.

The writing of nursing history has come under the powerful influence of new directions in historical analysis, shaped by French structuralism, Marxist history and above all by the feminist movement (Davies, 1980). These new perspectives are less concerned with questions of moral ideology and professional standing; instead the attention of historians is drawn towards issues of hierarchy, power and class. There is also less concern with the Nightingale mythology and a greater appreciation of the comparative analysis of nursing in different cultures and epochs. Alongside the history of nursing, there is an important role for comparative analysis and much interesting work has been done in this area. Historians have made important contributions to the study of women in health care in the USA in the nineteenth century (Ashley, 1976; Blake, 1965). These studies should be seen alongside a much wider debate about women in the medical and associated professions within the American context. Within this area, the analysis of the midwives' role is of particular interest and importance (Kobrin, 1966; Mongeau et al., 1961).

Related to the occupational sociology perspective, there has been a long debate about the professional or quasi-professional characteristics of nursing. Although nursing shows a number of common features with other so-called para-professional groups, limited practitioners and marginal practitioners, nursing is perceived to have a feature quite peculiar to its history, namely its female character. Thus in an influential article, Strauss (1966:61) noted that 'nursing is almost wholly a woman's province'; the professionalization of nursing was limited as a consequence of its association in popular ideology and myth with mundane bedside drudgery. Strauss went on to observe that nursing developed around a number of intensely sacred crises in life (death, illness and birth) and these have been traditionally associated with women's work. The characteristic features of nursing (low pay, low prestige, unsocial hours, high turnover of personnel, low income and lack of job autonomy) are seen to be determined by this single feature of its practitioners, namely their gender specificity. Thus, Davis (1972) and Davis and Olesen (1963) found that many nursing students did not see nursing as a continuous or dominant career, but as the precursor to a more permanent status in marriage and the family. These attitudes of student nurses appeared to be in direct contradiction to the values of their instructors and professional association. It was marriage, rather than other occupational aspirations which determined the career paths of nurses.

One problem for nursing as a profession is its subordination to the medical profession so that nurses in theory merely execute decisions arrived at by doctors. Nursing is subordinated within the technical division of labour surrounding medicine and the development of specialized educational programmes for nurses has not significantly improved their status in the medical hierarchy within the hospital context. Nurses suffer in particular from the dilemmas of professionalism versus bureaucracy, since within the hospital context it is often difficult for them to exercise initiative and autonomy (Davies, 1983). The evolution of the male nurse in this situation is paradoxical since, rather than improving the social status of nursing as a whole, it may merely function to diversify and divide nursing into rather separate grades and career paths (Brown and Stones, 1973; Hesselbart, 1977; Segal, 1962).

The occupational and professional dilemmas of nurses have been seen within the general perspective of occupational subordination and de-skilling (Freidson, 1970). Although these accounts of the problems of professionalization in nursing seem to follow directly from Weber's notion of social closure, the critical issue in the absence of professional status in the history of nursing has centred on the question of gender. The ultimate failure of nursing to achieve professional autonomy is explained in terms of the contradiction between family life and professional careers, bureaucracy and professionalism, the absence of the strong professional association and above all the absence of a continuous commitment to a career to the exclusion of domestic involvements.

The radical stream in the contemporary analysis of nursing has as a result been dominated by feminist writers. For feminist theory, nursing is *par excellence* an example of the subordination of women to patriarchy and the exploitation of women under ideologies which assert the naturalness of nursing as a feature of the female personality. Women are exploited as nurses because they are socialized into a doctrine which equates nursing with mothering and sees the hospital ward as merely an extension of the domestic sphere of labour. This trend in social analysis is well represented by Ehrenreich and English (1976), Gamarnikow (1978), and Game and Pringle (1983). For these writers, the secretary and the nurse are living representatives of the general problem of patriarchy and female subordination. The secretary plays the role of wife at work, while the nurse plays the role of mother in the hospital. Despite major changes in legislation and political organization, these authors assert that little has changed in reality with respect to female status, prestige and employment over the last fifty years.

The idea that nursing and mothering are natural activities of women is an ancient theme in western culture. The word 'nurse' is derived from 'nutririe' signifying to nourish and to suckle. A nurse was traditionally a person employed to suckle children and care for the household. In the eighteenth century, the idea of the nurse had been fully developed to include suckling, nourishing and caring as a special activity of housemaids (Reeder and Mauksch, 1979). Patriarchal relations in the delivery of care by nursing are explained by feminist theory in terms of the general ideology associating women with natural activities and men with cultural pursuits (Rosaldo and Lamphere, 1974). In addition to the argument from the ideology of nature, there is an important use of metaphor and homology in arguments about the status of nursing. It is common in the sociology of nursing to find arguments which point to the importance of emotion and affectual relations in the therapeutic tasks of nursing and for such studies to suggest that the nurse acts as a surrogate mother where the patient represents the child (Devereux and Weiner, 1950). A number of studies employ a form of Freudian language to describe the relationship between the nurse/mother and patient/child. Thus Thorner (1955:531) says

> the nurse like the mother in relation to the infant caters to the patient's needs and, therefore, presents the most convenient 'object of cathexis' on whom he may discharge his craving for response as well as aggressive impulses. The situation which predisposes the patient to the transference phenomena (falling in love) with the nurse.

The most systematic use of the argument from homology is to be found in an influential article by Gamarnikow (1978) in a critique of the Nightingale tradition which draws an exact parallel between the family and the nursing situation. She argues that the use of the family analogy as the major motif in nursing literature represents patriarchal ideology which legitimizes the nurse–doctor–patient triad in such a way as to block off any further analytical scrutiny. The nurse's authority is delegated in the same manner that the wife's authority is subsumed under that of the husband, while the subservience of the patient is a direct analogy to the subservience of the dependent and sick child. In compliance, the patient is literally one who exercises patience. Similarly, the knowledge of the doctor is scientific, while the actions of the nurse are merely manual and practical. Gamarnikow argues that this manual and mental division within nursing is simply a reproduction by analogy of the similar division within the family.

There is the additional argument that the dominance of women in nursing is simply another illustration of the use of female labour to cheapen the costs of production within a capitalist society. The predominance of women in nursing would be simply a duplication of a more general situation where women are located in occupations which are low in prestige and remuneration. Nursing is a sex-typed occupation with low unionization, high turnover and low prestige. In the USA, in 1900 94 percent of all nurses were female and in 1960 97 percent of all nurses were female. By contrast in 1910, 6 percent of all doctors were female and in 1960 6.8 percent of all doctors were female (Epstein, 1970; Lorber, 1984). In Australia in 1971, 94.3 percent of nurses were female and in 1976 94 percent of all nurses were female. By comparison, in 1971 11.8 percent of all medics and dentists were female and by 1976 this had risen to only 14.8 percent. In general, women represent approximately 50 percent of the staff in para-medical services in Australia (Western, 1983). The argument here is that female nurses cheapen the costs of labour and therefore help to ensure profitability, especially in the private health industry. In the USA what has been called the private health-care industry is one of the fastest growing sectors of the economy with a workforce of 5,500,000 people which is divided into an extreme income/skill dichotomy. At the top of this pyramid, there are 500,000 doctors (the highest paid in the world) and below them are 1,500,000 nurses who are the worst-paid college graduate professionals in the country; at the bottom of the pyramid there are 3,000,000 blue-collar clerical workers who represent the largest segment of low-wage labour in the society. Women as mothers and nurses contribute to the production and reproduction of human labour at the lowest possible market price and their low wage-rates contribute to the profitability of the private health-care sector.

Compliance and complaint at work

While there is an ideology of compliance and discipline within the nursing profession following from the Nightingale tradition, there is also resistance and conflict from nurses in opposition to traditional conditions of work, bureaucratic regulation and to the notion that nurses are wholly compliant to doctors' instructions. It is certainly the case that traditional discussion of the doctor–nurse relationship emphasizes total obedience. For example, while the trained nurse is to be intelligent and interested in her work, she has to bear in mind that it is her duty to follow the doctor's instructions without question. In addition physicians are typically older and from higher socio-economic groups than nurses and their authority is rarely challenged overtly as a result of these social conditions of subordination. Psychological studies of nurses' compliance to doctors' orders for medication have suggested that there was a tendency for nurses to be over-compliant when following instructions. Experimental studies showing that nurses would follow doctors' instructions even where these orders would endanger the life of the patient have been carried out (Hofling et al., 1966; Milgran, 1974). However, more recent studies of nurses' compliance suggest that nurses are no longer prepared to follow mindlessly medical instructions and this change in the level of compliance is probably associated with an increasing self-esteem amongst nurses and a fear of law suits and malpractice legislation (Rank and Jacobson, 1977). Within a broader perspective, there is evidence of a stronger militancy among some nurses, a greater willingness to defend their professional position and also a political will to take action in defence of their conditions of employment when necessary. These new features of conflict and lack of compliance appear to fit a conceptualization of the nurse–doctor relationship which does not assume normative compliance within a system of patriarchy.

Some aspects of nurses' dissatisfaction with their work conditions can be located in the 'vocabularies of complaint' which characterize nursing. All occupations have an informal culture of attitude and practice, including conventional topics of complaint. There is a split in the occupational culture of nursing into a discourse of compliance and of complaint. While the student nurse acquires a formal occupational culture as part of her training, there is also the acquisition of and socialization into, a sub-cultural occupational ideology. This sub-cultural world-view is often acquired during apprenticeship. This alternative occupational ideology may be called the vocabulary of complaint. While the official occupational ideology specifies how in principle tasks are to be accomplished, the vocabulary of complaint outlines methods of survival on the job which have the consequence of de-legitimizing the authority of the formal structure of operations within the bureaucracy. Empirical studies of nurses have clearly identified the extent of discontent in the nursing occupation and a variety of studies have sought to identify the parameters of these complaints (Melia, 1984). These studies of nurses' complaints appear often to be rather individualistic, literal and descriptive. The complaint is reported as the individual observation of a nurse about her circumstances, where these utterances are also taken to be literally true and descriptive of objective conditions. The idea of a vocabulary of complaint points by contrast to the fact that these occupational discourses are socially produced and acquired as part of the training for the job.

These vocabularies of complaint have a number of important functions. The crucial complaint is focused on the experience of lack of autonomy in relation to the patient and health-care delivery within large bureaucratic settings. The crux of these complaints is perhaps summarized by the observation that

> nurses are near the patients around the clock and yet they have the least formal responsibility compared with attending physicians or house staff physicians. (Mumford, 1983:292)

Nurses constantly complain about this absence of control over their situation. Sharing these complaints is an important aspect of the informal organization of nursing as an occupation. Complaints give articulate utterance to this structural hiatus between their skill and their lack of autonomy within the medical bureaucracy of the modern hospital. The vocabulary of complaints for nurses has five main components which function to express the value and autonomy of the nurse against her superiors.

The first component of this vocabulary is a set of assertions which underline the independent contribution and importance of nursing to the therapeutic process. These complaints typically devalue the function and significance of the doctor in the therapeutic process, providing a negative view of the doctor's role. These complaints suggest that doctors in fact represent a threat to the health of the patients who need protecting from male medical intervention. The second function of the vocabulary of complaint is to de-legitimize the system of authority and hierarchy at the place of work within the hospital context. The third function of the complaint system deflates the unwarranted idealism of young nurses coming into the hospital. These complaints typically seek to describe the real nature of nursing as a laborious, tiring and unrewarding set of activities. The occupational sub-culture provides a cynical and negative view of nursing as mere drudgery. Much has been written in the past about the fate of idealism in nursing as a consequence of the formal system of training (Psathas, 1969), but relatively little has been written about the ward training of nurses into a more realistic view of their social role. These complaints see the activity of the ward as often irrelevant and useless for the real care of the patient and they describe a variety of activities which merely support the bureaucratic functioning of the hospital rather than the care of the patient.

The fourth function of the vocabulary is the most significant, namely to create a sense of solidarity of the workforce against the intrusion and dominance of the bureaucracy and the medical profession. The complaints exchanged on the ward reassert the unity and coherence of nurses as a social group against the authority of the hospital hierarchy. Since the majority of nurses are female, the complaint system operates to unite female nurses often against male superiors. The vocabulary of complaint has a distinctly feminist character. It is here that reference to the 'doctor–nurse game' seems to be significant as deflating and critical. Complaining is therefore a crucial feature of occupational sub-cultures where solidarity becomes an important aspect of resistance (Salaman, 1986).

The final consequence of the vocabulary of complaint is however somewhat conservative. Complaining acts as a safety valve which lets off emotion and frustration against the contradictions and tensions of the work place. Once released in a collective way, the solidarity of the group is reasserted but the complaining does not lead to systematic changes in objective conditions. Complaining is symbolic and consists of collective gestures against authority. They do not necessarily lead to organized forms of conflict designed to change and transform the nature of the tasks which confront nurses in a modern hospital. Despite the nurse's symbolic encroachment on the space of medical authority, the objective situation of nursing is maintained and her powerlessness preserved. The ritual nature of the complaint system is reminiscent of Goffman's (1961) description of subordinate rituals of rebellion within total institutions which periodically overthrow the hierarchical structure of the asylum at the level of a symbolic critique.

In summary, these complaints have the functions of uniting nurses together as an occupational group with a common experience and language. The complaints de-legitimize the authority structure of the hospital especially with respect to the doctor–nurse relationship, but paradoxically the outcome of this form of complaining is conservative. Because the nurse occupies a subordinate position within the hospital and has little prestige in the market place, she is relatively ineffectual in challenging the structure of the hospital system. Nursing has the traditional weaknesses which are often characteristic of feminized labour, namely the presence of a vicious circle where low job satisfaction results in broken careers and inadequate career structures produce low occupational commitment.

Conclusion
Professionalization can be seen as an occupational strategy to maintain certain monopolistic privileges and rewards. It has been argued that an adequate sociological approach to the professions can suitably combine the perspectives of Weberian and Marxist sociology. We need to see the professions in relation to the class structure and the economy, but we can only evaluate the detailed features of

occupations by considering their relationship to the market. The professional dominance of certain occupational groups is clearly grounded in the possession of a body of knowledge which is a crucial feature of the exercise of professional power. A systematic body of knowledge however is ambiguous because it points simultaneously in the direction of routinization and interpretation. It has been argued that a systematic body of knowledge can undermine the privileges of a group because routine knowledge lays the basis for de-skilling through the fragmentation of tasks within the division of labour. Medicine and law are clear illustrations of bodies of professional knowledge which are not entirely subject to routine and systematic procedures. Both medicine and law allow a space for interpretation.

We have also seen how it is important for a profession to maintain open access to its clients and to maintain this access in competition with other groups. One important function therefore of medical dominance is to preserve and extend the medical access to its clientele by limiting and subordinating adjacent occupations. The possession of a knowledge base and access to patients as clients leads in the work place to considerable privileges in the form of occupational autonomy and control over the process by which the service is delivered. In these various dimensions, the medical profession has been relatively successful in maintaining its position within the class structure and the professional hierarchy over the last 100 years by regulating and controlling access to health-care delivery. A number of examples from pharmacy, dentistry and nursing illustrate these conditions with some degree of clarity. Professions are not fixed social entities, but structured forms of occupational strategy. The exercise of these strategies can be seen in terms of the class, work and status situation of occupations. In these three areas, professionalization involves the exercise of social closure, the maintenance of autonomy and finally the development of bodies of knowledge which permit sufficient scope for interpretation with the result that the patient or client remains relatively ignorant and subordinate.

It is equally important to see occupations within a historical perspective. Medicine as a professional activity was a specific product of late nineteenth-century social conditions – a rising middle-class clientele, the emergence of germ theory, the availability of state support through legislation and technical changes in the nature of medical practice which made medical intervention less dangerous for the patient. The ethos of medical professionalism was in both the UK and the USA in tune with the prevailing norms of liberal individualism. Before this late professionalism, the medical practitioner had relatively low social status because medicine itself had only a limited therapeutic efficacy for the patient (Rosen, 1983; Starr, 1982). Without adequate professionalization, medicine as a practice was broken by internal, unregulated schism. The growth of medical dominance in the first half of the twentieth century was associated with urbanization, the development of health insurance, improvements in medicine and the expansion of the hospital as the site of scientific medicine.

8
Medical bureaucracies: the hospital, the clinic and modern society

Introduction
The hospital is a crucial institution within modern systems of health care, but it is also symbolic of the social power of the medical profession, representing the institutionalization of specialized medical knowledge. The bureaucratic, centralized hospital system has a significant part to play in the training of doctors and as an institution it controls the organized power of medical professions; it is the locus of contemporary political conflicts which are not simply economic, but ideological and cultural. The very existence of hospitals is a significant statement about the structure of modern societies, especially about the erosion of kinship structures and the household as the framework for the nuclear family. In many respects, the hospital is a crucial illustration of Weber's analysis of rationalization and Foucault's concept of panopticism. The hospital as a professional arena of medical power illustrates many of the most fundamental processes of industrial society, namely urbanization, secularization, the dominance of professional power, and the development of the service factor. In this chapter I shall argue that the contemporary extension of medical domination is bound up with the recent history of the hospital and that the impact of medical knowledge on society depends on the alliance between hospitals, universities and the medical profession (Larson, 1977). In short, in the modern period 'medical domination went hand in hand with increasing medical knowledge' (Mumford, 1983:363). The expansion of medical knowledge and its legitimacy in turn have accompanied the contemporary growth and specialization of hospitals as the principal settings of medical technology and practice.

The hospital was an institution (the 'hospitium') which emerged in medieval society, but there are a number of special features which distinguish the modern hospital from its primitive origins in rest-stations for pilgrims. The development of the modern hospital is firstly associated with a major change in the character of disease in contemporary societies, namely a shift from the prominence of acute to chronic illness. Secondly, the modern hospital has been transformed by the impact of medical technology on its structure and functions. Thirdly, the nature of hospital work has been transformed by the increasing specialization of medical activity resulting in a proliferation of new specialist occupations within the hospital setting. The consequence of these structural and technological changes has been that the hospital increasingly resembles a collection of workshops (Strauss et al., 1985).

Because the hospital resembles a bureaucratic collection of workshops, it has been criticized by a variety of writers who have suggested that the alienating environment of the hospital ward has a detrimental effect, not only on the patient's capacity for recovery, but on their emotional wellbeing. While it is often difficult to provide an exact measurement of the quality of care within hospitals, there is considerable evidence of various forms of patient dissatisfaction with the formal and bureaucratic character of medical care within hospital settings (Cartwright, 1983).

The sociological critique of the hospital as a bureaucratic institution was heavily influenced by the symbolic interactionist approach of writers like Goffman (1961) who described the hospital as a total institution. One important feature of the contemporary critique of the hospital is the convergence of radical criticism of the hospital as a degrading institution and the monetarist critique of the hospital as an expensive and ineffectual system of medical care. Therefore, the critique of the hospital has run parallel to the decarceration debate respecting mental illness and the asylum. Although these debates may well lead to a situation where there is less emphasis on the hospital as the focal point of medical care, the hospital remains an archetypal institution of secular culture (Rieff, 1961). Alongside the school and the penitentiary, the hospital as the site of technical medicine is a feature of the 'disciplinary society' (O'Neill, 1986). If medicine has to some extent replaced religion as that system of knowledge which defines deviance, then we can argue that:

> the hospital is becoming such an archetypal institution largely through a process whereby human behaviour is being reinterpreted. Disapproved behavior is more and more coming to be given meaning of illness requiring treatment rather than of crime requiring punishment, victimization requiring compensation, or sin requiring patience and grace. (Freidson, 1970:248)

The hospital is the central feature of professional influence for medical power and therefore the major element within the medical–industrial complex.

Hospitals and the theory of bureaucracy
The modern hospital provides a labour-intensive system of medical

care. The consequence has been a sharp increase in the number of persons who are employed in such institutions. In the USA in 1946 one in every 67 of civilian workers was employed by a hospital and by 1961 this ratio had increased to one in every 39 workers; these increases in the labour force reflect the growth and complexity of the services offered to patients by the modern hospital (Mumford, 1983:361). There has also been a rapid increase in the number of hospitals. In 1873 there were 178 hospitals and in 1909 there were 4359 hospitals in the USA. In Australia between 1861 and 1947 the supply of hospital beds increased from 1 per 1000 of the population to 6 per 1000. By 1982 there were 768 public and 341 private hospitals and the number of beds per 1000 of the population had increased to 7 (Sax, 1984).

In the UK the National Health Service in 1946 inherited a collection of ancient and obsolete hospitals, many of which had been built before 1861. However, there has been in the post-war period considerable expenditure on the modernization and development of hospitals in the UK. The growing size and complexity of hospitals as medical settings has been associated with the expansion of bureaucratic systems of professional administration. One indication of this development of bureaucratic administration was the development in the UK of a professional occupation of hospital administrators equipped with a system of entry by formal examination and a professional journal by 1945.

Following the bureaucratization of medical care, there has been a considerable discussion of whether hospitals conform to Weber's ideal type of rational bureaucracy. Weber (1978: Vol. 2, 956) defined bureaucracy in terms of the following dimensions. The bureaucratic structure consists of a number of distinctive offices with specialized duties which are formally defined. The authority structure of a bureaucracy requires that these duties should be performed in a stable and systematic manner. Officials within these offices are recruited according to general rules by competitive examinations and their employment is in terms of a system of salaries. The principle of office hierarchy is the basis for a line of command which is hierarchical. The official is expected to behave in a way which is universalistic, specific and neutral such that the bureaucrat does not question legitimate instructions descending from superiors. This public realm of rational conduct is completely separated from the private life of the official. Weber also argued that the modern system of management by bureaucratic offices presupposes the emergence of the modern state, a monetary economy and a universal education providing the basis for specialized training by competitive means. The modern bureaucracy also presupposes the development of a rational system of law which will provide a stable legal environment for the modern bureaucracy. Weber has often been misinterpreted as arguing that the bureaucracy provides the most efficient means for the achievement of known ends; the essential part of his argument by contrast is that the bureaucracy provides primarily for stable management rather than efficient management. The bureaucratic form of organization guarantees that activities will be uniformly performed in a stable and reliable fashion (Parkin, 1982). Bureaucratic procedures are the opposite of ad hoc decision-making by fiat.

Although the large complex bureaucratic hospital has a number of features which conform to Weber's ideal type, it has been suggested by many sociologists that the modern hospital diverges from Weber's type in a number of significant respects. Although the hospital has an administrative structure which is bureaucratic, the doctors retain considerable professional power and make decisions which are not determined by the professional administrative system. The hospital in fact has a dual system of authority, one following from the governing body of administrators and the other from the professional group of doctors (Goss, 1963). The hospital authority structure is fractured around the difference between the rational bureaucratic system and the professional autonomy of the doctor through a system of medical domination. The medical profession remains relatively autonomous and subject to few non-medical regulations; this situation arises because the private physician is not an employee of the hospital but in some respects a guest who utilizes the facilities available within the hospital. The medical practitioners also enjoy considerable social status outside the hospital setting and their professionalism is resistant to bureaucratic management (Georgopolous and Mann, 1972).

This dual system of authority has, as we have seen, a problematic impact on such occupations as nursing, because the nurse is subject to both bureaucratic and professional regulation. In fact we could regard hospitals generally as structures involving various columns of occupational prestige and authority versus the overall management structure which the board of governors through the hospital administrators attempt to impose. Given the competition between various professional groups within the hospital system, some sociologists have suggested that the hospital should be regarded as 'a negotiated order' where professionals, administrators and patients are forced to seek a compromise in order to maintain the round of everyday hospital duties and activities (Strauss et al., 1963).

The argument that Weber's ideal type of bureaucracy is an adequate framework for the analysis of hospitals has also been criticized on the grounds that hospitals, like other total institutions, generally develop an informal structure of authority and an informal culture specifically relating to the life of the patients, which are not compatible with the formal system of authority and its ideology. Blau (1963, 1974) has argued that in general social organizations will be structured by informal as well as formal patterns of authority, practice and culture. The formal system of rules of an organization can never cover every eventuality and, over a long period of interaction, we may expect the emergence of informal systems which are in fact functional for the continuity of the organization as a whole. Sociological research on penal institutions has shown convincingly that these correctional agencies typically develop an informal structure of control which is essential for the maintenance of order, but may well corrupt the pure form of authority within the prison (Sykes, 1956).

This approach to informal social structures was developed with great panache and success by Goffman (1961) in his study of total institutions; Goffman through empirical research noted that patients within total institutions typically develop an informal culture which functions as a survival strategy in an environment which is foreign and alienating. Other studies of mental hospitals (Stanton and Schwartz, 1961) have shown that inmates typically develop informal groups which contribute to the patient's sense of wellbeing and to the stability of such institutions. These informal systems are not part of the bureaucratic charter, but they are clearly significant in the therapeutic process which is experienced by the patients. Finally, large hospitals will have what Goffman called a backstage, that is various areas of work which are not highly visible and which are organized by norms and customs falling outside the line of command required by the official bureaucratic structure. For example, the kitchen areas of hospitals constitute backstages where the norms of the hospital may not be entirely appropriate or effective (Paterson, 1981). These backstages are places where 'dirty work' has to be accomplished by low-status staff.

There are as a consequence various ways in which Weber's bureaucratic model is not entirely appropriate as a perspective or framework for the study of the modern hospital. Research has shown that these institutions have multiple systems of authority and divisions of professional power which rule out the operation of a single line of command. The result is that hospitals are scenes of inter-occupational conflict and resemble negotiated orders rather than smoothly functioning machines. Para-medical professions and occupations in particular are subject to cross-cutting lines of authority which render their performance of tasks complex and frustrating. Although these criticisms of Weberian sociological models are entirely appropriate, there is another version of Weber's analysis of the bureaucracy which provides a powerful perspective for the historical analysis of the emergence of the bureaucratic hospital. We may conceptualize the modern hospital as the social vehicle for the rationalization of medical practice, the specialization of medical knowledge and the division of health-care systems into specialized units. In order to present a further application of Weber through the concept of the rationalization of medicine, we need to consider the history of the hospital in the development of western societies as an aspect of Weber's comparative sociology of the processes of modernization (Collins, 1986).

The hospital in history
The origins of the hospital lie in religious culture and religious needs; for example, many early hospitals were places of rest and protection for pilgrims travelling to holy shrines. The growth and development of the modern hospital provides a significant illustration of the secularization of religious cultures under the impact of urban industrial capitalism. The history of hospitals may be divided into three major periods. Religious foundations between 335 and 1550 provided the basis for most hospitals in the early history of European societies. This period of religious foundations begins with the decree of Constantine to close pagan temples and erect Christian hospitals and it closes with the collapse of monastic hospitals in the sixteenth century. The second period of hospital development was dominated by the evolution of charity hospitals beginning with the foundation of the first charity hospital in London in 1719 and closing with the National Insurance Act of 1913. Finally, the period of major expansion in the modern bureaucratic hospital was between 1913 and 1948 when in the UK the National Health Act came into operation.

The word hospital derives from the Latin adjective 'hospitalis' which relates to 'hospites' or guests. Other terms for the hospital include hospice and spital. This original meaning of the term is preserved in the notion of hospitality. The early hospitals were therefore general refuges or way-stations for those people who fell ill during religious pilgrimages. Hospitals grew very quickly after the Norman Conquest in Britain when there was an increase in the volume of pilgrims crossing the English Channel. These early hospitals were completely unspecialized and operated as open houses for the sick, the old, the poor and the infirm. A wide range of institutions in this period provided services for the poor and the sick. In addition to the hospitals for pilgrims there were alms houses, bede houses or Maisons Dieu. Most monasteries had a hospitium at the abbey gate for travellers. Those institutions which tended to concentrate on services for the sick were called spitals or spittle houses. Between 1066 and 1550, approximately 700 such spitals were established in Britain; most of these were very small institutions catering to a limited number of patients.

The earliest form of hospital specialization was the development of the spital devoted to the service of those suffering from leprosy. As we have seen in an earlier chapter these spitals came to be known as lazar-houses. In 1078 a leprosarium was founded at Rochester and in 1084 Archbishop Lanfranc built a spital for lepers at Harbledown near Canterbury for the care of 100 patients. From these early beginnings, lazar houses developed rapidly in the twelfth and thirteenth centuries. As leprosy increased dramatically, many old alms houses were converted for the use of lepers. There was an increase in the number of statutes controlling lepers and these regulations included measures to prevent lepers from entering city gates. Leprosy began to decline after 1315 when there was severe famine, but the real termination of leprosy as a significant disease coincided with the Black Death (1346–1350). There was no new leprosy legislation after 1348.

Another form of specialization related to the provision of accommodation for lunatics. St Mary of Bethlehem in London was founded in 1247 and became famous for its accommodation of the insane. By 1403 there was a note from a Royal Commission which observed that Bethlehem provided accommodation for 6 male lunatics and a further reference in 1453 noted that Bethleham or Bedlam (Allderidge, 1985) provided shelter for a great variety of men who had 'fallen out of their wits'. By the seventeenth century Bedlam provided accommodation for 40 'distracted persons'. This hospital was the origin of a common term for the insane, namely Bedlamites. By the middle of the sixteenth century, Bedlam was reorganized as a Royal Hospital of the city of London reserved specifically for lunatics. An official investigation of the hospital in 1633 showed that the inmates were poor, destitute and vagrant people from the London area. In 1675 the hospital was rebuilt in order to expand its provision to provide shelter for over 100 inmates who came to be admitted on a more selective and specialized basis. By the eighteenth century this hospital had further developed to offer shelter to over 300 inmates who by this time had acquired the label 'incurable lunaticks'. Other asylums for lunatics were opened in Norwich in 1724, at Newcastle in 1767 and at York in 1777. By

1845, the Lunacy Acts had made it mandatory for counties and boroughs to build asylums for the insane (Donnelly, 1983).

Another form of hospital specialization was the development of the lying-in hospital for pregnant women. A statute which dates from 1414 acknowledged the reception of lying-in women as an appropriate aspect of hospital charity. Two great medieval hospitals in London (St Mary-without-Bishopgate and St Bartholomew's) provided obstetrics and provided charitable support for children whose mothers had died during childbirth. In the nineteenth century the notion that a period of rest was required after labour became specific to middle-class women receiving the specialized attention of male doctors.

There is therefore a certain amount of evidence of hospital specialization around leprosy, lunacy and pregnancy, but these institutional developments were not extensive or based upon systematic knowledge. In general, pre-modern hospitals were places of last resort, where the inmates had a wide variety of illnesses which were not treated on a specialized basis. The aim was to provide care for patients rather than a cure and there was little professional development of nursing as a specialized occupation. These medieval institutions depended a great deal on patronage and ecclesiastical support, since there was obviously no state provision for hospital care. Hospitals also raised money through such mechanisms as an annual fair or by charging admission fees. In some cases hospitals had the power to raise money or taxes from the local population. Many of these religious institutions were dissolved during the Reformation by which time many of these religious hospitals had become corrupted by the abuse of patronage. In England many of these hospitals disappeared between 1536 and 1547 as a consequence of royal intervention in order to raise additional revenues for the monarchy.

The charity hospitals which developed in the seventeenth century were created for somewhat different reasons and by a different class of people. These hospitals were based upon the philosophical principles of utilitarianism established by writers like Locke in *Essay on Human Understanding* (1690) and by Bentham (1748–1832). These charity institutions arose from middle-class philanthropy rather than from a significant religious zeal for social reform. The new hospitals were patronized by a new class of rentiers rather than by rich merchants and capitalists. They were typically not supported by the Church, the state or by tax payers, but maintained their independence through the benefactions of individuals and they were often served by unpaid medical staff. A survey in 1719 revealed that twenty-three English counties had no hospital accommodation, but by 1798 nearly every county and large town had acquired an infirmary characteristically maintained by a private benefactor. For example, in 1719 Westminster hospital was founded by a group of London merchants. This hospital was quickly followed by Guy's (1725), the London Infirmary (1734), the Middlesex Hospital (1746) and Bath Hospital (1737). Between 1743 and 1787 twelve major hospitals had been created in the English provinces.

These hospitals were primarily concerned to provide shelter for the homeless, the sick, orphans and unemployed vagrants. Many of these hospitals were poorly ventilated, cold, unclean and over-crowded. Morbidity and mortality rates in these institutions were consequently very high, especially for young people and children. For example, the London Foundling Hospital in its first few years of existence provided accommodation for approximately 15,000 children of whom only 4500 survived hospitalization. These charity hospitals were therefore not places where middle-class people sought cure or rest; they were largely dumping grounds for those who were unable to support themselves.

The specialization of hospitals began to be a significant feature of nineteenth-century medicine when a number of hospitals began to specialize in terms of specific illnesses. For example, Moorfield's Eye Hospital was opened in 1805; the Royal Hospital for Diseases of the Chest began in 1814; the Royal Ear Hospital was developed in 1816 and St Mark's Hospital for Cancer was established in 1835. These were followed in 1848 by the Victoria Park Hospital for Diseases of the Chest, the London Smallpox Hospital in 1850 and the Hospital for Diseases of the Throat in 1863.

Although there was a significant increase in the number of charity hospitals, it became evident that these institutions were unable to cope with the needs of a society undergoing rapid urbanization and considerable population increase. Furthermore, they were unable to cope with the numbers of dislocated, unemployed poor in the middle of the nineteenth century. The voluntary hospital system was also inadequate as a system of provision in the context of large-scale, mass warfare. Medical provision, training and know-ledge were revolutionized by the Crimean War (1854–1856), the Boer War (1899–1902) and the First World War (1914–1918). Mass warfare demonstrated the fact that the male population of Britain suffered from a variety of disabling diseases and disorders such as tuberculosis, poor eyesight, respiratory diseases, diabetes and mental illness. In addition, these wars demonstrated that the medical provision for modern armies was totally underdeveloped and ineffectual. For example, during the Crimean War more men died from exposure than on the battlefield. The social outcome of these military disasters was a period of reform in nursing and medical care for the army, a movement towards a national scheme of insurance and the development of a more systematic form of national health care.

The development of the modern hospital as a centre for training doctors and promoting research (that is, the development of the hospital as a clinic) owed a great deal to the transformation of the hospital system by the French Revolution. This emergence of the hospital as a clinic was the topic of an influential study by Foucault (1973). Foucault recognized the existence of 'proto-clinics' from the seventeenth century (such as the clinic established by Boerhaave at Leyden in 1658), but he argued that it was the reforms undertaken by the Comité de Mendicité which paved the way for a new empiricism in medical training, namely the birth of the medical gaze.

Under the *ancien régime*, hospitals were primarily places of refuge for the poor and destitute; they had their origins in systems of charity which were the products of a feudal system. The revolutionary committees proposed the abolition of hospitals because they were the corrupt symbols of a decaying society (Forrest, 1981). In their place, the Revolution looked towards the family as the 'natural' location for the cure of the sick. The family offered protection and an emotionally supportive environment where a 'moral regime' could complement the medical regimen (Donzelot, 1979). However, for various political and economic reasons, the original plan of hospital reform and abolition failed, but what emerged from that failure of the revolutionary ideal was the modern clinic.

The new system provided for better education of doctors and the elimination of quacks by regulation of entrance to the profession by an examination which covered both practical and theoretical aspects. The reforms also created a new category of officers of health who would provide basic care to the poor. More importantly, the hospital transformed the sick patient into an object of medical training. The sick were to become useful as illustrations of disease. Since the sick were typically the poor, they also became useful in the fulfilment of science. As Foucault expressed this idea, through the clinical gaze, the sick now became a spectacle.

The reform of the hospital system throughout Europe was an important feature of late nineteenth-century medicine and laid the basis for the evolution of modern medical science. The growing importance of the hospital depended on the following factors. First, the medical profession had secured a growing status and prestige within the community as a consequence of its successful profes-

sionalization. In addition there had been a significant development
in the training of nurses and therefore there was available an occupational group equipped and ready to find employment within the
hospital service. Secondly, there had been improvements in hygiene
and sanitation within hospitals, thereby reducing the high morbidity
rates which had characterized the pre-modern hospital. Thirdly, the
modern development of the hospital was accelerated by the redistribution of incomes, the emergence of a middle-class clientele and
the discovery of psychosomatic medicine. The middle classes were
now prepared to enter the hospital in search of cures (Lewis and
Maude, 1952; Larson, 1977). Single rooms were provided for the
rich and the middle classes which separated them from the mass of
the population within the general hospital. Furthermore, there were
significant improvements and developments in the area of hospital
insurance which brought hospital care within the reach of the
middle classes through expanded insurance schemes. Finally, the
development and introduction of antibiotics meant that infection in
hospital was less prevalent; paying patients from the middle classes
provided the basis for medical specialization and increased the
medical dominance of the surgeon.

Reform, containment and rationalization
The 1960s were in the majority of industrial societies a period of
extended hospital reform and reconstruction. This period of rapid
development had come to an end by the late 1970s and the contemporary period has been one of containment and management rather
than extensive development. One obvious cause of this change of
approach has been the soaring cost of hospitals. One aspect of this
increasing cost of medicine has been the changing character of
disease from acute to chronic, associated with the aging population. However, there is a more fundamental aspect to this situation
of rising costs, which is that health and illness are not finite phenomena. Illnesses which are treated by institutionalized medicine
represent the peak of an iceberg which has no known base line.
Therefore, medical expenditure appears to be highly elastic
depending upon expectations of health and criteria of health.
    To take the British example, the assumption behind the 1948
Health Act was that there existed a backlog of illness which could be
removed by a short injection of funds aimed to restore the nation to
good health after the devastation of warfare. In practice, illness has
turned out to be in financial terms a bottomless pit. In 1942 the
estimated annual cost of national health in the UK was £170m. but
by 1949 the actual expenditure had risen to £305.2m. By 1950 actual
expenditure had risen to £336.5m. In dental expenditure alone, the

1942 estimate for a national system of dental health was £10m., but by 1949 the actual expenditure had risen to £46.4m. In the UK, social services expenditure as a percentage of gross national product rose from 4.7 percent in 1913 to 26 percent in 1968. National Health Service (NHS) expenditure as a percentage of social service expenditure rose from 13 percent in 1948 to 21.6 percent in 1958 (Brown, 1972). In the first full year of the NHS more than 200,000,000 prescriptions were dispensed under the National Health Insurance Scheme; by the early 1970s this had reached more than 300,000,000 prescriptions per annum (Watkin, 1978). By 1953 nearly 6,000,000 pairs of dentures had been issued under the NHS. The expansion of medical services had however not produced the final conquest of disease and illness in the UK as had been expected by the authors of the NHS; the system of post-war health had merely extended the range of medical activities parallel to the increasing importance of chronic and degenerative illness.

One problem with the economics of health is that it is by nature a labour-intensive industry. This assertion is clearly borne out by the employment figures associated with the NHS. In 1949 it employed approximately 500,000 people but by 1973 this had increased to almost 1,000,000 which represented 1 in 30 of the working population. The number of hospital doctors and hospital nurses doubled in the period between 1949 and 1973; hospital administrative and clerical staff also increased markedly. This increase in staff in both the professional and para-medical areas partly explains the rising cost of the hospital service.

Hospital expenditure increased not only because of capital expenditure, but because the UK in the 1970s was experiencing high rates of inflation and a sharp decline in the economy. In response to these financial problems, British governments have since 1973 reduced the absolute and relative expenditure on the NHS, adopted a managerial philosophy, closed small rural hospitals, and permitted an increasing privatization of hospital services (Widgery, 1979). Although in the UK the move to increase private medicine has been primarily associated with Conservative governments, managerialism and free-market principles may be dated from the Labour government of Harold Wilson. For example, it was under the Labour government that the Resource Allocation Working Party (RAWP) of 1975 came to argue that the supply of health-care services creates its own demand and therefore there can be no limit to expenditure on health services. It was in the late 1970s that the British government became more sympathetic to movements for a greater emphasis on preventive medicine and community care (Doyal, 1979).

The problems of inflation, labour costs and effectiveness were felt with equal force by other industrial western societies in the 1970s and 1980s (Rodwin, 1984). In the USA, the rising cost of hospitalization has been a critical issue. The increasing cost of health care in the USA is produced by an increase in personal disposal income, the expansion of insurance coverage through third parties, and the aging of the population. Thus in 1950, health-care expenditure was under $20bn. per annum but this had risen to almost $200bn. by the end of the 1970s and accounted for almost 10 percent of the gross national product. Another feature of this expansion in cost is the increase in doctors' salaries and fees (Mumford, 1983). Knowles (1973) has estimated that in 1925 the cost of one day's stay in the Massachusetts General Hospital at Boston was approximately $3; by 1977 the average cost of hospitalization for one day had risen to $230. Furthermore there has been a significant shift from a situation where in 1920 only 10 percent of the American population possessed health insurance to a situation in the 1970s where 90 percent of the population have some form of medical cover. The cost of mental illness in the USA is equally problematic. In 1977 it was estimated that Medicaid paid over $4bn. for mental health services.

We have seen therefore that there are growing economic problems with the existing system of health care and hospital provision in the advanced industrial societies. There have been powerful critiques of the public provision of health on the grounds that it is wasteful, ineffective and inefficient. In a number of societies as a result, there has been a drift towards the privatization of the health sector and an increasing dependence on private insurance schemes. This new emphasis on privatization has, in societies like the UK, been associated with the rejection of social Keynesianism in favour of a monetaristic policy. The policy of privatization has become attractive in societies which are experiencing significant economic downturn as a consequence of world recession.

While there has been a monetaristic critique of hospital provision, there was also in the 1960s and 1970s the development of a sociological critique of the large-scale bureaucratic hospital on the grounds that it created widespread alienation among the patients. From the perspective of Garfinkel (1956), we can regard even entry into such anonymous workplaces as a process of degradation, whereby our civil identity is progressively stripped from us through a series of public rituals. While the standardization of patient care produces important benefits in terms of bureaucratic efficiency, it does create a significant de-personalization of the healing experience. This de-personalization is brought about by stripping the patient of their personal items, regulating the resources available to the patient, and by restricting their mobility within the hospital (Coe, 1978). By means of these social rituals, the person is gradually converted into a full-time patient. Hospital patients are likely to develop the equivalent to recidivism which penologists have observed in criminal populations. For example, it has been found that the longer a patient stays in a hospital the more likely he or she is to wish to remain in the hospital, or to be indifferent about returning to their normal round of activities (Wing and Brown, 1970).

We have seen that a variety of criticisms of the hospital as a health-care institution point toward alternative systems. First, there is greater emphasis on preventive medicine which involves a new perception of the individual in relation to health. Secondly, there is a greater recognition of the continuing importance of the community hospital, community health-care systems and the smaller hospital unit. Thirdly, there is a greater willingness to criticize high-technology medicine and the use of the large general hospital as the primary site for such developments. Although there is a wide area of consensus about the desirability of health reform, achieving rationalization and reform has proved very problematic in the advanced industrial societies.

Rodwin (1984) in reviewing the problems of health planning identified three primary explanations for the barriers to health-care reform. First, there is the view that health is not a state of affairs which lends itself to rational technology and systematic planning of administrative structures which have been developed in the area of industrial management. The primary concepts of health management (such as hospital-bed/population ratios) are not entirely suitable in the area of health services. Unlike the concept of economic productivity, health is not a unitary phenomenon and is highly elastic as a cultural notion. Because there is no genuine agreement as to which criteria would be appropriate in the politics of health, achieving rational objectives and applying contemporary management strategies have proved to be elusive. Secondly, there is the view that health reform is difficult to achieve because of the clash of interests between physicians, administrators and consumers. The professional monopolies have a clear interest in maintaining their control over the hospital and health system, thereby blocking any attempt to achieve reform. Planning in this area tends as a consequence to be ad hoc and pragmatic, merely reflecting the dominant political and economic interests of the time. Thirdly, there is the view that under capitalism health reform and rationalization are frustrated by capitalist structures and interests, whereby health requirements are constantly transformed into commodities; health reform is seen to be subordinate to the primary interest of capital accumulation.

While Rodwin finds these three explanations only partly satisfactory, he does recognize three broad emerging trends in contemporary health legislation. These are the expansion of the goals of health systems which will have to address the problem of health rather than illness; he also believes that there will be a greater regionalization of health services, and finally he suggests that the period of health-care rationing will be a relatively permanent feature of modern governmental responses to increasing health costs. It is important to consider the question of hospital reform and the extension of the definition of health within the broader framework of medical power and social knowledge. In particular we should consider the contemporary phase of hospital reform within a more systematic overview of twentieth-century medical development with special reference to its primary institutional forms (Armstrong, 1983).

Conclusion
We might argue that the hospital has had no continuous historical evolution; the form of the hospital has corresponded to the peculiar features of the society in which it has been embedded. It has also reflected the dominant theory of 'disease' prevailing in given societies. As an aspect of Christian charity, the hospitium was a resting place for wayfarers; in the early modern period, it was a place of confinement and restraint. The point of Foucault's (1973) argument is that, under bourgeois utilitarianism and a regime of disciplines, the sick became useful as a spectacle under the clinical gaze. The emergence of the hospital as the focal point of health-care systems has, therefore, been bound up with the growth of medical dominance and professional power. As we have seen, however, the hospital is once more being transformed by the increasing importance of chronic illnesses which are not amenable to hospital-based care, by the overwhelming cost of modern medicine, and by the fragmentation of the medical profession with a growing division of labour. In order to understand these developments, we need to look more closely at the complex relationship between the nature of disease and the requirements of a capitalist economic system.

9
Capitalism, class and illness

Introduction

Contemporary medical sociology has been profoundly influenced by neo-Marxist sociology and by the perspective of political economy. The basic argument of these approaches is that the morbidity and mortality characteristics of contemporary societies are to be explained primarily by the nature of capitalist production. The demand for profitability in a capitalist enterprise results in the exploitation and alienation of a large section of the population; it is the character of work in capitalism which explains both the importance of occupational illness and also the problematic character of retirement and leisure. Because in capitalism health becomes a commodity like other commodities in the market place, the delivery of health in turn is shaped by the requirement for profit and efficiency. In general therefore, there is a permanent tension between the requirements of the economy and the requirements of a healthy existence. The critique of health, health delivery and professions in capitalist health systems has been dominated in recent years by the *International Journal of Health Services* and by the work of Navarro. In order to lay the foundations for a discussion of the relationship between capitalism, class and illness, it is useful to start with an outline of the basic argument of Navarro and his colleagues.

As an introductory comment, it is important to note that there is a complex and contradictory relationship between the requirements of capital accumulation in contemporary societies and the requirement for a healthy, disciplined and educated workforce. Where there is an abundant supply of labour, the owner of capital does not have to take responsibility for the health of the worker. Where the supply of human capital is highly elastic, the capitalist employer can readily replace the workforce with fresh supplies of labour. Although the requirement for continuous and regular production with a submissive and healthy workforce is a basic feature of capitalist production, the capitalist does not want to bear the burden of financing the health, education and welfare of the workforce. Given the requirement for profit, the capitalist seeks to avoid these social costs. Therefore in capitalism, the state has a role to play in regulating, educating and providing services to the workforce, since individual capitalists may be reluctant to provide the infra-structure which is required for the reproduction of labour. Navarro's (1976) argument is concerned with the complex relationship between capitalist accumulation, the role of the state and the health of the workforce.

According to Navarro, state intervention in contemporary capitalist societies is both negative and positive. Under the notion of negative functions or negative selection, Navarro includes all of those functions and activities of the state which exclude or regulate the conflictual nature of the class structure of capitalism. These negative strategies involve various state mechanisms such as structural selection, ideological functions, decision making and repressive–coercive activities. For example, the structural selective mechanisms are those processes by which under the auspices of the state, alternative medical systems are excluded in so far as they are threatening to the profitability of capital and to the accumulation of wealth. One illustration of these selective mechanisms would be the absence of adequate legislation to protect the worker from the dangers of capitalist production and the ineffectual application of existing legislation to render the production process safe for the worker. While there is considerable debate about the loss of work hours through industrial disruption (such as strikes), there is little public discussion or information about hours of work lost as a consequence of industrial injury and occupational hazard. The protracted political struggle to regulate the use of asbestos in order to prevent the spread of asbestosis among workers handling asbestos would be a basic illustration of the weakness of legislation regulating industrial processes (Hunter, 1959).

Secondly, Navarro believes that the state has an important part to play in regulating the ideological debate over the cause and character of illness in contemporary capitalist society. For example, there is a clear tendency to see illness in individualistic terms rather than in terms of environmental and social causes. Illness is seen to be the personal problem of the worker often resulting from his or her moral failing. Illness is seen to be in individualistic terms the consequence of a failure to abide by appropriate diets, exercise and personal hygiene; the structural and environmental causes of illness are obscured by this individualistic approach, reflecting the individualism of capitalist society. Another feature of this ideological mechanism would be the focus on the cure of the individual rather than the prevention of illness through appropriate legislation and social change. The politics of the tobacco industry would be a common illustration of this argument. Although there is considerable research into cancer associated with cigarette smoking, there is relatively little systematic interest in preventing people from smoking. In the USA, the tobacco industry has proved to be a particularly effective pressure group against information concerning the health hazards of cigarette smoking not only for lung cancer but for coronary disease. In the UK, the major political parties have been equally slow to come to terms with the research evidence collected by Doll and Hill in the 1950s showing a significant relationship between smoking and the development of lung cancer (Cartwright, 1983; Inglis, 1981).

Thirdly, Navarro suggests that one important function for the state is to legitimize the continuing dominance of certain classes and interest groups in the decision-making processes relating to the development and maintenance of health-care systems. Navarro argues that the dominance of the planning and administrative agencies in the UK and the USA by upper-class groups and professionals clearly operates to support sectional interests against the general wellbeing of the lower, middle and working classes. We have seen in previous chapters how the state is particularly important in maintaining professional privilege and in expressing the interests of powerful groups through the medium of professional associations and related institutions (Larson, 1977).

Finally, Navarro argues that there are a number of 'repressive–coercive mechanisms' which either directly or indirectly serve the interests of the dominant class by, for example, cutting or undermining those health programmes which may conflict with the dominant sources of power. The drastic cuts in public hospitals under the economic policies of President Reagan and the growth of private–corporate medicine would be one particularly potent illustration of this argument (Salmon, 1985).

In terms of positive selection mechanisms, Navarro argues that the state also intervenes to develop certain positive responses to health problems which are favourable to the general growth of capital and the continuity of certain dominant classes. Following Offe (Lindberg et al., 1975), Navarro makes a distinction between allocative and productive policies of the state. Under the notion of allocative intervention, we should note the important role of the state in influencing and directing a variety of social activities which are important for the continuing accumulation of capital. Within the health area, the regulations requiring doctors to register and notify the authorities of contagious disease and for employers to adopt certain protective devices to limit the number of industrial accidents would be examples of such allocative functions. It is clearly in the interests of dominant groups for the medical profession to record the existence and development of epidemics, since the reproduction of the class system depends upon such administrative control of contagious diseases. Under productive interventions, Navarro refers to those processes by which the state directly participates in the production of social resources, such as the provision of medical education through public university courses, the development of research on drugs, the financial assistance to drug companies, the management of public hospital systems, and the promotion of medical research through various forms of financial assistance.

Although private industry typically adheres to the rhetoric of the free market, it is also the case that in the twentieth century there has been a significant increase in state intervention in capitalist societies. Navarro attempts to explain this growth of state intervention with special reference to health care by insisting that the state intervenes to facilitate the process of capital accumulation and to protect the interests of private property. Although the functions of private capital often require the institutional assistance of the state, Navarro also notes that in recent years there has been an invasion of corporate capital into a variety of social sectors. For example, he observes that there has been a significant invasion of private life by corporate capital through advertising, the circulation of commodities and various services provided for individual needs. Navarro also notes the increasing 'proletarianization' of the medical population as professional health workers are transferred from independent entrepreneurial units to medical corporations as salaried employees. There has also been a concentration of ownership and wealth within the medical system whereby private interests have gained a significant foothold in the provision of primary and secondary medical services.

It is evident from this brief overview of Navarro's account of the relationship between health and capitalism that a number of problematic theoretical issues arise from the political economy perspective. First we need to analyse the relationship between different forms of capitalism and health; for example, there are significant changes from early to late capitalism. Secondly, we need to consider how different forms of capitalism develop and what are the major causal mechanisms in bringing about changes in capitalism. Thirdly, we need to examine the development of the service sector and the growth of white-collar employment resulting in, for some social theorists, a new middle-class. Finally, we need to recognize the significant changes which have occurred in western capitalism over the last decade with the privatization of key medical functions. By examining these various issues, we can begin to perceive the limitations and unresolved dilemmas of the neo-Marxist and political-economy perspectives. These limitations indicate the need for new theoretical and empirical directions concerned with the elaboration of health inequalities in contemporary society.

Forms of capitalism

In mainstream sociology, it has been a standard practice to distinguish between early or competitive capitalism and late or monopoly capitalism (Poulantzas, 1973, 1975). More recently sociologists have considered the possibility of a different terminology namely disorganized capitalism (Offe, 1985). By early capitalism, sociologists mean the type of capitalist society described by Marx in *Capital* with particular reference to market-dominated capitalist society as it developed in England in the eighteenth and nineteenth centuries. Competitive capitalism represents the pure form of capitalism in which the cash nexus dominates the relationship between labour and capital. In this sense, capitalism involves the private ownership and control of the basic means of production, the organization of economic activity for the pursuit of profit, the existence of a market that regulates such activity, the social appropriation of economic profits by the personal owners of capital, and the provision of labour-power by workers who are regarded as free agents in the market place.

In this definition it should be noted that there is no requirement necessarily for state involvement, the relationship between the worker and the employer is not regulated by legal or moral mechanisms, and the criterion of economic success dominates all social relations. Considerable controversy surrounds this concept. There have been major debates over the origins, the character and the development of capitalism and capitalist society since the term first emerged in Marxist discourse in the nineteenth century. One important issue is whether capitalism in its pure form ever existed even in British society, since there is much debate surrounding the role of the state and other public institutions in the regulation of the market place in early capitalism. However, we may regard the concept as a useful heuristic device or ideal type in order to begin a discussion of the relationship between competitive capitalism, the working class and health issues.

In competitive capitalism, the working class is in a relatively weak position economically and politically in relation to the employer and the economic system as a whole. The model of competitive capitalism, at least in its historical form in the early UK, presupposes the absence of organized collective political action by the working class to transform its economic dependence on capital. The model also assumes that the working class has no option but to sell its labour, because the possibilities of self-sufficiency have been excluded by the decline of traditional peasant land holdings. The pure type of early capitalism would also assume an elastic supply of labour from a relatively young and expanding population as a consequence of the early stages of the demographic transition. Because the market is unregulated, the capitalist is not constrained by any legislation bearing upon the form of production or the nature of the commodity for sale.

Under the conditions of competitive capitalism we would assume the following range of consequences: a relatively high rate of industrial injury and accident; a high rate of labour turnover as a consequence of physical exhaustion and accident; a high level of environmental pollution from the industrial process; and high levels of injury for the clients or customers of the products being delivered by this system of unregulated production. Under the conditions of competitive capitalism therefore one would assume a poor standard of health amongst the working class, high levels of environmental pollution and significant disease patterns related to the poor quality of the food supply, the lack of environmental regulation and the inadequacy of housing for the working class.

An illustration of the connection between exploitative work conditions under capitalism and illness would be provided by the study of black lung among American coal miners in the nineteenth century. The health conditions of miners were determined by the highly competitive and labour-intensive nature of the mining industry in the nineteenth century. Under these competitive circumstances, industrial health and safety procedures were very slow to become established and accepted; they were also relatively ineffectual as means of regulating the relationship between the employer and the employee. In the UK probably the first specific illustration of industrial medicine was Charles T. Thackrah's *The Effects of the Principal Arts, Trades and Professions, and of Civic States and Habits of Living, on Health and Longevity* in 1831. Thackrah, who was a general practitioner in Leeds, drew attention to a variety of disabilities and health problems of various occupational groups, but he was particularly concerned with the problem of occupational health and the employment of children. His publication was part of the growing public anxiety over the employment of children; the first piece of effective legislation in this area was the Factory Act of 1833 relating to the employment of children in mills and factories in the UK. The Act established minimal conditions of employment for children and created an inspectorate to administer the Act. By the beginning of the twentieth century and specifically as a consequence of the First World War, there was a significant expansion of state intervention in the market place and in the relationship between the employer and employee to regulate the conditions of work. These changes are associated with a fundamental transformation of capitalism in the twentieth century towards so-called monopoly capitalist conditions.

Monopoly capitalism has the following characteristics. There is a growing separation between the ownership and control of capital with the rise of a special managerial class which controls the organization of capitalist production. There is a tendency for capitalist ownership to become more impersonal with the rise of institutionalized ownership through pension funds, banks and other collective agencies. These changes followed from the expansion of the joint stock company in the nineteenth century. There is also a growing concentration of ownership with a rapid growth of mergers, takeovers and other forms of consolidation (Scott, 1979). With the development of monopolies, prices are no longer fixed by competition between capitalist units. In addition, the state interferes to organize wage levels, profits and prices by negotiating deals with labour and capital. Some writers (Panitch, 1980) have suggested that capitalism assumes a corporatist form in which political decisions are made by corporate bodies such as trade unions, professions, political pressure groups, lobbies and voluntary associations. Under monopoly conditions, it is also the case that the state assumes a number of important welfare functions, providing educational and health services for the population where these services are not measured or dictated solely by market or profit principles.

A number of theories have been developed to explain the emergence of monopoly capitalism, the decline of the market principle and the increasing involvement of the state in the productive process. For example, one explanation is that certain functions are important for capitalism (such as the development of roads, policing, military functions and the development of communication systems) but these functions cannot be provided in a profitable manner by private capital or the development of these services involves a financial risk which individual capitalists are unable to sustain. The state intervenes to guarantee the general conditions of competition and economic expansion, by developing the infra-structure and providing expenditure on human capital. Another explanation is that the state intervenes to regulate the business cycle and to guarantee a general rate of profit where social and technical circumstances have made the rate of profit uncertain and unstable.

Where a number of governments accepted social Keynesianism (Weir and Skocpol, 1983), the intervention of the state was associated with responses to the Depression when it was assumed that public investment was the main procedure by which demand and investment could be stimulated. The crises of competitive capitalism are seen to be about profit and continued accumulation, where only the state can provide the injections of capital which are required to stimulate economic growth.

An alternative explanation suggests that, following the crises of the First and Second World Wars, the working classes had a number of political advantages by which they could force governments to provide improvements in health, welfare and education. In this approach, it was the weakness of post-war governments which allowed the working classes to gain a momentary advantage over capital through the development of reformist politics. The political success of radicalism in the post-war period varied considerably between societies, but in general the post-war period was one of significant social reconstruction which involved a new set of principles, which were expressed in the development of the welfare state (Gallie, 1983). These developments in social welfare meant that the pure cash nexus between employer and employee no longer operated without institutional restraint. Marx had argued in the nineteenth century that the worker was controlled by the dull compulsion of economic relations which faced the worker with a choice between employment or starvation. By the middle of the twentieth century in a number of European societies, the development of welfare and the transformation of capitalism meant that the worker was not wholly controlled by the cash nexus. A number of key developments (social Keynesianism, state intervention and the welfare society) brought about a significant improvement in the general health of the working class in the 1950s (Susser and Watson, 1962).

The sociological explanation of these changes is in fact complex and the subject of considerable controversy. The explanation can assume a functionalist character by arguing that the development of the state apparatus was necessary to maintain the general profitability of capital; the implication is that there is a symmetrical relationship between state requirements and capital accumulation. This explanation gives rise to considerable difficulties, because there is a certain contradiction between the taxation required to maintain the state and the quest for profitability as a basis of private enterprise and economic growth. Secondly, the explanation for the emergence of monopoly capitalism can give a special place to the importance of class struggle, suggesting that working-class conflict through the trade unions and other political institutions controlled and curtailed the dominance of private profit (Turner 1986a). Against this argument, it has been suggested by a number of Marxist and radical theorists that reformism in capitalist societies will never be sufficient to transform radically the relationship between the worker and the employer (Maravall, 1979). Finally, the argument may give special attention to contingent and historical features of the development of monopoly capitalism, such as the financial crisis of the Depression, the rise of fascism and the necessity for state intervention in economic production during the Second World War.

Because this type of historical explanation gives prominence to specific and accidental circumstances, it does not suggest any logic to capitalist development. In order to understand the problems associated with these explanations, it is interesting to consider the emergence of a service class as a feature of the decline of competitive capitalism. The social functions of a service class are of particular interest to medical sociology, because the development of such a class is associated with the modern dominance of the health professions, the social functions of the hospital and the dominance of scientific knowledge.

The service class
The concept of the service class was first used by Renner in an attempt to understand the changing character of capitalism (Bottomore and Goode, 1978). He identified three components of this service class, namely employees in the public sector, employees in private business enterprises (the managerial section) and employees in social services whom he regarded as the distributive agents of social welfare. The service class arises from the increasing scale of social organization (especially in government), the development of technology in a variety of occupational areas requiring specialized skills, and finally the specialization and rationalization of work patterns in contemporary capitalism (Goldthorpe, 1982). The social implications and political consequences of the development of this intermediate class have been of special interest to sociologists in recent years (Abercrombie and Urry, 1983; Wright, 1985).

The most useful survey of the explanations of the rise and functions of this service class has been presented by Offe (1985). Offe considers four types of explanation, namely the systemic requirements of the capitalist system, the employment deficits arising from changes in the demand for labour, changing requirements of productivity in capitalism and the supply-side interests of workers themselves.

The first type of explanation is a functionalist account of the growth of service labour in response to social-system requirements in advanced capitalism. These systemic requirements consist of regulative and coordinating activities in the context of a complex division of labour and the structural differentiation of the system as a whole. The service class provides for planning, regulation, control and coordination of productive activities. The tertiary sector emerges to satisfy certain requirements of the social system which is increasing in complexity and diversity. In sociological terms the social services emerge in response to the decline of the traditional household, the urbanization of society, the participation of women in the workplace, the changing age structure of the population, the transformation of disease towards chronic and degenerative illnesses, and the demands for regional and occupational mobility. At the level of the total society, there is the need for regulation and control, but also within the firm there is a clear tendency towards managerial bureaucracy and the dominance of planning through rational services. There is considerable specialization of these services, many of which are directed towards the regulation and control of conflicts between wage, labour and capital. The service class is a feature of the rationalization of modern societies.

The second form of explanation is addressed to the problem of unemployment and the transfer of surplus labour to the tertiary sector. The rapid mechanisation of production creates a labour surplus, because the demand for labour is never sufficient to guarantee full employment. The growth in services and white-collar employment functions to mop up this surplus labour force. The middle strata are therefore constituted by this unproductive layer of workers who provide administrative and control functions for the accumulation process. Although these groups may contribute relatively little to real production, their role is often seen to be as a consumption class, since a decline in the general level of employment creates problems for the absorption of commodities produced by private capital. In Keynesian terms, the service class stimulates supply because its relatively high wages maintain a stable level of demand for goods.

The third explanation of the growth of the service sector is related to the character of changing demands and is called the 'three-sector hypothesis'. The argument has three components. Following from improvements in economic productivity within the secondary sector, there is a corresponding increase in the real incomes of private households. As real incomes increase, the consumption of goods is subject to saturation and the demand for social services rises to compensate for this decline in the demand for consumer durables. Because the production of social services cannot be entirely rationalized and because service production is labour intensive, there is a tendency for a continuous increase in service employment. In addition, the demand for social expenditure on health, entertainment, education and culture will increase with the aging of the population and legislation for compulsory retirement. There is also a demand for household services associated with the participation of women in the labour force. With the growing complexity of economic and social arrangements, there is an increase in demand for such services as taxation advice, legal consultations, personal insurance and banking facilities. In summary, there are a variety of demands which bring about the growth of the service sector.

The fourth perspective explains the dynamism of the service sector by arguing that there is a strong demand within professional and quasi-professional groups for the continuity and expansion of service activities. There are status interests on the part of service workers to promote and expand opportunities within the personal service sector. There is a strong preference especially among women for white-collar jobs in the service economy rather than employment in manufacturing. White-collar employment is associated with the benefits and attractions of a middle-class lifestyle, associated with mental as opposed to manual labour. Credentialism and social control will function to protect the career prospects and lifestyles of professional and quasi-professional groups. There is an internal logic to the expansion of such occupations, since they are seen to be more desirable than alternative forms of employment. There are therefore significant social forces, associated with status, for employment in health-care occupations to expand exponentially.

Although Offe did not find these arguments, considered separately, as entirely convincing explanations for the growth of the service class, his outline of the arguments is useful in considering the expansion of health-care services in the second half of the twentieth century. Health-care occupations as a component of the service class provide important functions of surveillance and control over the workforce. The health industry has been significant in absorbing labour, because by its nature it is labour intensive and certain activities such as nursing cannot be easily rationalized. There is also an internal pressure towards an expansion of these occupations, since health occupations, considered as status communities, exert strong pressure to maintain their monopolistic control over their employment and the supply of labour. These occupations and activities can be easily legitimized in terms of the needs of clients and, given the aging of the population and the elasticity of the concept of illness, there is strong pressure towards an expansion of the health service. Finally, with the decline of the nuclear family and the general weakness of the household as a health agency, there is, as it were, a gap in the social structure whereby healing occupations can expand. In the health economy, supply creates demand.

Although there was indeed a major expansion of the service sector in the post-war period, there has been since 1973 a political and social movement against Keynesianism in favour of greater economic regulation of public provision. In disorganized capitalism, the conflicts between the public provision of services and the private accumulation of profit have become increasingly overt and protracted. While in the 1960s Marxists argued that private capital depended upon state services for key functions with respect to regulation and control, in the late 1970s and the 1980s there has been a general move towards privatization. In the contemporary view of disorganized capitalism, the contradictions between the private and the public, and between service and profit, have become the principal focus of theoretical discussion and analysis.

The crises of capitalism
Since the oil crisis of 1973, there has been a serious decline in commodity prices, an increase in world indebtedness, a spiral of inflation and unemployment, and a crisis in the world monetary system (Johnson, 1985). One common response to the economic crisis has been the adoption of monetaristic policies, or in a more popular terminology 'Reaganomics' and 'Thatcherism'. The general aim of these policies has, at least officially, been opposed to Keynesianism in seeking to curtail government expenditure, reduce welfare payments, control the money supply, lower personal taxes and stimulate private industry by tax concessions (Frank, 1983). In the area of social services, these monetaristic policies have involved the reduction of expenditure on welfare services, and also a privatization of services and institutions which previously had been controlled by the state.

A number of sociologists have seen the crisis of capitalism in terms of a conflict between the political demands of the electorate for greater social services and the economic interests of the owners of capital who seek private profit and further accumulation. There is in this perspective a necessary conflict between the taxation basis of the state as the source of social security payments and the private profit required by industry to reinvest for future production. Habermas (1976) developed a model to conceptualize this conflict as a set of contradictory exchanges between the economic, political and social systems. Given the problems of the economic system as a competitive organization of production and distribution, the state provides 'steering performances' as a form of regulation and support for the economy in exchange for which the state requires a fiscal return in the form of taxation.

With respect to the socio-cultural system, the polity offers social

welfare performances in return for voter loyalty and political commitment to the system. The rising expectations of the electorate put
continuous pressure on governments to improve and increase welfare performances as the basis for political commitment from the
electorate. However, these increases in welfare performances
threaten the viability of the economic system which requires unrestrained profitability. In the recession of the 1970s and 1980s, the
political problems of democratic governments have been intensified
since, with the decline of profitability and investment opportunities,
the state finds itself in a persistent economic crisis where securing
the loyalty of the electorate is constantly undermined by the poor
performance of the economic system. In the view of Habermas, this
is the economic basis of the crisis of legitimation which has characterized contemporary democracies in capitalist societies.

The ability of governments to respond to this cross-pressure from
business and the electorate is further reduced and complicated by
divisions within the economic system. The economy is divided into
competitive, monopolistic and state sectors which have different
and occasionally conflicting interests. The monopoly sector can
tolerate higher wage levels resulting from greater unionization of
labour than is the case for small-scale business. By setting relatively
high wage levels in the monopoly sector, there is a general encouragement for workers in other areas to demand comparability of
wages thereby bringing about a wage-push form of inflation
(O'Connor, 1973).

In response to this inflationary and fiscal crisis, western governments have adopted various programmes of rationalization and
privatization of their welfare schemes. Rationalization has in theory
three important consequences for the social system (Hirschhorn,
1978). Firstly, as expenditure on services and government bor-
rowing decline, private capital is injected back into the private
sector from the public sector. Secondly, reductions in social services
increase the size of the supply of labour especially low-wage labour
by forcing people into the market place. Thirdly, reductions in
expenditure on social services compel the managers of the service
sector to rationalize and streamline their welfare programmes in
order to achieve minimal standards of social welfare. The aim of
rationalization in the social services sector is to change the relationship between welfare payments and wages from employment in
order to make unemployment increasingly unattractive and punitive. Reductions in welfare expenditure are therefore a political
instrument for reducing the resistance of the working class to capitalist regulation. Although it can be argued that the social services
in fact represent a productive contribution to capital growth by

increasing the quality of human capital, the contemporary context of the world recession is unfavourable to the working class, since capitalist enterprises can be located in societies where social security and social service benefits are minimal and profits consequently more available. While national governments respond to local and indigenous problems, monopoly capital can locate its enterprises in any sector of the globe, where labour is plentiful and profitability guaranteed by governments seeking to attract overseas investment with the promise of a disciplined labour force and investment incentives.

To summarize the discussion so far, the state in capital society is forced to fulfil two fundamental but often contradictory functions, namely accumulation and legitimation. Under the first function, the state has to maintain and promote those social and economic circumstances in which profitable private capital accumulation can take place. However, under the function of legitimation, the state must attempt to preserve and promote the general conditions of social harmony. By supporting the interests of a property class, the state runs the risk of losing its political legitimacy because of its biased and one-sided activity. However, by seeking to create the general conditions of social harmony, the state may be unable to fulfil the requirements of private economic accumulation.

Corresponding to these two forms of social activity, state expenditures illustrate these contradictory requirements. Following O'Connor (1973:7), we can define social capital as the expenditures required to maintain profitable accumulation. This social capital can be further divided into social investment and social consumption. The former refers to those projects and services which increase the productivity of labour and thereby bring about an improvement in the rate of profit. Social investment expenditure includes the construction of roads, sewerage systems, and research and development. Social consumption consists of those government projects that reduce the reproduction costs of labour and again increase the rate of profit on investment. O'Connor distinguishes these forms of social capital from what he calls social expenses which exist to fulfil the state's function of legitimizing the social system. These social expenses are not, at least directly, productive investments; they produce social harmony through expenditure on the welfare system. O'Connor argues that all government agencies have these dual functions of accumulation and legitimation, and it is the contradictory relation between these functions which explains the complexity of much government activity (O'Connor, 1984).

Three theories of state expenditure

We have considered a number of explanations for the emergence of state interventionism in contemporary capitalism. The underlying theme of these explanations is that various crises in capitalist society require solutions which can only be provided by some central agency, specifically the state. These theories draw attention to two important functions which are related, namely the contribution of the state (1) to economic problems whereby the state aids the accumulation of capital and (2) to problems concerned with the legitimacy of society where the state provides some element of social harmony. These theories while useful are still somewhat vague with respect to explanations of state expenditure. We have seen that the historical circumstances for the growth of state intervention in the twentieth century included the economic crisis of the 1930s, the military requirements of state intervention during the Second World War and the organization of working-class movements in association with electoral reform to achieve a better or more equitable distribution of resources (Skocpol, 1980).

In reviewing various theories of state expenditure, Devine (1985) has usefully identified three broad traditions for explaining the increase of state expenditure in the twentieth century. The first explanation is economic structuralism which has been illustrated by the work of O'Connor. These arguments see the state's provision of social investment as a function of cyclical patterns of accumulation within the economic system. In order to sustain economic growth over long periods, the state becomes involved, not only to level out the crisis of the business cycle, but also to provide essential human capital investments to sustain the quality of the labour force. The economic role of the state is to absorb the increasing costs of production and reproduction in an advanced capitalist economy. During periods of economic decline, the state provides new investment incentives and creates employment through issuing contracts to private capital.

This explanation of state expenditure is distinguished from those analyses which emphasize the causal importance of political class struggle. In their classical study of state responses to civil disturbance, Piven and Cloward (1971) argued that relief expenditure by governments was a response to civil disorder and that these governmental responses were short term, because once the threat of order had been removed the level of government expenditure would be reduced. There was considerable expansion of government intervention to relieve the poor following the economic crisis of the Depression, but destitution of itself is insignificant as a lever for government involvement. Governments intervene when destitution produces 'a massive electoral convulsion' (Piven and Cloward, 1971:77). In their more recent study, Piven and Cloward (1982) have suggested that some forms of social disturbance such as the urban uprisings of the 1960s have produced more permanent and lasting forms of welfare such as job training, housing, health and education. As a minor change to the argument, it is interesting to note that in the USA organized working-class struggle has been relatively less important than racial conflict and urban riots in bringing about an expansion of government support for welfare (Isaac and Kelly, 1981). As a more general hypothesis, we can argue that there is a close relationship between the level of social protest and conflict, and the expansion of citizenship rights from merely political forms to substantive rights of welfare and redistribution (Lash, 1984; Turner, 1986a).

The third theory of state expenditure may be called state managerialism. This argument suggests that state elites, rather than being simply a section of the capitalist class or property owners, constitute a class for themselves with distinctive interests, consciousness and political power. This class has a relative autonomy from the economic power of the dominant class (Block, 1977). The managers of government agencies acquire a distinctive interest in expanding, or at least maintaining, existing levels of government expenditure in order to sustain their own political significance and control over resources. Of course these managers cannot be entirely independent or indifferent to the economic circumstances of the state and the wider society. In order to maintain existing levels of government expenditure, they must seek to maintain business confidence in state policies. The interests of these state managers are closely associated with the owners of capital, since the decline of the economy threatens the tax basis of the state and the continuity of managerial power. The argument is that state expenditure increases because there is a logic to bureaucratization which creates a spiral of expenditure, given the interests of state managers in an expanded power base.

Although Devine regards these as distinct theories of state expenditure, they are not incompatible and indeed it would be possible to develop a more general theory of the state in terms of these three themes. There is no incompatibility for example between an emphasis on political conflict as the basis of the state expansion and a structuralist view of the economic requirements of the capitalist mode of production. Given the contradictory clash of interests between business, the state and subordinate social groups, we may expect government policies to be relatively unstable because they are caught between the contradictory demands of economic accumulation and political legitimacy.

The USA: the medical industrial complex

The impact of the profit motive in capitalism on health care and illness has been unambiguously condemned by political economists and Marxists. For example, Waitzkin and Waterman (1974:15–16) have argued that it is not self-evident that

> a humane health care system is possible in a capitalist society. The institution of medicine is intimately tied to the broad socio-political framework of a society. Under capitalism, the right of individual citizens to decent health care remains an ambiguous principle. Despite widespread concern about the costliness, maldistribution and poor quality of services, the medical profession and larger American corporations continue to exploit illness for profit. In addition, political struggles in relation to welfare rights are often unstable and contradictory. While welfare relief is a form of regulating the poor, it is also an important political victory for subordinate social groups.

While this has a prima facie validity, there are significant variations within and between various capitalist societies depending on the type of health-care delivery system available, the political organization of these societies and their historical development as economic systems. In addition, as Mechanic (1968) has shown, some form of rationing of medical care appears to be inevitable in all modern societies. The only question is how that rationing is to be achieved. In this comparative approach, the history of health care in the USA is of particular interest.

The USA, by comparison with other industrial democratic societies, was exceptionally late in developing a public system of welfare and social security. West Germany, which has a decentralized system of funding for sickness benefit, began to develop a system of social insurance as early as 1883. Other societies developed social insurance schemes by the end of the nineteenth century; for example Austria established a scheme in 1883. The UK and Switzerland created social insurance schemes for health care in 1911. However, the USA did not organize a comprehensive system of public care through social insurance until 1965 through Medicare and Medicaid under the Social Security Act (Stevens and Stevens, 1974; Stevens, 1971). Throughout most of its history, the USA has depended upon various forms of private, individual and voluntary systems of health and welfare provision. There was some elementary welfare provision under the New Deal programmes of the 1930s which were a direct response to the social and economic problems following from the Wall Street Crash of 1929. Under Franklin Roosevelt there were a number of important developments which provided a framework of welfare for the destitute and deprived. The Social Security Act of 1935 created a national framework for old-age insurance in which employees were compelled to contribute. The Federal Government was committed to share with the states in the care of the destitute over the age of sixty-five who would not be able to participate in the insurance scheme. The Act also included an element of unemployment insurance and established a national system of aid to the states for the social provision of services to dependent mothers and the handicapped. Although the Act had a number of serious limitations, it was a new departure in the history of American social policy (Leuchtenburg, 1963).

Various explanations have been provided for the late development of American social security and welfare systems; these explanations are closely related to the explanation of the absence of socialist and radical political parties in the USA. In reviewing the history of social policy and welfare in the USA, Higgins (1981) considered a number of factors which might explain the weak and late development of a welfare state in the USA. First, ideological factors may have played a significant role in denying legitimacy to state intervention. In particular, American individualism tends to emphasize the moral value of self-help and self-reliance (Bellah et al., 1985). Since de Tocqueville published *Democracy in America* in 1835, social commentators on American life have been impressed by the force of moral ideology on social and cultural life. This emphasis on the individual has underlined the importance of voluntary activity and voluntary associations in the public life of contemporary America. The emphasis on voluntarism in welfare activity was also associated with a fear of state intervention and bureaucracy; democratic individualism emphasized the importance of local activity and personal responsibility against the intervention of the state. Towards the end of the nineteenth century, this tradition of individualism became associated also with the racial doctrines of social Darwinism which were imported from European social philosophy especially in the evolutionary thought of Herbert Spencer. Social Darwinism as an ideology rejected all welfare policies and institutions on the grounds that they would protect the weak, the degenerate and the morally corrupt. Evolutionary progress required the pure mechanism of the survival of the fittest in order to guarantee the most efficient social system. The protection of the weak by the state could only harm social survival in the long term. These doctrines of individualism and self-reliance continue to be important and influential in American society and they are not conducive to the development of social welfare programmes (Feagin, 1975; James, 1972).

The ideological importance of localism versus the state was also associated with the constitutional separation of powers and the establishment of local autonomy and state rights. The lack of centralization in American public activity and government structures has prohibited the development of a coherent and centralized policy for a national system of social welfare (Wilensky, 1975, 1976). These constitutional and governmental arrangements have permitted the continuity of significant regional variations in the provision of social benefits and services. This fragmentation of the political system has encouraged local elites to protect vested interests and particularistic objectives against the possibility of a centralized reform of the system.

Another feature of the weakness of a welfare system is the absence of strong unionization and working-class militancy expressed through a socialist party in the USA. Whereas, for example, at the end of the 1970s, in the UK approximately half of the workforce had union membership, in the USA this was below 22 percent. Again the importance of the ideology of individualism should not be underestimated as an alternative to a commitment to egalitarianism among the poor, the unemployed and minority groups. In the USA which is clearly unequal in terms of the distribution of resources, even the poor do not typically support the notion that there should be greater social equality through a redistribution of personal income. For example, among black Americans in the lowest income groups, less than one-third supported egalitarianism in the distribution of wealth (Turner, 1986b). As we have seen in an earlier discussion, Piven and Cloward (1971) have suggested that while the political mobilization of the poor may produce certain temporary measures to reform the social distribution of wealth, these advantages have been relatively short lived and welfare institutions, from this perspective, are at least covertly concerned to achieve the political docility of the poor rather than to meet their welfare needs.

Finally, the development of social welfare reform was hindered and opposed by various pressure groups, professional associations and business interests who saw centralized health care and welfare as a direct threat to their professional standing, their monopolistic control over services or their professional authority in relationship to the patient or clients. The American Medical Association has been successful in preventing the development of a centralized, public system of health-care delivery. The interests of the Medical Association have often coincided with those of the private health insurance business which has opposed all moves to introduce a compulsory national insurance scheme.

As in the UK and other industrial capitalist societies, the medical profession has proved to be particularly significant in the develop-

ment or otherwise of health-care systems. In Australia, the Australian Medical Association has opposed the National Health and
Pensions Insurance Bill in the 1930s, the introduction of Medibank
during the Whitlam Government and the development of Medicare
under the Hawke Government, because these schemes threatened
medical dominance, professional autonomy and the fee-for-service
arrangements (Opit, 1983; Scotton, 1978, 1980). Two recent studies
of the American medical profession throw considerable light on the
politics of welfare in the USA.

Rosen (1983) and Starr (1982) both draw attention to the social
context within which the medical profession and associated institutions developed in the USA towards the end of the nineteenth
century from a position of social weakness to one of medical dominance. The medical profession in the mid-nineteenth century was
demoralized and lacked any significant professional organization or
status. Medicine lacked any demonstrable therapeutic efficacy and,
given the absence of urbanization, it did not have a concentrated
clientele for even this limited service. The profession did not enjoy
scientific security and there were many intra-occupational con-
troversies which further diminished the doctor's status in society.
General hospitals had not been developed and most patients
received medical care in their own homes. However, between 1875
and 1920 the status of the general practitioners was transformed by
a number of social developments. Starr argues that the expansion in
the market for medical services was an effect of economic growth,
urbanization and the development of urban transport systems. The
sovereignty of the medical profession was reinforced by the
development of licensing laws with the backing of the state.

With the professional development of medicine, physicians came
to oppose alternative forms of practice which departed from the
fee-for-service model. They claimed that innovations in the delivery
of health would undermine individualism, self-help and self-
reliance. Any development of diagnostic and preventive medicine
by public health departments would have been a direct economic
threat to the medical profession, and would have in addition challenged their professional autonomy and their control over the relationship with the patient.

However, Starr claims that the private development of medicine
on the fee-for-service model in the USA does not necessarily lend
unambiguous support to Marxist interpretations since

> capitalism is compatible with many diverse systems of medical care, and
> it is not entirely clear whether the development of American medicine
> followed the 'objective' interests of the capitalist class or the capitalist
> system. (Starr, 1982:16–17)

Welfare programmes in the USA did not develop in the same direction as they had done in Europe, partly because working-class movements were relatively weak and did not significantly threaten the existing economic and social system in the USA. There was relatively little continuous and organized political agitation for state-welfare systems such as health insurance. However, in the mid-1930s following the Depression era, the American Medical Association came eventually to see that some features of private insurance schemes could support their monopoly of medical care. By securing the maximum provider control, the professional association was able to convert third-party insurance to its financial advantage. In the post-war period the organized medical profession has also been able to secure significant political and financial advantages from the development of Medicaid, Medicare and other medical programmes.

The interesting feature of Starr's historical account of the rise of the medical profession as an interest group which has opposed public provision of welfare is that he believes the modern development of corporate control over medical care may eventually result in a decline of professional autonomy, initiative and status. The renewal of an emphasis on the free market and entrepreneurship has, through the medical industrial complex, brought about a certain proletarianization of the medical profession by converting them into the hired employees of profit-making, private-sector health systems. The professional physician who is hired by a commercial enterprise has to make a profit in addition to providing an adequate system of health care. Furthermore, the contemporary development of health care in the USA has brought about a new emphasis on specialism; specialization has undermined, or at least, threatened the professional coherence and solidarity of medicine as a whole. In addition to this internal division, with the growth of consumer groups, malpractice legislation and public alarm with technological medicine, there has been a renewed interest in more holistic forms of medical service through alternative systems. The commercialization of medicine and the dominance of free-market principles may in the long term bring about the decline of the traditional autonomous professional physician; these developments have given rise to an extensive debate over the character of professional employment in medicine (Derber, 1984).

While the pursuit of monetarism may in the long run curtail or destroy the traditional autonomy of the medical profession, these policies have had serious consequences for users and consumers (Davis, 1984; Salmon, 1985). Rationalization, privatization and deregulation of the economy have been achieved by transferring income from the less advantaged sectors of the community to the more privileged, by reducing the level of support to the poor, by reducing funding for basic programmes in education, housing and health services, by removing the funding necessary for the enforcement of social rights, and by cutting funds for the development of appropriate health standards in the area of occupational health (Milio, 1985).

The consequences of these policies have become apparent in a variety of areas of welfare. For example, poverty has increased by 30 percent among children since 1979. Between 1981 and 1982, 11 states in the USA showed increases in the infant mortality rate and also showed considerable differences between black and white mortality rates. In Michigan for example, infant mortality rates rose for the first time in over 30 years to over 13 per 1000 live births. These increases in the infantile mortality rate are associated with the increase in poverty, unemployment, decline in nutrition and the loss of health insurance coverage through the new limitations on Medicaid. While there are significant indicators of increasing poverty, the private health sector has enjoyed buoyant profitability and expansion. The economic and political importance of the tax cuts under the Reagan administration is that, by reducing revenue to the state, they curtail the ability of future governments to introduce new social welfare programmes to remove hardship, stimulate employment schemes and restore welfare measures. The consequences of these changes in public provision have reinforced the class divisions within the health system, resulting in a marked division between the privileged and the non-privileged.

Conclusion: capitalism, class and crisis

We have seen that the relationship between illness, health care and capitalism is complex. For a number of writers, the predominant forms and content of illness in modern society are directly explained by the character and requirements of capitalism. For Navarro, the modern hospital with its highly technical delivery of health care reflects the current requirements of capital accumulation and the political level of struggle within the capitalist system. He also claims that the legislation which protects the enjoyment of rights of private property stands in stark contrast to the absence of adequate legislation on health at work, occupational hazards and stress-related illnesses. Furthermore, the medical model and its aetiological categories reflect the underlying assumptions of capitalism in which health is a commodity and responsibility for illness is increasingly seen to be the individual's problem. The distribution of health resources also reflects the medical dominance enjoyed by professional medicine as a section of the dominant class. The current crisis in the welfare system in societies like the UK and the call for a reduction of state expenditure and privatization simply reflect the contemporary requirements for capital growth given the limitations on profits and the restriction of the market place (Navarro, 1978). Major reductions in expenditure on the National Health Service in the UK are seen to be responses to the crisis of capitalism which attempt to redistribute wealth from the disprivileged to the privileged; therefore, expenditure cuts are regarded as characteristically in the interests of private capital rather than in the interests of the sick, the unemployed and the destitute.

There are a number of problems with this explanatory framework. First, it fails to distinguish adequately between different types or stages of capitalism, namely competitive and monopoly capitalism. The relationship between capitalist production, health and health-care delivery systems will vary considerably according to the prevailing form of capitalism and its specific requirements. Secondly, these explanations often fail to provide a clear and systematic account of the precise causal mechanisms which require different types of health care and produce different distributions of illness. For example, it is important to distinguish between structural approaches and those which give a particular emphasis to the autonomy of political conflict. Thirdly, the Marxist analysis of capitalism and health often fails to provide a clear and systematic account of why and how capitalist societies have very different patterns of disease and health-care delivery. In short, these political-economy approaches are often inadequate from the point of view of a comparative and historical sociological study. There are major differences between the USA, the UK and Sweden, despite the fact that all three societies are quite distinctively capitalist. Finally, Marxist critics have often failed to recognize the positive and progressive features of welfare systems, because they tend to regard welfare as merely reformist. However, as Piven and Cloward (1982) insist, welfare benefits are an essential element of democracy, regardless of their economic consequences.

The problem with these radical approaches can be illustrated by a consideration of the relationship between illness and social class. The political-economy approach normally emphasizes the importance of class difference in capitalism, but the exact relationship between capitalism, illness and class is frequently implied rather than systematically elaborated. For example, in the United Kingdom in a useful review of the Black Report (*Inequalities in Health*, Department of Health and Social Security, 1980), Blane (1985) identified four possible types of explanation of class differences in health. The first suggests that the relationship between health and social class may be an artifact, which is the outcome of the way in which the Registrar General's classification is used as a form of social measurement. For example, as the proportion of the employed population in semiskilled and unskilled manual jobs declines as a result of de-skilling and mechanized production, new recruits to the work force are compelled to move directly into skilled and white-collar jobs. The inferior health of social classes IV and V may be simply a function of their greater average age. This problem can be avoided by the use of age-standardized crude mortality rates.

The second form of explanation is the social selection approach which argues that the poor health of the lower classes is a function of downward social mobility by those who are ill. In a study of maternal health, Illsley (1955) argued that the inferior health of working-class mothers was a product of their downward social mobility at marriage rather than of the social factors connected with a mother's social class. In a classic study of schizophrenia (Goldberg and Morrison, 1963) it was argued that schizophrenics are downwardly mobile and this accounts for the disproportionate representation of schizophrenia in social class V. These studies can be criticized for the narrow and unrepresentative character of the populations which they study. For example, the study of schizophrenia employed subjects from hospital patients and the downward mobility of these samples may be simply a reflection of hospitalization.

In assessing the Black Report we should also consider the cultural/behavioural explanation of illness. It is possible to accept a close relationship between social class and health, but to treat health as the dependent variable. Within this framework the class character of health is the product of different social class behaviours such as the use of tobacco and alcohol, differences in leisure and differences in nutrition. Differences in the rates of morbidity with respect to cancer may be explained by differential use of tobacco by different social classes. The cultural/behavioural explanation of class differences is favoured by the medical profession; it reflects the assumption that many aspects of illness are the products of individual variations in lifestyle and that the pattern of illness could actually be controlled by improvements in personal behaviour. This approach can be challenged on the grounds that we cannot separate cultural/behavioural activities from the broader social environment within which they are located and produced. We need to ask a more challenging set of questions, namely how different social structures produce different forms of personal behaviour.

The final explanation therefore of the relationship between health and social class is the materialist explanation. Class differences in health within this perspective are the consequence of the competitive character of capitalism. Health is directly related to the distribution of fundamental resources (income and wealth) and illness is the outcome of poverty, poor housing, low educational attainment and the level of business activity. In capitalism, class differences in health statistics are the outcome of differentials in occupational conditions, where a number of significant diseases are associated with the chemical hazards of certain types of employment. Poor housing is another significant variable in the explanation of class differences in respiratory disease, domestic accident and life expectation. There is no simple or constant connection between illness, capitalism, class and personal behaviour.

The problem of health in capitalism can be seen finally as a fundamental issue of citizenship with capitalism. The rights to health, like those for education, housing and other benefits, are the outcome of political action, class organization and democratic representation. The contradictory relationship between citizenship and class has been a fundamental feature of the modern political analysis of contemporary capitalism. The economic recession of the 1970s and 1980s has resulted in an important decline in citizenship rights as a consequence of privatization, government policy, welfare cuts, economic recession and the application of free-market principles. However, the relationship between economic recession and the decline of health is not direct, since it is mediated by political conflict. The success, at least in political terms, of Reaganomics and Thatcherite politics has been made possible by the political weakness of opposition, the decline of the urban working class, the political incapacity of trade union organizations, and the transformation of global capitalism in the contemporary period.

10
Comparative health systems: the globalization of medical power

Health-care systems

There are a number of ways in which health-care systems can be classified. For example, Roemer (1977) draws a valuable distinction between free enterprise systems, welfare-state forms of health care, the health systems of the underdeveloped societies, the health systems of transitional societies and finally socialist systems of health care. In this chapter I shall be solely concerned with free enterprise, welfare state and socialist forms of health care with special reference to the USA, the UK and Soviet Bloc societies. To simplify the discussion, we can argue that health-care systems vary along a continuum from private to public provision, but in practice the majority of health-care systems will be mixed, combining both private and public forms of delivery. Basically private provision is characteristic of capitalist societies, while public delivery is usually associated with state socialism. It is also valuable to differentiate the various levels of health systems; these would include the economic base for the support of health care, the organization of manpower resources, the health-care facilities, the numerous systems by which medical care is delivered, the system of preventive services, the political regulation of health care, and finally the various methods for the planning and administration of health systems.

We can also within each health-care system consider the various levels of medical delivery. It is, for example, conventional to distinguish between primary, secondary and tertiary care. Primary care includes the ordinary forms of out-patient care which are provided conventionally on the basis of a clinic by professional practitioners who represent, as it were, the first point of call. Then we may consider the secondary levels of care which would include various specialized services; finally, there is tertiary care which embraces the more complex systems of specialized hospital treatment, such as open-heart surgery (Mechanic, 1968).

There are a number of important theoretical reasons for expecting the emergence of a mixed delivery system, combining a private market and public regulation of health care. These pressures towards a mixed system are associated with the problem of rationing in health delivery (Mechanic, 1976, 1977b). In principle the demand for medical care appears to be unlimited for at least two reasons. First, in contemporary societies as a consequence of various democratic movements, the demand for health is part of a system of rising expectations with respect to the state's role in society. Secondly, the notion of illness is essentially infinite and the circumstances, phenomena and behaviour which can fall into such a category are highly elastic. Therefore, every health-care delivery system requires some principle of rationing in order to contain the exponential growth of medical care. Mechanic identifies three forms of rationing, namely rationing by a system of fee-for-service, implicit rationing and explicit rationing. Under a system of rationing by the fee, the physician appears as an entrepreneur in the market place where the use of medical services is clearly limited by the financial ability of the patient to pay for the service. He argues that a fee-for-service system tends to collapse over time or at least to be regulated by governmental agencies, because of the great expansion of medical technology leading inevitably to higher costs, the growth of insurance schemes which allow a wider use of medical services, the adoption of expensive diagnostic techniques by the physician, and a greater commitment to a technological imperative in the medical system (Wolf and Berle, 1981). For various reasons, there-fore this set of arrangements tends to lead to an overconsumption of services. The problem with such a system is not only the growing costs of medical care, but the inequalities which it brings about through the inability of certain sectors of the community to pay for the service.

Implicit rationing takes place through the means of a centralized system of budgetary controls as in the UK or through the limited financial provision of charity institutions or sickness associations. Under these conditions, the professional physician is still left rela-tively free to determine the price of services and the specific use of medical facilities. Implicit rationing depends primarily upon the existence of the queue, limited medical resources, and restrictions on the availability of manpower. While medical provision may be relatively free under such a system, the length of the queue for surgery and other services may drive wealthier people into the private market for medical provision. Implicit rationing does not therefore overcome the problem of inequalities of provision and use.

Because of the problems associated with the fee-for-service sys-tem and implicit rationing, there is a tendency for governments to intervene to bring about an explicit system of rationing with the aim of controlling total expenditure and of establishing a more rational and egalitarian system of medical provision. One problem with rational planning and explicit rationing, however, is that it has in practice proved to be very difficult to measure which exact form of health-care delivery has the most significant cost effectiveness with respect to the impact of the system on the health status of any given society. As we have seen in previous chapters, it is in practice very difficult to impose an explicit system of rationing because of the political opposition of organized professional medicine. While there were significant attempts to impose forms of explicit rationing in the 1960s, we have also seen in more recent times under Reagan's government in the USA and Thatcher's government in the UK the development of privatization to bring about a reduction in the level of demand for public provision of health care. However, Mechanic's approach to the problem of rationing is an important way of conceptualizing the relationship between the fee-for-service system, the prominence of client control in the professional relationship, and the development of an entrepreneurial role for the physician. By contrast, under a system of implicit rationing, the professional relationship assumes the form of colleague control where the physician develops his formal relationship under the expert role. Finally, with explicit rationing, the relationship between the professional and the client is organized under bureaucratic control where the physician adopts an official role.

From these arguments, we can develop the thesis that firstly, the defects of private medicine will be adjusted by the use of public regulation and that the problems of public delivery will be regulated by privatization. This oscillation between the private and public can be illustrated by the French health-care system (Cullis and West, 1985). In France, the health system has been predominantly a private market form of medicine in which physicians are principally in private practice under the system of 'La Médecine Libérale' (Webb, 1982). The clients are free to select their own doctors and the physician is free to determine the price of the service. Although the French constitution provides each citizen with protection of health, as a result of the market-dominated form of health care there have been major inequalities within the French system. For example, in Paris there are twice as many doctors per capita as in Picardy. Although the system is largely private, the French government has brought about a number of changes in recent years to regulate the system. For example, fees are now established as the outcome of a set of negotiations between the social security funds and the medical profession. The government has also attempted to control significant geographical inequalities resulting from a private medical system regulated by professional norms. Following Mechanic, Cullis and West argue that health-care systems tend to evolve from fee-for-service systems to implicit rationing, and finally to state regulation of the market in order to control medical costs and to bring about some redistribution of services in the interests of an egalitarian principle. As we have seen however, the development of disorganized capitalism has indicated an alternative trajectory for health systems whereby the enormous cost of explicit rationing will be occasionally regulated by a period of privatization and cut-backs.

The free enterprise system
The underlying problem in the organization of health care is the apparent contradiction between efficiency and equality (Daniels, 1985). It is typically argued that a free market system produces greater efficiency, whereas a public system of health attempts to guarantee equality. It is normally assumed that it is impossible to achieve both a radically egalitarian system of health and an effective and efficient form of delivery which will bring about a cost-effective service. In order to understand this apparent contradiction, we need to look more closely at the economic arguments which are utilized to justify a free market system. Behind the economic argument for free market systems, there are the usual assumptions of demand-and-supply economics concerning consumer choice. It is assumed that each consumer has perfect knowledge of the market, that there is a perfect supply by competitive means and finally that there is consumer sovereignty in the choice of goods and services. The argument suggests that this system in the health market would produce an efficient cost-effective supply of medical services (Le Grand and Robinson, 1976).

The disadvantages and advantages of economic models for the analysis of social welfare functions have been cogently outlined in a variety of directions by Arrow (1951, 1983). Arrow has been specifically concerned with the problem of applying utility models from economic theory to the systems of medical care in mixed economies (Arrow, 1963). In Arrow's critique, the particular character of medical information as a commodity departs significantly from the classical assumptions of economics. In medicine the product and the activity of production are often identical and furthermore the consumer cannot test the medical product before consumption. Unlike motor cars, we cannot try out surgery before purchase. In addition, the decision to seek medical services is, as we have seen in the discussion of the sick role, a complex social process. Often the client does not know what their wants or needs are before the visit to the doctor. It is in this situation that trust in the physician is an essential feature of the medical service; within a Parsonian analysis, trust is an important component of professional values and norms. Associated with these conditions of ignorance, there is the problem of the uncertainty of the medical product itself. Because of patient ignorance, the patient is not in a position to judge the effectiveness of the service against other forms of treatment. Given the uncertainty of the medical encounter, the physician defines the clinical situation and controls the evaluation of the product. It is this uncertainty which underlines the notion of the docile patient role in relation to the doctor's intervention. In short, uncertainty is an essential component of patient compliance within the sick role. The patient has relatively little control over the norms of treatment in terms of the length, form and outcome of the service.

There are various reasons why this uncertainty in the medical context and the professional norms of the physician should have the consequence of increasing the cost of medical services. According to Mechanic, there is a professional norm to treat the patient without regard to the patient's ability to pay. Physicians therefore take actions in the interests of their clients without significant consideration for the cost or long-term economic consequences of medical treatment. Another feature of professionalism is the absence of price competition and advertising of professional services. Because of the existence of professional control, there is little specific advertising of medical services; and as a result, medical prices are not significantly responsive to changing consumer demand. Professionalism also restricts entry into the medical market place which is controlled by professional associations via a system of formal examinations. Professional medicine attempts to regulate the market and to prevent the introduction of alternative systems of care. These controls on entry bring about limitations on competition which means that there is a strong pressure for the maintenance of medical costs. In short, there is little public regulation of prices and the supply of services because of the existence of medical dominance.

It is not clear that medical institutions or health behaviour can be understood appropriately in terms of economic models of efficiency. On the other hand, there will always be an element of rationing for the reasons which we have outlined. It is not clear how the supply of medical services relates to the general health of the population. It is difficult to evaluate the specific contribution of professional medicine to the general health status of a community by comparison for example with improvements in the environment, an expansion of education, a development of the food supply and the control of pollution.

Despite the theoretical arguments of classical economics, it appears that most western societies possess health systems which are neither efficient nor egalitarian. In free market circumstances and in states dominated by a welfare system, there has been an important continuity of class inequalities in terms of morbidity and mortality rates. During the period of post-war reconstruction, there was a general improvement in the health of populations generally as measured by longevity and infant mortality rates. However, the differences between the social classes have remained relatively constant. For example, the Black Report of 1980 in the UK found that during most of the 1960s and 1970s there was no significant improvement in the health experience of the unskilled and semi-skilled manual classes (Class I and IV). While the infant mortality rate of the lowest classes had declined, the gap between the upper and lower classes had increased (Townsend and Davidson, 1982). Because of inequalities and inefficiencies in both free market and welfare systems, a number of writers have argued that by comparison socialist health-care systems are egalitarian and relatively effective. The argument in favour of socialist health-care systems has to assume that a comparative sociology of health care is possible and feasible.

A comparative approach to health care
The comparison of health-care systems is complex for a number of reasons. For example, the socio-cultural settings of health-care systems are clearly variable. Some societies such as Australia have comparatively young populations, while others such as France have a high proportion of elderly in the population. There are other significant variations within the wider setting of health care, such as the levels of urbanization, industrialization and literacy. More importantly, as we have seen in previous chapters, cultural attitudes towards illness vary considerably between societies. For example, attitudes towards the desirability of hospitalization are significantly different in Japan and the UK.

In addition, there are major differences in the classificatory and diagnostic frameworks between societies. This problem is particularly acute in the case of mental illness. A patient of any age admitted to a mental hospital in the UK would be ten times more likely to be diagnosed as manic depressive than a patient exhibiting the same symptoms in the USA. In the age group over sixty with the same symptoms, manic depression was diagnosed twenty times more frequently in the UK than in the USA (Inglis, 1981). Furthermore, at least some disease entities are the outcome of political processes; these would include repetitive strain injury and black lung. Other sickness categories have largely disappeared (for example, hysteria) while others (for example, anorexia) have become increasingly prevalent. These problems of comparison are well known in general sociology and could be illustrated by the debate which has surrounded Durkheim's study of suicide (Atkinson, 1978). Are suicide rates the effect of different classificatory procedures?

The other difficulties are that countries record diseases in different classificatory systems and obviously some societies have inadequate health records or fail to make their records widely available. In general, the recording of health statistics in state-socialist societies is poor by comparison with the detailed information available from the majority of the industrial capitalist societies of the West.

An important sociological issue is the different functions of health-care systems. Only some of these functions are narrowly confined to medical and health issues in a direct way. Following Parsons (1951), we can suggest that health-care systems are also institutions of social control and that they provide an institutional legitimation of the sick role as a form of social deviance. Mechanic (1975) noted that the health-care systems of modern societies can function with respect to social control, as a means of social support and as the institutional setting in which the social conflicts of the wider system can be informally resolved in a manner which is at least overtly apolitical. Because health-care systems have different social functions, the boundaries which circumscribe these systems are often unclear, because they shade off in one direction towards policing and in the other towards welfare.

Health-care systems also differ significantly in terms of the relative emphasis they give to either prevention or cure. Much epidemiological and demographic research suggests that in developing societies an emphasis on preventive medicine and social welfare will be more effective and relevant than curative approaches (McKeown, 1965). In evaluating curative and preventive approaches to medicine, there are methodological problems in achieving adequate measures of the impact of such systems in terms of the eradication of specific diseases, the increase in life-expectancy, the improvements in the infant mortality rates, and the reduction of days of work lost from serious illness. Finally, in evaluating the effect of health-care systems we should keep in mind a strange paradox outlined cogently by Mechanic in his review of health-care delivery systems:

> to the extent that medical care identifies more illness, sustains life among chronically ill persons, and allows the survival of persons with congenital and other defects, it contributes to higher levels of recognized morbidity and disability in the population. (Mechanic, 1975:55)

It is in this sense that we can argue that health-care delivery systems create illness or at least amplify illness in society. This is parallel to the issue of contrology in the sociology of deviance (Ditton, 1979).

Health and state socialism

Although Marxist authors have commented extensively on illness as a consequence of the special features of capitalist exploitation, there is relatively little literature spelling out in a clear and precise way the specific goals of a socialist health programme. There are many critiques of capitalist health-care systems, but few valuable discussions of socialist objectives for health care. In this lacuna, Deacon (1984) has provided a valuable outline of the principles of socialist medicine. Basically Deacon argues that socialism would remove health care from the centre point of discussion in order to put greater emphasis on the importance of changing social conditions in order to attack avoidable illness. Secondly, socialism would break the dominance of the medical profession in order to, for example, change the status relationship between the doctor as expert and the patient as client. Thirdly, a socialist approach would change the sexual division of labour which is a regular feature of western, technical medicine. Fourthly, a socialist strategy would seek to ensure an equality of access to health and equality of outcome, at least in terms of avoidable illness.

From these general principles, Deacon generates sixteen specific objectives for socialist health-care systems including higher expenditure of gross national product on health, significant reductions in mortality and morbidity rates, a reduction in the status of doctors, a transformation of patriarchy in medicine, a greater equality of distribution and free, universal access to health care rationed democratically on the basis of work and need.

Deacon then compares three state-socialist systems (the Soviet Union, Hungary and Poland) with a number of European societies, specifically those within the European economic community. His results (Table 5) suggest that state-socialist societies have been relatively unsuccessful in achieving major socialist goals in medical care.

We can add further statistical information (Table 6) to support the evidence in Deacon's argument from a wider range of societies to argue that the achievements of socialist societies have been far below the ideals of a socialist system. Deacon's general conclusion is that state-socialist societies fail to achieve the desired goals of a socialist system. In terms of the percentage of gross domestic product spent on medical care, infantile mortality rates and life-expectancy rates, western European societies show better results

TABLE 5

Indicator	Year	Soviet Union	Hungary	Poland	Non-socialist countries
Percent of GDP on medical care	1974	2.5	3.3	3.9	5.1–6.7 (EEC)
Population/ physician	1977	289	435	606	455 (West Europe)
Population/ hospital bed	1977	82	114	113	105 (West Europe)
Infant mortality/ 1000 live births	1975	27.8	24.3	22.4	11.4–17.6 (EEC)
Life expectancy Male Female	1975	66.5 74.3	66.1 72.8	66.5 74.9	70.2 76.3

Source: Deacon, 1984:461.

TABLE 6
Life-expectancy

Country	Year	Male	Female	Infant mortality rate	Neonatal mortality rate
Australia	1980	71.0	78.1	10.7	7.1
England and Wales	1979	70.2	76.2	12.8	8.2
France	1977	70.3	78.6	10.0	6.0
Netherlands	1979	72.5	79.2	8.7	5.9
Poland	1978	66.5	74.9	21.1	13.8
Rumania	1978	67.3	72.4	31.6	11.2
Sweden	1979	72.6	78.9	7.5	5.3
USA	1978	69.6	77.4	13.0	9.5
Yugoslavia	1977	67.8	73.0	32.2	17.1

Source: Commonwealth Department of Health, *Annual Report of the Director-General of Health, 1981–1982*, AGPS, 1982:163

than Soviet Bloc societies. More specifically, state-socialist medicine is in many respects convergent with free market and welfare systems. For example, the medical curriculum in the Soviet Union is still dominated by the medical model and is clinically oriented. Disease patterns in the Soviet Union increasingly resemble those of the capitalist West. As deaths from infectious diseases have declined, they have been replaced by mortality resulting from cancer and cardiovascular diseases.

The control of the medical system in the Soviet Union is overwhelmingly dominated by the professional medical elite. The Soviet health-care system is being developed to satisfy the requirements of industrialization and the professional interests of the medical and academic institutions rather than to achieve egalitarian socialist objectives (George and Manning, 1980). A limited private market exists in the Soviet Union where a financial payment secures a better medical service. There are also significant inequalities between regions and status groups in the Soviet Union. For example, in Moscow in the early 1970s there were 76 physicians per 10,000 members of the population whereas the ratio for the whole society was 29 physicians per 10,000. Finally, there has been little democratization of medical or clinical relations, and there is no complaint system whereby patients can bring complaints about their physicians.

The major conclusion to be drawn from these studies is that, while there was a significant improvement in medical facilities, equality of access to health and improvements in health status in the years following the socialist revolutions (Parkin, 1969; Matthews, 1978; Szelenyi, 1978; Watson, 1984), over a period of time the health-care systems of state-socialist societies come eventually to share many of the characteristics of western medicine within a capitalist environment.

Similar conclusions may be drawn from the history of medicine and medical reform in China, since the revolution (Sidel and Sidel, 1982). Although the health status of the Chinese population was improved dramatically in the period of social reform after the revolution, there are, especially in the rural areas, high rates of infectious disease and an increase in certain communicable illnesses such as hepatitis. For example, the infant mortality rate was improved in China as a consequence of a redistribution of wealth and a major improvement in the social environment. In 1949 the infant mortality rate for Peking City was 118 per 1000 live births, but by 1980 this had been reduced to 10 deaths per 1000 live births. These figures compare favourably with the non-white infant mortality rate of New York City which in the 1980s was 18 deaths per 1000 live births.

However, there are also certain important signs of a convergence of contemporary Chinese health-care systems with those of the West. There are in contemporary China three systems of medicine, namely the traditional, a socialist form based upon the principles of Maoism and an emergent system of western medicine (Unschuld, 1985). There is also a significant integration of western and traditional pharmaceutics (Unschuld, 1986). While China compares relatively favourably with other developing and socialist societies (Table 7), it is important to note that China, like other socialist societies, is converging in epidemiological terms towards the western pattern, whereby degenerative diseases are the most significant causes of death. In Shanghai the leading causes of death in order of frequency are cancer, stroke and heart disease. In the USA the order is heart disease, cancer and stroke. The principal causes of death in Peking in 1978 were reported to be the diseases of the heart, blood vessels and cancer. The paradox is that in aggregate terms the illness profile of socialist societies appear to be converging on those of the West. We live in a world characterized by aging populations and significant environmental pollution which are associated with these forms of disease.

TABLE 7

Country	GNP per capita ($, 1979)	Infant mortality/ 1000 live births (1978)	Life expectancy at birth 1979
India	190	125	52
China	260	56	64
USSR	4110	36	73
UK	6320	14	73
USA	10,630	14	74
Sweden	11,930	8	76

Source: Sidel and Sidel, 1982:92–93.

The convergence thesis
In the 1960s the notion that the industrial societies of the West and the Soviet bloc were converging on a common pattern of development enjoyed some degree of support (Kerr et al., 1962). The central argument of the convergence thesis was that the common process of industrialization would result in uniform political, cultural and social characteristics in societies which before industrialization may have had rather different historical and social

backgrounds. These societies are converging towards a common point, because the process of industrialization requires certain basic features in order to develop effectively. The common features of industrialism are an extended social division of labour, the separation of the household, the enterprise and the workplace, a mobile workforce, the rational organization of economic calculation and the development of a rational system of distribution and consumption. The 'logic of industrialism' will produce industrial societies which have in common a secular democratic and urban culture.

The thesis was criticized on a number of grounds. Firstly, it is not entirely clear that a common process of industrialization will necessarily produce a common institutional and cultural superstructure. Secondly, the thesis was criticized because it assumed a form of technological determinism which did not allow for the impact of the cultural systems on the process of change. Finally, the convergence thesis was seen to be the product of an optimistic political environment in the USA in the 1960s. The recent development of industrial societies in terms of their disorganization, inflation, unemployment and indebtedness has not supported the optimistic assumptions of the original theory. While the optimistic and naive premises of the original convergence thesis look distinctively outdated, it is possible to provide a modest defence of the 'logic of industrialism' (Hall, 1985).

In empirical terms there appear to be a number of common features to health-care delivery systems, regardless of their social and political context (Mechanic, 1975). Firstly, the medical profession has been relatively successful in adapting to a variety of political circumstances and its medical dominance is a significant feature of both Soviet state-socialism and American capitalism. However, in capitalist societies, the development of market medicine under monetaristic conditions may paradoxically bring about a reduction of professional power and a proletarianization of medical activity. Secondly, there are important continuities of social inequality in health care, health experience and access to medicine in both capitalist and socialist societies. In the Soviet Union, we have noted the continuity of a private market in medicine and significant regional inequalities, despite radical political change in the twentieth century. Thirdly, in all forms of medical delivery, there will be the necessity for some system of rationing. Fourthly, in all health systems we have noted an increasing secularization of religious authority and its replacement by medical values and medical persons. Contemporary health care is essentially secular in its ideology and organization. Fifthly, modern health-care systems have replaced the care functions of the traditional kinship group, the family and the local community. Sixthly, in association with the growing importance of the hospital as the key institution of technical medicine, there has been a growing bureaucratization of medical practice and physicians are increasingly subject to the conflicting pressures and expectations of a professional system stressing autonomy and a bureaucratic administration stressing uniformity and administratively dominated practice. Finally, there is a significant epidemiological convergence towards the same patterns of morbidity and mortality, regardless of political contexts, in which the degenerative diseases have become the primary causes of death in aging populations. Mechanic (1975:62) consequently argues that:

> the basic pattern of practice in modern society is increasingly dominated by the imperatives of the emerging technology, the objective pattern of morbidity in the population, and growing public expectations which are a world phenomenon.

There is a globalization of medicine in the modern period whereby a world-economic system has become the basis for a number of common institutional responses to illness and mortality. In Weberian terms, we could also see this development as a feature of the progressive rationalization of medical practice and knowledge with the exclusion of distinctively religious beliefs and attitudes towards illness. This rationalization process also involves the increasing bureaucratization of health-care delivery systems which are now international. The expansion of medical knowledge and medical dominance as the primary forms of social regulation and control are also common features of contemporary political systems.

Conclusion: the paradox of state socialist medicine
Within radical sociology, it is commonly argued that medicine is a major institution of social control which in contemporary society has to some extent replaced the traditional institutions of law and religion (Zola, 1972). The expansion and development of health-care delivery systems has consequently brought about a more profound if hidden framework of social regulation in which there is often no court of appeal or system of complaints, unlike the older systems of law and religion. Involuntary hospitalization for the mentally disturbed has been a prominent target of radical criticism in the modern period, but medical social control can take far more subtle and insidious forms.

Although the overt aims of socialist reform of medicine may well be laudable and morally valuable, the unintended consequences of socialist reform may be less desirable. In so far as socialism proposes more medicine, it brings about a greater medicalization of society and potentially a greater expansion of medical dominance. While medical dominance in socialism would not be exercised by a medical profession as such, dominance would be exerted through lay practitioners of a medical bureaucracy which would be far more expansive and regulating than similar systems in western capitalist societies. The result would be a policing of society by the state via bureaucratic personnel in the state-run medical system. Primary care would become a form of primary regulation via local community workers acting on behalf of the state. Under such circumstances, social deviance would be minutely controlled under a system of bureaucratic surveillance. The regulation of bodies would be complete. We are converging on a global system of regulation, albeit under different political systems. In the framework of Foucault, this would be global panopticism.

While different societies will undergo rather distinctive forms of change which largely correspond to their political and economic context, there are in conclusion a number of general trends within the world health systems (Roemer, 1977:232). Firstly, there is in most societies a tendency for the economic support for health services to become more regulated by collective agencies such as the state. Insurance schemes and general revenues have largely replaced the traditional pattern of private payment. Secondly, the supply of trained doctors in relation to the population of all countries is steadily increasing. These trends are also associated with the specialization and differentiation of the medical profession. Thirdly, the range and numbers of allied health personnel has been expanding both in relation to the population and to professional medicine. Fourthly, health facilities are increasing in number and in their technical character. Fifthly, the forms of health delivery at all levels of care are becoming gradually systematized. Health centres have become a significant feature of contemporary health-care systems and services in hospitals are typically provided by salaried specialists within a bureaucratic framework. Sixthly, the importance of preventive medicine has become widely acknowledged, giving rise to greater concentration on nutritional and educational issues together with a concern for environmental regulation to control contemporary levels of pollution. Finally, the technological and bureaucratic imperatives of modern medicine have resulted in the search for more effective administration of health-care systems and a more rational approach to the organization and rationing of health care. These trends clearly point to a widening of medical control and the medicalization of deviance and disease under the common bureaucratic policing of society. There is a convergence on a new global pattern of population regulation and management. This is the bio-politics of the modern period of rational capitalism and state-socialism.

IV
CONCLUSION

11
The regulation of bodies

Towards a general theory in medical sociology
Medical sociology is a complex and diverse component within contemporary sociology, covering and addressing a variety of issues and
topics related to medical institutions, health-care systems and illness
behaviour. In recent years this sub-discipline has been considerably
expanded both in subject matter and in terms of perspectives. In
addition, as we have seen, there is considerable dispute as to whether
this area of inquiry should be called 'medical sociology' or 'the
sociology of health and illness' (Conrad and Kern, 1985). Furthermore, I have added the complication that to some extent we can
regard medical sociology as a form of applied medicine, and we can
regard social medicine as an aspect of applied sociology. There is
clearly a convergence between clinical sociology and clinical medicine, in which there is a strong argument for an integration of the
medical and sociological curricula. Given this complexity of subject
matter and perspectives, in this text-book on medical sociology I
have taken a specific slice out of the subject to consider medical
institutions, forms of social power and social control.

Although the focus of this study has been defined by certain
necessary parameters, I have attempted to provide a general
approach to the problems of health, illness and health-care systems
which is an adequate reflection of contemporary concerns in
sociological theory, methodology and applied sociology. An adequate sociology of sickness and medical institutions has to work at
three levels, namely the level of individual experience, the level of
social values and institutions, and finally at the macro-societal level.
Corresponding to these three levels of analysis, this text has
attempted to develop three theoretical perspectives, namely the
phenomenology of sickness, the sociology of the sick role, and a
political economy of health-care systems.

While sociology may be defined as the scientific study of social
groups, institutions and processes of social change, sociology also has
to address the nature of individual behaviour and experience. Start-

ing with the assumption that individuals are necessarily social individuals, sociology may be defined as the study of social action where action involves notions of choice, selection and interpretation. These acts of choice and interpretation may be treated collectively as social phenomena; therefore some approaches in sociology are often referred to as 'action–systems approaches' because they are concerned both with social action and the character of social systems.

In this study in medical sociology, I have insisted that we should adopt an interpretive sociology of action in order to understand sickness and illness behaviour at the level of the social individual. It has been argued therefore that medical sociology should be interested in health and illness as aspects of social action rather than considering illness merely as behaviour, where behaviour is understood to be devoid of meaning, significance or voluntarism. This particular approach to sociology was first developed by writers like Weber and Simmel, and was subsequently expanded within the voluntaristic theory of action by Parsons (Holton and Turner, 1986). From this perspective, there is a sense that sickness is something we do rather than simply something we have. Being sick involves interpretation, choice and action. Being sick has, for human beings as social actors, a meaning.

We can see part of the activity of medicine, and more specifically of psychoanalysis, as an attempt to understand the meaning of illness for the social actor. Often the meaning and significance of sickness may be disguised from the sufferer and therefore the role of counselling is to present an acceptable meaning to the patient. In arguing that sociology should be concerned with the meaning and significance of illness at the level of the individual and individual experience, this study has been influenced by the Freudian tradition especially represented in the work of Groddeck (1977), the analytical tradition of Lacan (Lemaire, 1977) and by the work of Sacks who in his investigation of migraine (Sacks, 1981) has provided a model of inquiry into the complex interaction between body, body-image and consciousness. Following Sacks, we can regard illness as a text or story which requires interpretive skills, because illness rather like a novel suggests multiple or indeed infinite interpretations all of which may be plausible. This suggests the possibility of what he has called 'neurographies', an inner story of personal experience of neurological realities.

To regard illness as a text open to a variety of perspectives is a radical approach to sickness, because it points to some of the problems in the medical model which underlies the basis of institutionalized, scientific, technologically directed medicine. As we have seen, the medical model as the principal paradigm of modern medicine is derived from the positivistic philosophy of Descartes who established an unbridgeable gap between the life of the mind and that of the body. Modern medicine, treating the body as a sort of machine, regards illness and disease as malfunctions of the body's mechanics. All 'real' diseases have specific causal mechanisms which can be ultimately identified and treated. Such an approach rules out the centrality and importance of experience, feeling, emotion and interpretation in the phenomenology of sickness and disease. A classic illustration of the medical model is the germ theory, derived from the scientific medical work of Pasteur and Koch in the nineteenth century; their work established a scientific basis for the emergence of medicine as a profession equipped with a satisfactory knowledge basis. The medical model is not concerned primarily with questions of prevention since it approaches the problem of disease through the experience of germ theory which involves a highly interventionist and specific form of medical practice. Germ theory was simply one component within a wider scientific revolution in Victorian medicine (Youngson, 1979).

There are a number of problems with the medical model. The first is that many major disorders, particularly in contemporary society, have no known causal basis in pathologies of the biochemistry of the body. Quite simply, many crucial problems in contemporary patterns of sickness are not deducible to physiological malfunctioning; these problems would include a wide range of so-called 'behavioural disorders' such as anorexia nervosa. Furthermore, many problems in chronic illness (such as diabetes) cannot be treated adequately simply by recourse to therapies based on the medical model. Other major changes in contemporary patterns of illness such as addictions and aging are for very different reasons not amenable to conventional medical intervention. There is also the problem of cross-cultural variations in disorders. For example, in contemporary Japan a number of neuroses have appeared (menopausal syndrome, school refusal syndrome and the kitchen syndrome) which are thought to be the product of the breakdown of traditional values under the impact of economic individualism, where many forms of stress are experienced by housewives and their children caught in the contradictory pool of different value systems (Lock, 1980).

The development of a scientific medicine based upon a medical model was part of a medicalization of society in the late nineteenth century. Following the work of Foucault, I have treated medicalization as an aspect of the rationalization of society through the dominance of scientific categories. Since sickness can be regarded as a form of social deviance, the medical profession has a policing function within society. Medicine as a form of social control involves the standardization of illness into phenomena which can be managed by bureaucratic agencies. Behind the philosophy of Foucault, there stands the work of the German philosopher Nietzsche. Nietzsche regarded the role of the state and the growth of professional men as part of a new pattern of power and control in contemporary societies. Modern medical practice, for Nietzsche, represented a normalization of health in the interests of professional power. Nietzsche (1974) criticized this regularization of health in the following terms:

> for there is no health as such, and all attempts to define a thing that way have been wretched failures. Even the determination of what is healthy for your body depends on your goal, your horizon, your energies, your impulses, your errors, and above all on the ideals and phantasms of your soul. Thus there are innumerable healths of the body; and the more we allow the unique and incomparable to raise its head again, and the more we abjure the dogma of the 'equality of men', the more must the concept of a normal health, along with a normal diet and the normal course of an illness, be abandoned by medical men. (Nietzsche, 1974, Section 120)

This argument of Nietzsche's about the variability of health and illness followed from his view of language, namely that scientific theories are simply forms of language which provide an interpretation of the world. Nietzsche argued that there are no 'facts' but only interpretations, and therefore an illness is simply an interpretation of reality. Whether we call homosexuality a disease, deviance or a personal preference depends upon our standpoint or perspective. Similarly, to call cancer a pathology is to impose a particular interpretation upon natural processes (King, 1954). Such a position calls into question the whole notion that one can approach the diseases of human beings as if they were neutral facts rather than aspects of human interaction, social organization and culture.

It is possible therefore to approach the sociology of health and illness from the perspective of an individual's system of interpretation, whereby sociology would focus upon the signs of disorder manifest in the speech and behaviour of the individual. However, what I have called the 'phenomenology of sickness' leads naturally into a discussion of illness and health as aspects of social interaction and organization at the level of social values and historical processes. The argument here is that we need to consider the relationships between action and structure in the character of illness and health-care institutions. I have approached this level of analysis through the work of Parsons on the sick role.

The way in which an individual interprets or understands their disorders will depend, not upon individual whim or fancy, but significantly upon the classifications of illness which are available within a culture and by reference to general cultural values concerning appropriate behaviour. It is for this reason that Parsons's concept of the sick role is particularly useful within sociology. This concept indicates not only that illness behaviour is structured and patterned according to specific expectations in the interaction between doctor and patient, but also that disease and sickness are products of general values relating to that which is esteemed significant within a given society. Parsons's approach enables us to compare and contrast the dominant assumptions within a given society where these dominant assumptions are indicated by distinctions between health and sickness. Parsons's discussion of the sick role can therefore be regarded as a modern analytical version of Durkheim's distinction between the sacred and the profane in the sociology of religion. The notion of sickness is fundamental to the ways in which we evaluate things (people, experiences, societies or events) as desirable, important or appropriate.

In western societies, there is a particular emphasis on activism and individualism so that being sick in terms of the sick role involves the absence of individual responsibility, activism and achievement. Quite simply, to be sick is to be not at work. Forms of sickness, their diagnosis and their treatment will reflect the prevailing values of society; for example, the absence of a strongly individualistic culture in Asia means that the form of illness behaviour is radically different from that existing in the West where there is a long tradition of individualism in terms of culture and social organization (Abercrombie et al., 1986; Marsella et al., 1985).

In this respect, for sociologists it is important to compare and contrast sickness and crime as two forms of deviance. From the legal point of view, crime is related to theories of responsibility and in particular to the notion of criminal intention. People are typically punished for crimes for which they are held to be individually responsible. Therefore, the grounds for the reduction of responsibility are of great philosophical and practical interest to legal theory and practice (Wootton, 1963). By contrast, the sick role legitimizes deviant behaviour by removing responsibility, since within the medical view one does not in fact choose to be sick in the same way that one might choose to commit a crime. However, sickness legitimizes withdrawal from everyday expectations only on the assumption that sickness will be a short episode of behaviour under the regulation of the doctor. The sick-role complex is therefore seen within Parsons's sociology to be functional for the social system, since commonsensically not everybody can be sick simultaneously.

By approaching sickness through the sick role, the sociologist necessarily raises questions about the character of professions and professional values within modern society. We have seen that within

contemporary sociology the nature of professionalism and professionalization has been hotly disputed. For example, Parsons's
account of the professions was criticized for being a reflection of the
dominant values of the profession itself, thereby precluding any
significant critical evaluation of the professions. Contemporary
sociology is as a consequence more likely to regard professionalization as a growth in power and status. In this respect, the history of
the medical profession over the last century represents an interesting
illustration of the growth of medical dominance under the auspices of
the state, associated with the development of a professional body of
knowledge through for example, the germ theory of disease.

The dominance of the medical profession represents an interesting
combination of knowledge and power in relation to the untutored
consumption of medical services by the lay patient. It is in this area of
analysis that the sociology of knowledge has proved to be particularly
important and prominent within contemporary medical sociology
(Wright and Treacher, 1982). The power of the professions depends,
at least in part, on the ability to make claims successfully about the
scientific value of their work and the way in which their professional
knowledge is grounded in precise, accurate and reliable scientific
information. Therefore the way in which disease categories are
socially constructed is of critical importance to the status and role of
professions in contemporary society. In this respect, medical professionals have become the moral guardians of contemporary society,
because they have a legitimate domination of the categorization of
normality and deviance.

The discussion of professional power and knowledge leads eventually to a third level of analysis, namely the level of macro-societal
processes. This level of analysis has been of particular interest to
Marxist theories of illness and health, and to the political economy of
health-care systems (McKinlay, 1984). We may regard health rather
like other forms of wealth as a basic social resource which is une-
qually distributed within society. Furthermore, this unequal distribution of health and health care is closely correlated with a major axis in
the social structure, namely the division between the owners of
labour power and the owners of productive wealth. However, there
are other dimensions which may be significant in the distribution of
health, such as age and gender. In addition, the distribution of health
on a global scale closely corresponds to the distribution of political
and economic dominance. There are health inequalities both within
and between social systems.

As we have seen, a Marxist medical sociology argues that the
prevalence and shape of sickness in contemporary society is largely
an effect of the exploitative character of capitalist production. Just as

capitalism is associated with the destruction of the environment through exploitative systems of production, so capitalism is associated with the production of illness through the exploitation of labour. Marxists argue that there is a tendency for medicine to emerge as a global system of colonial or neo-colonial power, whereby the diseases of western capitalism are exported to Third World societies. Finally, the political economy of health argues that only through a socialist redistribution of resources can the problems of sickness and health care be resolved.

The regulation of bodies

In this approach to medical sociology, I have therefore adopted a self-consciously diverse and eclectic approach to sociological explanation and perspective. I have borrowed critical perspectives from Marxists like Navarro, sociological perspectives from inter-actionists like Goffman, while also adopting and developing Parsons's approach to the sick role. This theoretical eclecticism can be justified on a variety of grounds. For example, I have suggested that different levels of analysis might require rather different approaches. However this diverse approach within this text book has been held together by a central interest in the work of Foucault, whose sociological and historical analyses of knowledge and power have proved to be extremely useful in the area of medical sociology. From Foucault, I have developed a particular focus on the body and populations.

The problem of the body in medical sociology is especially interesting, because it raises in an acute form the whole debate on the relationships between body and mind, culture and nature, self and society. Following Foucault, I have argued that the body has been subject to a long historical process of rationalization and standardization. The body has become the focus of a wide range of disciplines and forms of surveillance and control, in which the medical profession has played a critical part. The birth of the clinic and the growth of the teaching hospital have been significant institutional developments in the development of what Foucault has called the medical gaze. This framework provides an organizing principle for looking at the problem of sickness at the level of the individual body, the growth of institutional regulation and control at the level of the clinic and hospital, and finally at the emergence of a bio-politics of populations whereby the state through its various local and national agencies constantly intervenes in the production and reproduction of life itself. With technological change in the production and termination of life processes, the state has become increasingly involved in the legal dispute over the character of life – its origins, shape and destiny.

To some extent these conflicts raise at an acute political level the features of modern patriarchy, since the state is now involved in the technical, political and ideological battle over women's bodies.

This bio-politics also represents a stage in the secularization of health and sickness in which the state has gradually replaced the Church as that central institution having control over life processes at the level of the individual and the household. In this study I have as a consequence made the argument that secularization involves not only the decline of the Church, but also that the medical profession has replaced the traditional clergy as that group in society which manages normal social relations. Through preventive medical regimens, we are encouraged to jog, to diet, to rest, to avoid stress and to manage our sexuality in the interests of social normality. With the changing pattern of contemporary sickness (that is from acute to chronic problems), the question of management and regulation of patients has become an important issue not only within social medicine but also in geriatric medicine. The medicalization of society involves therefore a regularization and management of populations and bodies in the interests of a discourse which identifies and controls that which is normal (Conrad and Schneider, 1980).

Critical appraisals

In this introductory study of medical sociology, I have been mainly concerned to provide a general explanation of the character of sickness and medical dominance through a variety of perspectives. In order to develop those perspectives, I have not been primarily concerned with either exegesis or with criticism. One argument in favour of eclecticism is that no single paradigm or perspective can ever be theoretically adequate. Each of the major traditions within medical sociology can be criticized for its limitations and lacunae. In this study I have advocated the use of a phenomenological perspective on illness, since it is clearly important for sociologists to obtain an account of how individuals are conscious of their sickness and how knowledge of illness is constituted in everyday life. Such a programme of research would have important and beneficial consequences not only for sociologists, but also for practitioners in health care. For example, we know very little about the phenomenology of diabetes, since most sociological and medical accounts of illness are content with second-order descriptions. One criticism of Parsons's sociology of the sick role would be that the analysis of social roles often fails to grasp the phenomenological construction of consciousness in everyday interaction.

However, while a phenomenology of illness is important, phenomenology by itself does not provide an adequate basis for a general medical sociology. Phenomenology as a whole has been criticized for being too descriptive, restricted to minor or trivial issues, and unable to provide an account of social structure. A phenomenology of sickness would simply be a description of the actor's consciousness of sickness, but it would not provide an account of the social distribution of illness in relation to questions of power and social structure. A phenomenological description of sickness does not provide the basis for a critique of modern medicine, since phenomenology seeks primarily to describe the taken-for-granted knowledge which constructs the everyday world. Phenomenology merely places events and descriptions in a context which is made meaningful by an apprehension of everyday descriptions.

In addition to phenomenology therefore, it is important to look at sick roles, the interaction between lay people and professionals, and the role of professional values in structuring everyday interactions within clinics, hospitals and other medical settings. However, as we have seen, there are major limitations to this Parsonian model. One problem with Parsons's analysis of the sick role is that the sick role is taken out of the context of everyday referral. In simple terms, the visit to the doctor should be seen as the outcome of a long process of interaction and exchange between lay people as to the character of the disorder in question. In addition, the professional doctor is not the only figure within the system of lay medicine. The existence of folk healing and folk practitioners may be an important part of help-seeking behaviour even in advanced industrial societies. For example, shortly before Henderson and Parsons were developing the idea of the medical encounter as a social system, Robert and Helen Lynd undertook their famous study of Middletown in 1929. In their chapter on keeping healthy in an American community, they noted the presence of a great variety of folk medicine and lay practitioners. The Lynds observed that Middletown was still relatively close to its pioneer origin and that the citizens of this community were still dependent upon or involved in a variety of non-scientific forms of lay medical practice:

> some people still treasure incantations for curing erysipelas and other ills, carefully passed down from generation to generation, always to one of the opposite sex. A downtown barber regularly takes patients into a back room for magical treatment for everything from headache to cancer. Some people still believe that an old leather hatband wrapped about each breast of the mother at child-birth will prevent all forms of breast trouble. An old leather shoe-string wrapped about a child's neck will prevent croup... If one rubs a wart with a bean picked at random from a sack of beans and then drops the bean back into the sack the wart will disappear. (Lynd and Lynd, 1929:435)

This quotation from the study of Middletown reminds us not only of the extent of the lay referral system and folk medicine, but also of the often precarious character of medical dominance through the professional organization of medicine even in North America. It also points to the historical limitations of the professionalization model, since one argument against Parsons is that the one-to-one relationship between patient and doctor has been obliterated by the development of contemporary, bureaucratic, hospital-centred medical practice.

We need therefore to supplement the analysis of sick roles with a Marxist analysis of medical dominance and a political economy of health inequalities. These perspectives provide us with a macro-sociological view of social structures, political processes and economic conditions, all of which in various complex ways shape the nature of health in modern societies. The political-economy perspective has been especially useful in tracing the emergence of multinational corporations concerned with health issues, especially the pharmaceutical industry. While the political-economy perspective offers us a grasp on the major political processes which lie behind health-care institutions, this approach is weak and under-developed at the level of individual experiences of illness and health. Indeed the Marxist framework is largely indifferent to the phenomenology of illness and does not attempt to provide an account of the consciousness of sickness at this level. The experience of illness largely falls outside the range of Marxist interest.

While Marxism has no particular need to examine the phenomenology of sickness, it is strange that Marxism has really no theory of the body; such a theory should be an important feature of materialism. Indeed only Timpanaro (1975) has noticed the curious absence in Marxism of a theory of the body, since at one level the birth and death of human beings and of populations is a fundamentally materialistic issue. In the work of Engels in classical Marxism, there was an interest in and concern for the complex relationship between economic production and human reproduction, but these concerns have dropped out of view within contemporary Marxist theory. It was Foucault who pointed out this strange absence in Marxist theory, when he noted that it would be more materialistic to present the question of the body prior to questions of ideology.

There are in addition a number of basic problems within the political economy and Marxist paradigms. The sharp distinction which is drawn between health in capitalism and in socialism is not in practice so clearly borne out. As we have seen the promotion of health and alternative systems of medicine, at least under state socialist societies, have been less than successful. Often industrial socialist societies compare rather badly with the development of progressive measures under capitalism. In addition, many health problems are now global and it is not possible to explain differences in sickness simply by reference to different modes of production. In general, Marxism tends to deny or ignore real improvements in health care and the health status of populations in capitalist societies as a consequence of expanding citizenship and popular political struggles for better health. Furthermore, the problem of patriarchy has been both a theoretical and political problem within Marxism, and currently there is no really adequate Marxist analysis of gender in relation to health issues. In short, the inequalities between men and women in health terms appear to persist within state-socialist health systems. Marxism has not been able to explain significant variations within and between capitalist and socialist societies. There is a tendency to deny the significant contributions of the welfare state to the health status of the working-class and minority groups inside industrial capitalist societies.

Because Marxism is often unable to provide an appropriate theory of the body in relation to the interests of medical sociology, many sociologists have recently turned to the work of Foucault to provide an alternative, and indeed a critical alternative to Marxist frameworks. This turning to Foucault has been of particular importance in the understanding of mental illness and in the analysis of the asylum. Foucault provides a significant understanding of the development of medical institutions in relation to scientific bodies of knowledge and to the new professional organization of health-care institutions.

There are however problems within Foucault's perspective. First, he tends to provide what we would call a structuralist theory of the body; that is, he treats the body as the outcome, or effect of changes in social organizations and thereby does not provide a phenomenology of the lived body. Foucault tends to deny the importance of consciousness at the phenomenological level, being more concerned with the effects of medical discourses. Furthermore, Foucault has found it difficult to provide an analysis of opposition and resistance to medical power, since he paints a picture of society in which bureaucracy and organization are paramount. It is quite obvious that lay people resist medical control, form consumer groups to oppose professional medicine and challenge medical authority through alternative approaches. Indeed within contemporary industrial societies alternative medicine has flourished in opposition to the medical model and medical professionalization. While medical power is all pervasive and predominant, it does not mean that opposition and resistance to such power is precluded or rendered ineffectual. Rather we need a perspective on health care which will take into account the conflicts between lay groups and professional associations, and the reconciliation of the conflicts to either co-optation or to successful opposition. While Foucault's account of medicine is in many respects critical, Foucault did not attempt to provide a significant alternative to medical dominance and therefore there is a gap between his theoretical account of society and its political implications.

Since these various perspectives have problems and limitations, in this text-book on medical sociology I have adopted an eclectic strategy, combining various elements from existing frameworks in order to provide a general approach in medical sociology which would consider various levels of illness and health care from the individual through to global considerations (such as environmental pollution). While sociology often proceeds by destroying para-digms, I have recommended a theoretical strategy which builds upon existing approaches and research. I have adopted a position of evolutionary growth in sociological theory rather than constant radical transformation (Wagner, 1984).

Medicine and social change

From a comparative and historical viewpoint, it is clear that medi-cine is deeply embedded in the culture and social structure of human societies. Medicine, like religion and other human activities, reflects the overall pattern of values and institutions within a given society. For example, we have noted that in classical Chinese medi-cine the dominant metaphors of medical explanation and the domi-nant forms of medical practice were very closely related to the organization of the political and economic institutions of China. In this study, I have tried to show how medicine and medical practice have been influenced by large and significant changes in the organ-ization of human societies, particularly with reference to the secu-larization and rationalization of modern cultures under the impact of bureaucracy, scientific medicine and industrial technology.

These long-term changes in medical models and medical power are also closely related to important changes in the character of disease and sickness in human society. Prior to the emergence of the germ theory, the development of vaccination and the capacity of society to control epidemics through improvement in sanitation and the water supply, life-expectancy was very limited and the primary causes of mortality were infectious diseases. Pre-modern societies in Europe were characterized by both high rates of infant mortality and high birth rates. Within this context, medicine was primarily concerned with the treatment of acute illness which was life-threatening. This situation was radically transformed in the late nineteenth century with the development of modern medical practice, the organization of the general hospital and the growing professional dominance of doctors within the health-care system. Within contemporary societies, we are now faced with a range of long-term medical problems which at present are not amenable to easy resolution in either medical or economic terms. Disorders related to stress and lifestyle do not lend themselves to simple solutions through what we might call 'heroic medicine'. Medical intervention now requires the complicated back-up of social workers, health visitors, social-policy units and psychiatry. We might call these new problems diseases of lifestyle which reflect profound changes in social organization and values, such as the relationship between men and women and between different age groups. There is a paradox that the more successful medicine is in delaying death, the more we suffer from an increase in morbidity. This consequence follows from the aging of populations. We have longer life but worsening health (Verbrugge, 1984).

It appears increasingly obvious that existing medical curricula and medical practices are not appropriate to the problems faced within the health field. Unfortunately the general practitioner is often poorly trained in the social sciences and ill-equipped to deal with the interactional and social problems presented by patients. In particular, doctors have been criticized by feminists for their lack of understanding of, and empathy with, the problems faced by women in contemporary society. However, it is also the case that sociologists have often lacked an empathy for the dilemmas faced by the general practitioner in a world of limited resources and rising health expectations. Given the economic constraints on health-care systems, the commentaries of medical sociologists have often been naive in their appreciation of the structural limitations on contemporary health practice. Too often the sociologist has not been sufficiently aware of the paradox of their own position. On the one hand, they criticize the medicalization of society as a form of medical dominance, and on the other they recommend more intensive and interventionist medicine in the management of lifestyles and everyday interaction by arguing a case for extensive preventive approaches. Preventive medicine is clearly far more interventionist than conventional curative medicine, yet sociologists have been on the whole advocates of preventive medicine in response to the social causation of chronic disease in modern societies. Medical sociology clearly has a major contribution to make to medical practice, but this contribution has to be modest, judicious and circumspect.

Conclusion: health as citizenship

If we regard health as a desirable but limited resource, then we can perceive improvements in health standards as an aspect of the expansion of citizenship rights in contemporary societies (Turner, 1986a). In the post-war period of social reconstruction in Europe and the USA, governments have been subject to the pressure of rising expectations of health standards and health care, in a situation where social and economic inequalities continue to persist. There is in modern societies therefore a contradictory pull between the political process of democracy with respect to citizenship rights and the continuity of economic inequality which is closely related to the character of capitalist society, namely the existence of social classes. The problem for modern governments, at least in the 1980s and into the foreseeable future, is that the capacity to provide high standards of health care is being gradually eroded as a consequence of world economic recession. The contradiction between these health expectations and the possibilities of delivering an adequate health-care system in a period of recession means that modern democratic governments are unstable. In the theory of Habermas (1976), modern industrial democracies have severe crisis-tendencies, especially in terms of the legitimization of political office.

While there have been rising expectations of health care, there has also been a persistent demand for equal access to health-care services. In other words, expectations have been rising, but they have also been within the context of a broader demand for social equality. Modern governments are forced to take seriously regional inequalities in infantile mortality rates which are a strong indication of the underlying social inequalities of democratic capitalist systems. While the welfare system on the whole provides for greater equality of opportunity in health care, these welfare provisions have been threatened by the recession in the modern period. While a democratic system could provide for equality of opportunity, it is very difficult to provide for equality of outcome in health terms without a serious invasion of personal liberties, or without a significant degree of instability within the political and economic arena. There is a paradox in modern societies that the greater the demand for personal equality, the greater the requirement for surveillance and regulation of society. That is, the provision of citizenship tends to require the expansion of regulation, control and surveillance from the state. We could call this 'the Foucault paradox', namely the contradiction between individual rights and social surveillance. The medicalization of society involves a detailed and minute bureaucratic regulation of bodies in the interests of an abstract conception of health as a component of citizenship.

As a result of these processes, we can predict with a great deal of confidence that medical politics will be the subject of criss-crossing and contradictory pressure groups with their own specific and separate interests and agenda. These pressure groups in the area of medical politics would include the environmentalist lobby with its critique of medical technology, the feminist movement with its critique of patriarchal medicine, the movement towards a greater concern for the health and social status of children especially in the area of domestic violence, a broad pressure group to reform the legislation relating to medical malpractice, a variety of progressive groups concerned with alternative medical systems, and a variety of socialist groups in search of a greater equality of health care and a control, or the elimination of the profit motive in medical systems. The various professional and para-professional groups in health-care systems will be caught in the cross currents of these various political movements. The result is that we would expect health-care systems to become increasingly politicized towards the end of the twentieth century given the global character of both medicine and the economic system. These contradictory pressures will come to bear upon the medical curriculum; they will also require and bring about profound changes in the education of nurses and social workers; they will also require a radical rethinking of the role of pharmacy in modern medical practice. We may also hope that these changes will bring about necessary reforms in the sociology curriculum both in terms of theory and methodology, to reflect a more profound interest in health and sickness as basic contours of the social fabric.

References

B. Abel-Smith (1960), *A History of the Nursing Profession*, London, Heinemann.

N. Abercrombie and J. Urry (1983), *Capital Labour and the Middle Classes*, London, Allen and Unwin.

N. Abercrombie, S. Hill and B.S. Turner (1986), *Sovereign Individuals of Capitalism*, London, Allen and Unwin.

M. Abrams (1979), 'The Future of the Elderly', *Futures*: 178–184.

P. Allderidge (1985), 'Bedlam: fact or fantasy?' in W.F. Bynum, R. Porter and M. Shepherd (eds) *The Anatomy of Madness*, London, Tavistock, 2:17–33.

R. Andorka (1978), *Determinants of Fertility in Advanced Societies*, New York, Free Press.

P. Ariès (1962), *Centuries of Childhood*, Harmondsworth, Peregrine Books.

P. Ariès (1974), *Western Attitudes towards Death, from the Middle Ages to the Present*, Baltimore, Ma. and London, Marion Boyars.

P. Ariès and A. Bejin (eds) (1985), *Western Sexuality, Practice and Precept in Past and Present Times*, Oxford, Basil Blackwell.

D. Armstrong (1983), *Political Anatomy of the Body, Medical Knowledge in Britain in the Twentieth Century*, Cambridge, Cambridge University Press.

K.J. Arrow (1951), *Social Choice and Individual Values*, New York, John Wiley.

K.J. Arrow (1963), 'Uncertainty and the Welfare Economics of Medical Care', *The American Economic Review*, 53(5):941–973.

K.J. Arrow (1983), *Social Choice and Justice*, Cambridge, Ma., Harvard University Press.

T. Asad (1983), 'Notes on Body Pain and Truth in Medieval Christian Ritual', *Economy and Society*, 12(3):287–327.

R. Asher (1951), 'Munchausen's Syndrome', *Lancet*, 1:339–341.

J.A. Ashley (1975), 'Nurses in American History, Nursing and Early Feminism', *American Journal of Nursing*, 75:1465–1467.

R.C. Atchley (1977), *The Social Forces in Later Life*, Belmont, California, Wadsworth.

J.M. Atkinson (1978), *Discovering Suicide, Studies in the Social Organization of Sudden Death*, Pittsburgh, University of Pittsburgh Press.

R. Badgley and S. Bloom (1973), 'Behavioural Sciences and Medical Education: The Case of Sociology', *Social Science and Medicine*, 7: 927–941.

H. Bakwin (1945), 'Pseudocia Pediatricia', *New England Journal of Medicine*, 232:691–697.

J.A. Banks (1969), *Prosperity and Parenthood*, London, Routledge and Kegan Paul.

J.A. Banks and O. Banks (1964), *Feminism and Family Planning in Victorian England*, Liverpool, Liverpool University Press.

V. Barnouw (1979), *Culture and Personality*, Homewood Ill., The Dawsey Press.

C.R.B. Barrett (1905), *History of the Society of Apothecaries*, London, Stock.

F. Basaglia (1967), *L'istituzione Negata*, Turin, Einandi.

F. Basaglia (1981), 'Breaking the Circuit of Control' in D. Ingleby (ed.) *Critical Psychiatry*, Harmondsworth, Penguin.

E.L. Bassuk (1986), 'The Rest Cure: Repetition or Resolution of Victorian Women's Conflicts' in S.R. Suleiman (ed.) *The Female Body in Western Culture*, Cambridge,

228   *Medical power and social knowledge*

Ma., Harvard University Press, pp. 139–151.

H. Becker (1963), *The Outsiders*, Glencoe, Ill., Free Press.

H.S. Becker (ed.) (1964), *The Other Side, Perspectives on Deviance*, New York, The Free Press.

H. Becker, B. Geer, E.C. Hughes and A. Strauss (1961), *Boys in White: Student Culture in Medical School*, Chicago, Chicago University Press.

D. Bell (1974), *The Coming of Post-Industrial Society*, New York, Basic Books.

R.N. Bellah, R. Madsen, W.M. Sullivan, A. Swidler and S.M. Tipton (1985), *Habits of the Heart, Individualism and Commitment in American Life*, New York, Harper and Row.

J. Ben-David (1963–4), 'Professions in the Class System of Present Day Societies: A Trend Report and Bibliography', *Current Sociology*, 12.

N. Ben-Yehuda (1980), 'The European Witchcraze of the 14th to 17th centuries: a sociologist's perspective', *American Journal of Sociology*, 86(1):1–32.

P.L. Berger and T. Luckmann (1967), *The Social Construction of Reality*, London, Allen Lane, The Penguin Press.

A. Berman (1966), *Pharmaceutical Historiography*, Madison, American Institute of the History of Pharmacy.

C.A. Bishop (1975), 'Northern Algonkian Cannibalism and Windigo Psychosis' in T.R. Williams (ed.) *Psychological Anthropology*, The Hague, Mouton, pp. 237–248.

J.B. Blake (1965), 'Women and Medicine in Ante-bellum America', *Bulletin of the History of Medicine*, 39:99–123.

D. Blane (1985), 'An Assessment of the Black Report's Explanations of Health Inequalities', *Sociology of Health and Illness*, 7(3): 423–445.

P.M. Blau (1963), *The Dynamics of Bureaucracy*, Chicago, University of Chicago Press.

P.M. Blau (1974), *On the Nature of Organizations*, New York, Wiley.

Z.A. Blau (1973), *Old Age in a Changing Society*, New York, Franklin Watts.

F. Block (1977), 'The Ruling Class Does not Rule: Notes on the Marxist Theory of the State', *Socialist Revolution*, 7:6–28.

M. Bloor and G. Horobin (1975), 'Conflict and Conflict Resolution in Doctor–Patient Interactions' in C. Cox and A. Mead (eds) *A Sociology of Medical Practice*, London, Macmillan.

T. Bottomore and P. Goode (eds) (1978), *Austro-Marxism*, Oxford, Clarendon Press.

H. Braverman (1974), *Labor and Monopoly Capital: The Degradation of Work in the Twentieth Century*, New York, Monthly Review Press.

S.N. Brody (1974), *The Disease of the Soul, Leprosy in Medieval Literature*, New York, Ithaca.

M.B. Brown (1972), *From Labourism to Socialism*, London, Spokesman Books.

T.M. Brown (1985), 'Descartes, Dualism, and Psychosomatic Medicine', in W.F. Bynum, R. Porter and M. Shepherd (eds), *The Anatomy of Madness, Essays in the History of Psychiatry*, London and New York, Tavistock, 1:40–62.

G.W. Brown and J.L.T. Birley (1968), 'Crises and Life Changes and the Onset of Schizophrenia', *Journal of Health and Social Behaviour*, 9: 203–214.

G.W. Brown and T. Harris (1978), *Social Origins of Depression*, London, Tavistock.

R.G.S. Brown and R.W.H. Stones (1973), *The Male Nurse*, London, Bell.

H. Bruch (1978), *The Golden Cage*, Cambridge, Ma. Harvard University Press.

I.C. Buchan and I.M. Richardson (1973), 'Time Study of Consultations in General Practice', *Scottish Health Service Studies*, No. 27, Scottish Home and Health Department.

B. Bucher (1981), *Icon and Conquest, A Structural Analysis of the Illustrations of De*

Bry's Great Voyages, Chicago and London, University of Chicago Press.

M. Bulmer (1982), 'The Research Ethics of Pseudo-patients Studies: A New Look at the Merits of Covert Ethnographic Methods', *The Sociological Review,* 30(4):672–646.

G. Burrows (1984), 'Mental Health Research' in M. Tatchell (ed.) *Perspectives on Health Policy,* Canberra, ANU, pp. 102–110.

J. Busfield (1986), *Managing Madness, Changing Ideas and Practice,* London, Hutchinson.

W.J. Cahnman (1968), 'The Stigma of Obesity', *The Sociological Quarterly,* 9(3):283–299.

D.J. Callen and M.B. Sussman (ed.) (1984), *Obesity and the Family,* New York, Haworth Press.

A.L. Caplan (1981), 'The Unnaturalness of Aging – A Sickness unto Death?' in A.L. Caplan, H. Tristan Engelhardt, J.J. McCartney (eds) *Concepts of Health and Disease, Interdisciplinary Perspectives,* London, Addison-Wesley, pp. 725–738.

G. Carchedi (1977), *On the Economic Identification of Social Classes,* London, Routledge and Kegan Paul.

A. Cartwright (1967), *Patients and their Doctors,* London, Routledge and Kegan Paul.

A. Cartwright (1983), *Health Surveys in Practice and in Potential,* London, King's Fund Publishing Office.

A. Cartwright, L. Hockey and J.L. Anderson (1973), *Life Before Death,* London and Boston, Routledge and Kegan Paul.

A. Cartwright and M. O'Brien (1976), 'Social Class Variations in Health Care and in the Nature of General Practitioner Consultations' in M. Stacy (ed.), *The Sociology of the NHS, Sociological Review,* monograph, No. 22.

N. Caskey (1986), 'Interpreting Anorexia Nervosa' in S.R. Suleiman (ed.), *The Female Body in Western Culture, Contemporary Perspectives,* Cambridge Ma., Harvard University Press, pp. 175–189.

J. Cawte (1974), *Medicine is the Law, Studies in Psychiatric Anthropology of Australian Tribal Societies,* Honolulu, The University Press of Hawaii.

K. Chernin (1981), *The Obsession, Reflections on the Tyranny of Slenderness,* New York, Harper and Row.

J.N. Clarke (1983), 'Sexism, Feminism and Medicalism: A Decade Review of Literature on Gender and Illness', *Sociology of Health and Illness,* 5(1):62–82.

J.A. Clausen (1979), 'Mental Disorder' in H.E. Freeman, S. Levine and L.G. Reeder (eds), *Handbook of Medical Sociology,* Englewood Cliffs, New Jersey, Prentice Hall, pp. 97–112.

J.A. Clausen (1980), 'Some Current Issues in Medical Sociology' in H.M. Blalock (ed.), *Sociological Theory and Research: a Critical Appraisal,* New York, Free Press, pp. 361–372.

R.M. Coe (1978), *Sociology of Medicine,* New York, McGraw-Hill.

W.C. Cockerham (1982), *Medical Sociology,* Englewood Cliffs, New Jersey, Prentice-Hall.

R. Collins (1986), *Max Weber, a Skeleton Key,* Beverly Hills, Sage.

P. Conrad and R. Kern (eds) (1985), *The Sociology of Health and Illness, Critical Perspectives,* New York, St. Martin's.

P. Conrad and J.W. Schneider (1980), *Deviance and Medicalization, from Badness to Sickness,* St. Louis, C.V. Mosby.

C.H. Cooley (1902), *Human Nature and The Social Order,* New York, Scribners.

D. Cooper (ed.) (1968), *The Dialectics of Liberation,* Harmondsworth, Penguin Books.

C.J.O. Corcoran (1957), 'Thomistic Analysis and Cure of Scrupulosity' *American Ecclesiastical Review*, 137:313–29.

R.G. Corwin (1961a), 'The Professional Employee – a Study of Conflict in Nursing Roles', *The American Journal of Sociology*, 66:604–615.

R.G. Corwin (1961b), 'Role Conception and Career Aspirations: A Study of Identity in Nursing', *Sociological Quarterly*, 2:69–86.

M. Cousins and A. Hussain (1984), *Michel Foucault*, New York, St. Martin's Press.

M.W. Cranston (1975), *John Locke, A Biography*, New York, Macmillan.

V. Crapanzano (1973), *The Hamadsha, a study in Moroccan Ethno-psychiatry*, Berkeley, University of California Press.

A.H. Crisp, R.L. Palmer and R.S. Kalucy (1976), 'How Common is Anorexia Nervosa? A Prevalence Study', *British Journal of Psychiatry*, 128: 549–554.

J.G. Crowther (1960), *Francis Bacon, the First Statesman of Science*, London, The Cresset Press.

J.G. Cullis and P.A. West (1985), 'French Health Care: a Viewpoint A-system X', *Health Policy*, 5:143–149.

E. Cumming (1963), 'Further Thoughts on the Theory of Disengagement', *International Social Science*, 15:377–393.

E. Cumming and W.E. Henry (1961), *Growing Old, the Process of Disengagement*, New York, Basic Books.

N. Daniels (1985), *Just Health Care*, Cambridge, Cambridge University Press.

B. Davies (1966), *Introduction to Clinical Psychiatry*, Melbourne, Melbourne University Press.

C. Davies (ed.) (1980), *Re-writing Nursing History*, London, Croom Helm.

C. Davies (1983), 'Professionals in Bureaucracies: The Conflict Thesis Revisited' in R. Dingwall and J. McIntosh (eds), *Readings in the Sociology of Nursing*, Edinburgh, Churchill and Livingstone, pp. 177–194.

G. Davies (1959), *The Early Stuarts 1603–1660*, Oxford, The Clarendon Press.

M. Davies (1982), 'Corsets and Conception: Fashion and Demographic Trends in the Nineteenth Century', *Comparative Studies in Society and History*, 24:611–641.

F. Davis (1960), 'Uncertainty in Medical Prognosis, Clinical and Functional', *The American Journal of Sociology*, 66:41–47.

F. Davis (ed.) (1966), *The Nursing Profession, Five Sociological Essays*, New York, Wiley.

F. Davis (1972), *Illness Interaction and the Self*, Belmont, Ca., Wadsworth.

F. Davis and V.L. Olesen (1963), 'Initiation into the Woman's Profession: Identity Problems in the Status Transition of Coed to Student Nurse', *Sociometry*, 26:89–101.

K. Davis (1976), 'The World's Population Crisis' in R.K. Merton and R. Nisbet (eds) *Contemporary Social Problems*, New York, Harcourt Brace Jovanovich, pp. 363–406.

K. Davis and W. Moore (1945), 'Some Principles of Stratification', *The American Sociological Review*, 10:242–249.

M. Davis (1984), 'The Political Economy of Late-Imperial America', *New Left Review*, 143:6–38.

P. Davis (1980), *The Social Context of Dentistry*, London, Croom Helm.

B. Deacon (1984), 'Medical Care and Health under State Socialism', *International Journal of Health Services*, 14(3):453–480.

S. de Beauvoir (1972), *Old Age*, London, Weidenfeld and Nicolson.

C. Derber (1984), 'Physicians and their Sponsors: the New Medical Relations of Production', in J.B. McKinlay (ed.), *Issues in the Political Economy of Health*,

London, Tavistock, pp. 217–254.

A. de Swaan (1981), 'The Politics of Agoraphobia', *Theory and Society,* 10:359–385.

G. Devereux and F.R. Weiner (1950), 'The Occupational Status of Nurses', *The American Sociological Review,* 15:628–634.

J.A. Devine (1985), 'State and State Expenditure: Determinants of Social Investment and Social Consumption Spending in the Postwar United States', *The American Sociological Review,* 50(2):150–165.

K. Dewhurst (1958), 'Locke and Sydenham on the teaching of anatomy', *Medical History,* 2:1–12.

R. Dingwall and J. McIntosh (eds) (1983), *Readings in the Sociology of Nursing,* Edinburgh, Churchill and Livingstone.

J. Ditton (1979), *Contrology, beyond the new criminology,* London, Macmillan.

B. Dohrenwend (1975), 'Socio-cultural and Socio-psychological Factors in the Genesis of Mental Disorders', *Journal of Health and Social Behaviour,* 16(4):365–392.

M. Donnelly (1983), *Managing the Mind, Study of Medical Psychology in Early Nineteenth Century Britain,* London and New York, Tavistock.

J. Donnison (1977), *Midwives and Medical Men,* London, Heinemann.

J. Donzelot (1979), *The Policing of Families,* New York, Pantheon.

M. Douglas (1970), *Purity and Danger, an Analysis of the Concepts of Pollution and Taboo,* London, Routledge and Kegan Paul.

M. Douglas (1973), *Natural Symbols, Explorations in Cosmology,* Harmondsworth, Penguin Books.

J.J. Dowd (1975), 'Aging as Exchange: A Preface to Theory', *Journal of Gerontology,* 30:584–594.

J.J. Dowd (1980), 'Exchange Rates and Old People', *Journal of Gerontology,* 35:596–602.

L. Doyal (1979), *The Political Economy of Health,* London, Pluto Press.

H.L. Dreyfus and P. Rabinow (1982), *Michel Foucault, Beyond Structuralism and Hermeneutics,* Brighton, The Harvester Press.

R. Druss and J. Silverman (1979), 'The Body Image and Perfectionism of Ballerinas', *General Hospital Psychoanalyst,* 1:115–121.

G. Duby (1978), *Medieval Marriage – Two Models from Twelfth-century France,* Baltimore and London, John Hopkins University Press.

E. Durkheim (1951), *Suicide, a Study in Sociology,* Glencoe, Free Press.

G. Dussault and A. Sheiham (1982), 'Medical Theories and Professional Development, the Theory of Focal Sepsis and Dentistry in early Twentieth-century Britain', *Social Science and Medicine,* 16:1405–1412.

G. Eaton and B. Webb (1979), 'Boundary Encroachment: Pharmacists in the Clinical Setting', *Sociology of Health and Illness,* 1:69–89.

B. Ehrenreich and D. English (1972), *Witches, Midwives and Nurses: A History of Women Healers,* New York, Feminist Press.

B. Ehrenreich and D. English (1976), *Complaints and Disorders: The Sexual Politics of Sickness,* London, Writers and Readers Publishing Cooperative.

B. Ehrenreich and D. English (1978), *For Her Own Good: A Hundred and Fifty Years of the Experts' Advice to Women,* New York, Anchor Press.

S.N. Eisenstadt (1956), *From Generation to Generation, Age Groups and Social Structure,* New York, The Free Press.

M. Eliade (1964), *Shamanism, Archaic Technique of Ecstasy,* London, Routledge and Kegan Paul.

N. Elias (1985), *The Loneliness of the Dying,* Oxford, Blackwell.

J. Elinson (1980), 'Medical Sociology, Theoretical Underdevelopment and Some

Opportunities' in H.M. Blalock (ed.), *Sociological Theory and Research, a Critical Appraisal*, New York, Free Press, pp. 373–387.

H.F. Ellenberger (1970), *The Discovery of the Unconscious: The History and Evolution of Dynamic Psychiatry*, London, Allen and Unwin.

A.J. Enelow and S.N. Swisher (1979), *Interviewing and Patient Care*, New York, Oxford University Press.

G.L. Engel (1981), 'The Need for a New Medical Model: A Challenge for Biomedicine' in A.L. Kaplan, H.T. Engelhardt and J.J. McCartney (eds), *Concepts of Health and Disease, Interdisciplinary Perspectives*, London, Addison-Wesley Publishing Company, pp. 589–608.

H.T. Engelhardt (1974), 'The Disease of Masturbation, Values and the Concept of Disease', *Bulletin of the History of Medicine*, 48: 234–248.

F. Engels (1952), *The Condition of the Working Class in England in 1844*, London, Allen and Unwin.

A. Enthoven (1984), 'Reforming US Health Care: The Consumer Choice Health Plan' in N. Black et al. (eds), *Health and Disease: A Reader*, Milton Keynes, Open University Press, pp. 335–340.

C.F. Epstein (1970), 'Encountering the Male Establishment: Sex Status Limits on Women's Careers in the Professions', *The American Journal of Sociology*, 75:965–982.

M. Esslin (1976), *Artaud*, London, Fontana.

C.L. Estes (1979), *The Aging Enterprise*, San Francisco, Jossey-Bass.

A. Etzioni (ed.) (1969), *The Semi-Professions and their Organisation*, New York, Free Press.

R. Evans (1982), *The Fabrication of Virtue, English Prison Architecture 1750–1840*, Cambridge, Cambridge University Press.

J. Feagin (1975), *Subordinating the Poor*, N. J., Englewood Cliffs, Prentice Hall.

H. Feifel (ed.) (1959), *The Meaning of Death*, New York, McGraw-Hill.

R.H. Felix (1967), *Mental Illness: Progress and Prospects*, New York, Columbia University Press.

D. Ferguson (1984), 'The "New" Industrial Epidemic', *Medical Journal of Australia*, 140:318–319.

K. Figlio (1982), 'How does Illness Mediate Social Relations: Workmen's Compensation and Medico-legal Practices 1899–1940', in P. Wright and A. Treacher (eds), *The Problem of Medical Knowledge, Examining the Social Construction of Medicine*, Edinburgh, Edinburgh University Press, pp. 174–224.

R.C. Finucane (1982), *Appearances of the Dead, A Cultural History of Ghosts*, London, Junction Books.

D.H. Fischer (1978), *Growing Old in America*, Oxford, Oxford University Press.

R. Fitzpatrick, J. Hinton, S. Newman, G. Scambler and J. Thompson (1984), *The Experience of Illness*, London and New York, Tavistock.

R. Fletcher (1962), *Britain in the Sixties, the Family and Marriage*, Harmondsworth, Penguin Books.

B. Ford (1979), *The Elderly Australian*, Ringwood, Penguin Books.

A. Forrest (1981), *The French Revolution and The Poor*, Oxford, Basil Blackwell.

M. Foucault (1971), *Madness and Civilisation*, London, Tavistock.

M. Foucault (1973), *The Birth of the Clinic*, London, Tavistock.

M. Foucault (1974), *The Order of Things*, London, Tavistock.

M. Foucault (1977), *Discipline and Punish, The Birth of the Prison*, London, Tavistock.

M. Foucault (1979), *The History of Sexuality, Volume One, an Introduction*,

London, Allen Lane, Penguin Books.

M. Foucault (1980), *Power/Knowledge, Selected Interviews and Other Writings 1972–1977*, Brighton, The Harvester Press.

R. Fox (1957), 'Training for Uncertainty', in R.K. Merton, G. Reader and P.L. Kendall (eds), *The Student-Physician*, Cambridge, Ma., Harvard University Press.

R.G. Fox (1981), 'The Welfare State and the Political Mobilisation of the Elderly' in S.B. Kiesler, J.N. Morgan and V.K. Oppenheimer (eds), *Aging, Social Change*, New York, Academic Press. pp. 159–182.

A.G. Frank (1983), 'After Reaganomics and Thatcherism, What?', *Thesis Eleven*, 4:33–47.

E. Freidson (1961), *Patients' Views of Medical Practice*, New York, Russell Sage Foundation.

E. Freidson (1970), *Profession of Medicine, a Study of the Sociology of Applied Knowledge*, New York, Harper and Row.

E. Freidson (1983), 'Viewpoint: sociology and medicine: a polemic', *Sociology of Health and Illness*, 5(2):208–219.

S. Freud and J. Breuer (1974), *Studies on Hysteria*, Harmondsworth, Penguin Books.

P.E.S. Freund (1982), *The Civilised Body: Social Domination, Control and Health*, Philadelphia, Temple University Press.

D. Gallie (1983), *Social Inequality and Class Radicalism in France and Britain*, Cambridge, Cambridge University Press.

E. Gamarnikow (1978), 'Sexual Division of Labour: The Case of Nursing' in A. Kuhn and A. Wolpe (eds), *Feminism and Materialism, Women and Modes of Production*, London, Routledge and Kegan Paul, pp. 96–123.

A. Game and R. Pringle (1983), *Gender at Work*, Sydney, Allen and Unwin.

H. Garfinkel (1956), 'Conditions of Successful Degradation Ceremonies', *The American Journal of Sociology*, 61:420–424.

E. Gellner (1983), *Nations and Nationalism*, Oxford, Basil Blackwell.

V. George and N. Manning (1980), *Socialism, Social Welfare and the Soviet Union*, London, Routledge and Kegan Paul.

B.F. Georgopoulos and F.C. Mann (1972), 'The Hospital as an Organisation', in E. Jaco (ed.), *Patients, Physicians and Illness*, New York, Macmillan, pp. 304–311.

G. Gereffi (1983), *The Pharmaceutical Industry and Dependency in the Third World*, Princeton, Princeton University Press.

J.P. Gibbs and W.T. Martin (1964), *Status Integration and Suicide*, Eugene, University of Oregon Press.

D. Gill (1977), *Illegitimacy, Sexuality and the Status of Women*, Oxford, Basil Blackwell.

D. Gill and A. Twaddle (1977), 'Medical Sociology: What's in a Name?', *International Social Science Journal*, 29(3):369–385.

B.G. Glaser and A.L. Strauss (1965), *Awareness of Dying*, Chicago, Aldine.

B.G. Glaser and A.L. Strauss (1968a), *The Discovery of Grounded Theory, Strategies for Qualitative Research*, London, Weidenfeld and Nicolson.

B.G. Glaser and A.L. Strauss (1968b), *Time for Dying*, Chicago, Aldine.

F. Godlee (1985), 'Aspects of Non-conformity: Quakers and the Lunatic Fringe' in W.F. Bynum, R. Porter and M. Shepherd (eds), *The Anatomy of Madness, Essays in the History of Psychiatry*, London and New York, Tavistock, II:73–85.

E. Goffman (1961), *Asylums*, Harmondsworth, Penguin Books.

E. Goffman (1964), *Stigma, Notes on the Management of the Spoiled Identity*, New Jersey, Englewood Cliffs, Prentice Hall.

M. Gold (1977), 'A Crisis of Identity: The Case of Medical Sociology', *Journal of*

Health and Social Behaviour, 18:160–168.

E.M. Goldberg and S.L. Morrison (1963), 'Schizophrenia and Social Class', *British Journal of Psychiatry,* 109:785–802.

M.S. Goldstein (1979), 'The Sociology of Mental Health and Illness', *The Annual Review of Sociology,* 5:381–409.

J. Goldthorpe (1982), 'On the Service Class, Its Formation and Future', in A. Giddens and G. Mackenzie (eds), *Social Class and the Division of Labour, Essays in Honour of Ilya Neustadt,* Cambridge, Cambridge University Press, pp. 162–185.

J. Goody (1962), *Death, Property and the Ancestors,* Stanford, California, Stanford University Press.

N.E. Goss (1963), 'Patterns of Bureaucracy Among Hospital Staff Physicians' in E. Freidson (ed.) *The Hospital in Modern Society,* New York, Free Press, pp. 170–194.

W.R. Gove (1970), 'Societal Reaction as an Explanation of Mental Illness: An Evaluation', *The American Sociological Review,* 35:873–884.

W.R. Gove (1972), 'Sex Roles, Marital Status and Suicide', *Journal of Health and Social Behaviour,* 13:204–213.

W.R. Gove and M.R. Geerken (1977), 'The Effect of Children and Employment on the Mental Health of Married Men and Women', *Social Forces,* 56:66–77.

W.R. Gove and J.F. Tudor (1973), 'Adult Sex Roles and Mental Illness', *The American Journal of Sociology,* 78:813–835.

H. Graham (1984), *Women, Health and the Family,* Brighton, Wheatsheaf Books.

S. Graham and L.G. Reeder (1979), 'Social Epidemiology of Chronic Diseases' in H.E. Freeman, S. Levine and L.G. Reeder (eds) *Handbook of Medical Sociology,* Englewood Cliffs, New Jersey, Prentice Hall, pp. 71–96.

G.N. Grob (1977), 'Rediscovering Asylums: The Unhistorical History of the Mental Hospital', *The Hastings Center Report,* 7:33–41.

G. Groddeck (1977), *The Meaning of Illness, Selected Psychoanalytical Writings,* London, The Hogarth Press.

D. Grylls (1978), *Guardians and Angels, Parents and Children in Nineteenth Century Literature,* London and Boston, Faber and Faber.

G. Gurvitch and W.E. Moore (eds) (1945), *Twentieth Century Sociology,* New York, The Philosophical Library.

J. Habermas (1970), 'On Systematically Distorted Communication', *Inquiry,* 13:205–218.

J. Habermas (1972), *Knowledge and Human Interests,* London, Heinemann.

J. Habermas (1976), *Legitimation Crisis,* London, Heinemann.

J. Habermas (1979), *Communication and the Evolution of Society,* London, Heinemann.

J. Habermas (1984), *The Theory of Communicative Action,* Boston, Beacon Press, 1.

J.A. Hall (1985), *Powers and Liberties, the Causes and Consequences of the Rise of the West,* Oxford, Basil Blackwell.

R.H. Hall (1968), 'Professionalisation and Bureaucratisation', *The American Sociological Review,* 33:92–104.

P. Halmos (1973), *Professionalization and Social Change, The Sociological Review* Monograph, No. 20, Keele.

R. Hassan (1983), *A Way of Dying, Suicide in Singapore,* Kuala Lumpar, Oxford University Press.

M.R. Haug (1973), 'Deprofessionalization: An Alternative Hypothesis for the Future' in P. Halmos (ed.), *Professionalization and Social Change,* pp. 195–212.

R.A. Havighurst (1963), 'Successful Aging', in R. Williams, C. Tibbits and W.

Donahue (eds), *Processes of Aging,* New York, Atherton, pp. 299–320.

T.H. Hay (1971), 'The Windigo Psychosis: Psychodynamic, Cultural and Social Factors in Aberrant Behaviour', *American Anthropologist,* 73: 1–19.

W.S. Heckscher (1958), *Rembrandt's Anatomy of Doctor Nicholaas Tulp, An Iconological Study,* Washington Square, New York University Press.

L.J. Henderson (1935), 'Physician and Patient as a Social System', *New England Journal of Medicine,* 212:819–823.

L.J. Henderson (1936), 'The Practice of Medicine as Applied Sociology', *Transactions of the Association of American Physicians,* 51:8–15.

M. Hepworth and B.S. Turner (1982), *Confession, Studies in Deviance and Religion,* London, Routledge and Kegan Paul.

S. Hesselbart (1977), 'Women Doctors Win and Male Nurses Lose', *Sociology of Work and Occupations,* 4:49–62.

M.A. Hewson (1975), *Giles of Rome and the Medieval Theory of Conception,* London, The Athlone Press.

J. Higgins (1981), *The States of Welfare, Comparative Analysis in Social Policy,* Oxford, Basil Blackwell and Martin Robertson.

C. Hill (1964), 'William Harvey and the Idea of Monarchy', *Past and Present,* 27:54–72.

J. Hinton (1967), *Dying,* Harmondsworth, Penguin Books.

J. Hirsch (1978), 'The State Apparatus and Social Reproduction, Elements of a Theory of the Bourgeois State', in J. Holloway and S. Picciotto (eds) *State and Capital, A Marxist Debate,* London, Edward Arnold, pp. 57–107.

L. Hirschhorn (1978), 'The Political Economy of Social Service Rationalization', *Contemporary Crises,* 2:63–81.

C. Hofling, E. Brotzman, N. Dalrymple and C. Pierce (1966), 'An Experimental Study in Nurse–Physician Relationships', *Journal of Nervous and Mental Disease,* 143:171–180.

R. Hofstadter (1955), *Social Darwinism in American Thought,* Boston, The Beacon Press.

A.B. Hollingshead and F.C. Redlich (1958), *Social Class and Mental Illness, a Community Study,* New York, Wiley.

T.H. Holmes and M. Masuda (1974), 'Life Change and Illness Susceptibility' in B.S. Dohrenwend and B.P. Dohrenwend (eds), *Stressful Life Events: Their Nature and Effects,* New York, Wiley, pp. 45–72.

T. Holmes and R. Rahe (1967), 'The Social Re-adjustment Rating Scale', *Journal of Psychosomatic Research,* 11:213–218.

R.J. Holton and B.S. Turner (1986), *Talcott Parsons on Economy and Society,* London, Routledge and Kegan Paul.

S. Holton (1984), 'Feminine Authority in Social Order: Florence Nightingale's conception of Nursing and Health Care', *Social Analysis,* No. 15:59–72.

D.C. Hoy (ed.) (1986), *Foucault, a Critical Reader,* Oxford, Basil Blackwell.

E.C. Hughes (1951), 'Studying the Nurse's Work', *The American Journal of Nursing,* 51:294–295.

E.C. Hughes (1958), *Men and their Work,* Glencoe, Ill. Free Press.

E.C. Hughes, H. Hughes and I. Deutscher (1958), *Twenty Thousand Nurses Tell Their Story,* Philadelphia, Lippincott.

D. Hunter (1959), *Health in Industry,* Harmondsworth, Penguin Books.

I. Illich (1977), *Limits to Medicine, Medical Nemesis: The Expropriation of Health,* Harmondsworth, Penguin Books.

R. Illsley (1986), 'Occupational Class Selection and the Production of Inequalities in

Health', *Quarterly Journal of Social Affairs*, 2: 151–165.

D. Ingleby (ed.) (1980), *Critical Psychiatry*, Harmondsworth, Penguin Books.

B. Inglis (1981), *The Diseases of Civilisation*, London, Hodder and Stoughton.

L. Isaac and W. Kelly (1981), 'Racial Insurgency, The State and Welfare Expansion: Local and National Level Evidence from the Postwar United States', *The American Journal of Sociology*, 86:1348–1386.

S.W. Jackson (1981), 'Acedia: The Sin and its Relationship to Sorrow and Melancholia in Medieval Times', *The Bulletin of the History of Medicine*, 55:172–185.

D.B. James (1972), *Poverty, Politics and Change*, New Jersey, Englewood Cliffs, Prentice Hall.

H. Jamous and B. Peloille (1970), 'Changes in the French University-Hospital System' in J.A. Jackson (ed.), *Professions and Professionalization*, Cambridge University Press, pp. 111–152.

M. Jay (1986), 'In the Empire of the Gaze: Foucault and the Denigration of Vision in Twentieth-century French Thought' in D.C. Hoy (ed.), *Foucault, a Critical Reader*, Oxford, Basil Blackwell, pp. 175–204.

E.S. Johnson and J.B. Williamson (1980), *Growing Old, The Social Problems of Aging*, New York, Holt, Rinehart and Winston.

R.W. Johnson (1985), *The Politics of Recession*, London, Macmillan.

T. Johnson (1972), *Professions and Power*, London, Macmillan.

T. Johnson (1977), 'The Professions in the Class Structure' in R. Scase (ed.), *Industrial Society: Class Cleavage and Control*, London, Allen and Unwin, pp. 93–110.

T. Johnson (1982), 'The State and the Professions: Peculiarities of the British' in A. Giddens and G. Mackenzie (eds), *Social Class and the Division of Labour*, Cambridge, Cambridge University Press, pp. 186–208.

K. Jones (1965), *Lunacy, Law and Conscience 1744–1845* (ed.) W.J.H. Sprott, London, Routledge and Kegan Paul.

R.S. Kalucy, A.H. Crisp and B. Harding (1977), 'A Study of 56 Families with Anorexia Nervosa', *British Journal of Medical Psychology*, 50: 381–395.

G.S. Kart (1981), *The Realities of Aging*, Boston, Allyn and Bacon.

P.L. Kendall and G.G. Reader (1979), 'Contributions of Sociology to Medicine' in H.E. Freeman, S. Levine and L.G. Reeder (eds), *Handbook of Medical Sociology*, Englewood Cliffs, New Jersey, Prentice Hall, pp. 1–22.

C. Kerr, J.T. Dunlop, F.H. Harbison and C.A. Myers (1962), *Industrialism and Industrial Man*, London, Heinemann.

N. Keyfitz (1982), *Population Change and Social Policy*, Cambridge, Ma., Abt Books.

L.S. King (1954), 'What is Disease?', *Philosophy of Science*, 21: 193–203.

L.S. King (1970), 'Empiricism and Rationalism in the Works of Thomas Sydenham', *The Bulletin for the History of Medicine*, 44 (1), pp. 1–11.

L.S. King (1982) *Medical Thinking, a Historical Preface*, Princeton, N. J., Princeton University Press.

J.H. Knowles (ed.) (1973), *Hospitals, Doctors and the Public Interest*, Cambridge, Ma., Harvard University Press.

S.E. Kobrin (1966), 'The American Midwife Controversy: A Crisis of Professionalisation', *The Bulletin of the History of Medicine*, 40: 350–363.

K.P. Koepping (1985), 'Absurdity and Hidden Truth: Cunning Intelligence and the Grotesque Body Images as Manifestation of the Trickster', *History of Religions*, 24(3):191–214.

E. Kubler-Ross (1970), *On Death and Dying*, London, Tavistock.

A. Kuhn and A. Wolpe (1978), *Feminism and Materialism, Women and Modes of Production*, London, Routledge and Kegan Paul.

K. Kumar (1978), *Prophecy and Progress, The Sociology of Industrial and Post-Industrial Society*, London, Allen Lane.

E. Kurzweil (1980), *The Age of Structuralism, Lévi-Strauss to Foucault*, New York, Columbia University Press.

J. Lacan (1977), *Ecrits, A Selection*, London, Tavistock.

R.D. Laing (1960), *The Divided Self, an Existential Study in Sanity and Madness*, London, Tavistock.

R.D. Laing (1961), *The Self and Others*, London, Tavistock.

G. Larkin (1981), 'Professional Autonomy and the Ophthalmic Optician', *Sociology of Health and Illness*, 3(1):15–30.

M.S. Larson (1977), *The Rise of Professionalism, A Sociological Analysis*, Berkeley and Los Angeles, University of California Press.

M.S. Larson (1980), 'Proletarianisation and Educated Labour', *Theory and Society*, 9:131–175.

S. Lash (1984), *The Militant Worker, Class and Radicalism in France and America*, London, Heinemann.

P. Laslett (1972), *The World We Have Lost*, London, Methuen.

P. Laslett (ed.) (1972), *Household and Family in Past Time*, Cambridge, Cambridge University Press.

M. Lawrence (1979), 'Anorexia Nervosa – the Control Paradox', *Women's Studies International Quarterly*, 2:93–101.

J. Le Grand and R. Robinson (eds) (1976), *The Economics of Social Problems*, London, Macmillan.

E. Le R. Ladurie (1980), *Montaillou*, Harmondsworth, Penguin Books.

A. Lemaire (1977), *Jacques Lacan*, London, Routledge and Kegan Paul.

C. Lemert and G. Gillan (1982), *Michel Foucault, Social Theory and Transgression*, New York, Columbia University Press.

E.M. Lemert (1951), *Social Pathology*, New York, McGraw-Hill.

E.M. Lemert (1962), 'Paranoia and the Dynamics of Exclusion', *Sociometry*, 25:2–25.

E.M. Lemert (1967), *Human Deviance, Social Problems and Social Control*, Englewood Cliffs, New Jersey, Prentice-Hall.

W.E. Leuchtenburg (1963), *Franklin D. Roosevelt and the New Deal 1932–1940*, New York, Harper and Row.

D.M. Levin (1985), *The Body's Recollection of Being, Phenomenological Psychology and the Deconstruction of Nihilism*, London, Routledge and Kegan Paul.

S. Levine and M.A. Kozloff (1978), 'The Sick Role: Assessment and Overview', *The Annual Review of Sociology*, 4:317–343.

E. Lewin and V. Olesen (eds) (1985), *Women, Health and Healing, Toward a New Perspective*, New York and London, Tavistock.

A. Lewis (1953), 'Health as a Social Concept', *The British Journal of Sociology*, 4:109–124.

I.M. Lewis (1971), *Ecstatic Religion, an Anthropological Study of Spirit Possession and Shamanism*, Harmondsworth, Penguin Books.

R. Lewis and A. Maude (1952), *Professional People*, London, Phoenix House.

Lief (ed.) (1948), *The Commonsense Psychiatry of Doctor Adolph Meyer*, New York, McGraw-Hill.

N. Lin, W.M. Ensel, R.S. Simeone and W. Kuo (1979), 'Social Support, Stressful Life Events, and Illness: A Model and an Empirical Test', *Journal of Health and*

Social Behaviour, 20:108–119.

L.N. Lindberg, R. Alford, C. Crouch and C. Offe (eds) (1975), *Stress and Contradiction in Modern Capitalism*, Lexington, Ma., Lexington Books.

C.R. Littler (1982), *The Development of the Labour Process in Capitalist Societies*, London, Heinemann.

M. Lock (1980), *East Asian Medicine in Urban Japan*, Berkeley, University of California Press.

D. Lockwood (1958), *The Blackcoated Worker*, London, Allen and Unwin.

J. Lorber (1984), *Women Physicians, Careers Status and Power*, New York and London, Tavistock.

C.F. Longino and G.S. Kart (1982), 'Explicating Activity Theory: A Formal Replication', *Journal of Gerontology*, 37:713–722.

R.S. Lynd and H.M. Lynd (1929), *Middletown, a Study in Contemporary American Culture*, New York, Harcourt Brace and Co.

W. McDermott (1980), 'Pharmaceuticals: their Role in Developing Societies', *Science*, 209:240–245.

S. Macintyre and D. Oldman (1984), 'Coping with Migraine' in N. Black et al (eds) *Health and Disease, A Reader*, Milton Keynes, The Open University Press: 271–275.

T. McKeown (1965), *Medicine in Modern Society*, London, Routledge and Kegan Paul.

J. McKinlay (1973), 'Social Networks, Lay Consultation and Help-seeking Behaviour', *Social Forces*, 53:275–292.

J.B. McKinlay (1984), *Issues in the Political Economy of Health Care*, London, Tavistock.

H. McLachlan and J.K. Swales (1980), 'Witchcraft and Anti-feminism', *The Scottish Journal of Sociology*, 4:141–166.

U. Maclean (1974), *Nursing in Contemporary Society*, London, Routledge and Kegan Paul.

S.P. Mangen (1982), *Sociology and Mental Health*, Edinburgh, Churchill Livingstone.

M. Mannoni (1973), *The Child, His 'Illness' and the Others*, Harmondsworth, Penguin.

J.M. Maravall (1979), 'The Limits of Reformism: Parliamentary Socialism and the Marxist Theory of the State', *The British Journal of Sociology*, 30(3):267–290.

A.J. Marsella, G. Devos and F.L.K. Hsu (1985), *Culture and Self, Asian and Western Perspectives*, New York and London, Tavistock.

T.H. Marshall (1985), *Social Policy*, London, Hutchinson.

M. Matthews (1978), *Privilege in the Soviet Union: A Study of Elite Lifestyles under Communism*, London, Allen and Unwin.

D. Mechanic (1968), *Medical Sociology*, New York, The Free Press.

D. Mechanic (1975), 'The Comparative Study of Health Care Delivery Systems', *Annual Review of Sociology*, 1:43–65.

D. Mechanic (1976), *The Growth of Bureaucratic Medicine*, New York, John Wiley.

D. Mechanic (1977a), 'Some Aspects of the Medical Mal-Practice Dilemma', *The Duke Law Symposium*, Cambridge, Ballinger: 1–18.

D. Mechanic (1977b), 'The Growth of Modern Technology and Bureaucracy: Implications for Medical Care', *Milbank Memorial Fund Quarterly*, 55(1):61–78.

K.M. Melia (1984), 'Student Nurses' Construction of Occupational Socialisation', *Sociology of Health and Illness*, 6:132–151.

R.K. Merton (1957), *Social Theory and Social Structure*, Glencoe, Ill., The Free Press.

R.K. Merton (1970), *Science Technology and Society in Seventeenth Century England*,

New York, Harper and Row.

S. Milgram (1974), *Obedience to Authority: An Experimental View*, New York, Harper and Row.

N. Milio (1985), 'US Public Policies Make You Sick', *Radical Community Medicine*, pp. 25–34.

G.L. Millerson (1964), *The Qualifying Association*, London, Routledge and Kegan Paul.

J. Mitchell and A. Oakley (eds) (1976), *Rights and Wrongs of Women*, Harmondsworth, Penguin Books.

B. Mongeau, H.L. Smith and A.C. Maney (1961), 'The "Granny" Midwife: Changing Roles and Functions of a Folk Practitioner', *The American Journal of Sociology*, 66:497–505.

D. Morgan (1975), 'Explaining Mental Illness', *Archives Europeennes de Sociologie*, 16:262–280.

S.A. Morsy (1978), 'Sex Differences and Folk Illness in an Egyptian Village' in L. Beck and N. Keddie (eds), *Women in the Muslim World*, Cambridge, Cambridge University Press: 599–616.

E. Mumford (1983), *Medical Sociology, Patients Providers and Policies*, New York, London House.

A. Murcott (1981), 'On the Typification of Bad Patients', in P. Atkinson and C. Heath (eds) *Medical Work, Realities and Routines*, London, Gower, pp. 128–140.

V. Navarro (1976), *Medicine Under Capitalism*, New York, Prodist.

V. Navarro (1978), *Class Struggle, The State and Medicine, An Historical and Contemporary Analysis of the Medical Sector in Great Britain*, London, Martin Robertson.

V. Navarro and D.M. Berman (eds) (1981), *Health and Work Under Capitalism: An International Perspective*, New York, Farmingdale, Baywood Publishing Co.

B. Neugarten (1964), *Personality in Middle and Later Life*, New York, Atherton.

F. Nietzsche (1974), *The Gay Science*, New York, Vintage Books.

A. Oakley (1984), *The Captured Womb, a History of the Medical Care of Pregnant Women*, Oxford, Basil Blackwell.

J. O'Connor (1973), *The Fiscal Crisis of the State*, New York, St. Martins Press.

J. O'Connor (1984), *Accumulation Crisis*, Oxford, Basil Blackwell.

C. Offe (1985), *Disorganised Capitalism, Contemporary Transformations of Work and Politics*, Oxford, Polity Press.

E. Ohnuki-Tierney (1984), *Illness and Culture in Contemporary Japan, An Anthropological View*, Cambridge, Cambridge University Press.

J. O'Neill (1985), *Five Bodies, the Human Shape of Modern Society*, Ithaca and London, Cornell University Press.

J. O'Neill (1986), 'The Disciplinary Society', *The British Journal of Sociology*, 47, 37(1):42–60.

L.J. Opit (1983) 'Wheeling, Healing and Dealing: the Political Economy of Health Care in Australia', *Community Health Studies*, 7(3): 238–246.

M. Oppenheimer (1973), 'The Proletarianization of the Profession', in P. Halmos (ed.), *Professionalization and Social Change*, pp. 213–228.

S. Orbach (1978), *Fat is a Feminist Issue*, New York, Paddington Press.

S.B. Ortner (1974), 'Is Female to Male as Nature is to Culture?' in M.A. Rosaldo and L. Lamphere (eds), *Women, Culture and Society*, Stanford, California, Stanford University Press, pp. 67–87.

R.L. Palmer (1979), 'The Dietary Chaos Syndrome: a Useful New Term', *British Journal of Medical Psychology*, 52:187–190.

R.L. Palmer (1980), *Anorexia Nervosa*, Harmondsworth, Penguin Books.

E. Palmore (1968), 'The Effects of Aging on Activities and Attitudes', *Gerontologist*, 17:315–320.

E. Palmore (1981), *Social Patterns in Normal Aging, Findings from the Duke Longitudinal Study*, Durham, N.C. Duke University Press.

L. Panitch (1980), 'Recent Theorizations of Corporatism', *British Journal of Sociology*, 31:159–87.

C.M. Parkes (1972), *Bereavement, Studies of Grief in Adult Life*, London, Tavistock.

F. Parkin (1969), 'Class Stratification in Socialist Societies', *The British Journal of Sociology*, 20(4):355–374.

F. Parkin (1979), *Marxism and Class Theory, a Bourgeois Critique*, London, Tavistock.

F. Parkin (1982), *Max Weber*, Chichester, Ellis Horwood and London, Tavistock.

N. Parry and J. Parry (1976), *The Rise of Medical Professions*, London, Croom Helm.

T. Parsons (1937), *The Structure of Social Action*, New York, The Free Press.

T. Parsons (1939), 'The Professions and the Social Structure', *Social Forces*, 17:457–467.

T. Parsons (1951), *The Social System*, London, Routledge and Kegan Paul.

E. Paterson (1981), 'Food-work: Maids in a Hospital Kitchen' in P. Atkinson and C. Heath (eds), *Medical Work, Realities and Routines*, London, Gower, pp. 152–170.

J.F. Payne (1900), *Thomas Sydenham*, London, Unwin.

R.D. Penn (1983), 'Theories of Skill and Class Structure', *The Sociological Review*, 31:22–38.

C. Phillipson (1982), *Capitalism and the Construction of Old Age*, London, Macmillan Press.

I. Pilowsky (1978), 'A General Classification of Abnormal Illness Behaviours', *British Journal of Medical Psychology*, 51:131–137.

R. Pinker (1971), *Social Theory and Social Policy*, London, Heinemann.

F.F. Piven and R.A. Cloward (1971), *Regulating the Poor, The Functions of Public Welfare*, New York, Pantheon Books.

F.F. Piven and R. Cloward (1977), *Poor People's Movements*, New York, Pantheon Books.

F.F. Piven and R. Cloward (1982), *The New Class War, Reagan's Attack on the Welfare State and its Consequences*, New York, Pantheon Books.

N. Poulantzas (1973), *Political Power and Social Classes*, London, NLB and Sheed and Ward.

N. Poulantzas (1975), *Classes in Contemporary Capitalism*, London, NLB.

F.N.L. Poynter (ed.) (1965), *The Evolution of Pharmacy In Britain*, London, Pitman.

G. Psathas (1969), 'The Fate of Idealism in the Nursing School', *Journal of Health and Social Behaviour*, 9:52–64.

S. Rank and C. Jacobson (1977), 'Hospital Nurses' Compliance with Medication Overdose Orders: A Failure to Replicate', *Journal of Health and Social Behaviour*, 18:188–193.

G. Rath (1961), 'Pre-Vasalian Anatomy in the Light of Modern Research', *Bulletin of the History of Medicine*, 35:142–148.

S.J. Reeder and H. Mauksch (1979), 'Nursing: Continuing Change' in H.E. Freeman, S. Levine and L.G. Reeder (eds), *Handbook of Medical Sociology*, Englewood Cliffs, New Jersey, Prentice-Hall, pp. 209–229.

P. Rieff (1961), *Freud: The Mind of the Moralist*, Graden City, Doubleday.

V.G. Rodwin (1984), *The Health Planning Predicament, France, Quebec, England and the United States,* Berkeley, University of California Press.

M. Roemer (1977), *Comparative National Policies on Health Care,* New York and Basel, Marcel Dekker.

M.A. Rosaldo and L. Lamphere (eds) (1974), *Women, Culture and Society,* Stanford, California, Stanford University Press.

G. Rosen (1979), 'The Evolution of Social Medicine' in H. Freeman, L. Levine and L.G. Reeder (eds), *Handbook of Medical Sociology,* New Jersey, Englewood Cliffs, Prentice Hall, pp. 23–50.

G. Rosen (1983), *The Structure of American Medical Practice 1875–1941,* Philadelphia, University of Pennsylvania Press.

D. Rosenhan (1973), 'On Being Sane in Insane Places', *Science,* 179: 250–258.

J. Rossiand (1985), 'Prostitution, Sex and Society in French Towns in the Fifteenth Century' in P. Ariès and A. Bejin (eds), *Western Sexuality,* Oxford, Basil Blackwell, pp. 76–94.

J. Roth (1962), 'Management Bias in Social Science Research' *Human Organisation,* 21:47–50.

J.A. Roth (1962), 'The Treatment of Tuberculosis as a Bargaining Process' in A.M. Rose (ed.), *Human Behaviour and Social Processes, an Interactionist Approach,* London, Routledge and Kegan Paul, pp. 550–574.

J.A. Roth (1963), *Timetables, Structuring the Passage of Time in Hospital Treatment and Other Careers,* Indianapolis, Bobbs-Merrill.

Royal Commission on Population Report, London, Her Majesty's Stationery Office, 1949.

C. Russell (1981), *The Aging Experience,* Sydney, Allen and Unwin.

O. Sacks (1976), *Awakenings,* Harmondsworth, Penguin Books.

O. Sacks (1981), *Migraine, Evolution of a Common Disorder,* London, Pan Books.

O. Sacks (1986), *A Leg to Stand on,* London, Pan Books.

G. Salaman (1986), *Working.* Chichester, Ellis Horwood and London, Tavistock.

J.W. Salmon (1985), 'Profit and Health Care: Trends in Corporatization and Proprietization', *International Journal of Health Services,* 15(3): 395–418.

M. Sargent (1979), *Drinking and Alcoholism in Australia, a Power Relations Theory,* Melbourne, Longmans Cheshire.

S. Sax (1984), *A Strife of Interests, Politics and Policies in Australian Health Services,* Sydney, Allen and Unwin.

A. Scambler, G. Scambler and D. Craig (1981), 'Kinship and Friendship Networks and Women's Demand for Primary Care', *Journal of the Royal College of General Practitioners,* 26:746–750.

T.J. Scheff (1963), 'Decision Rules, Types of Error and their Consequences', *Behavioural Science,* 8:97–107.

T.J. Scheff (1966), *Being Mentally Ill, A Sociological Theory,* London, Weidenfeld and Nicolson.

N. Scheper-Hughes and A.M. Lovell (1986), 'Breaking the Circuit of Social Control: Lessons in Public Psychiatry from Italy and Franco Basaglia', *Social Science and Medicine,* 23(2):159–178.

S. Schulman (1958), 'Basic Functional Roles in Nursing: Mother Surrogate and Healer', E.G. Jaco (ed.) *Patients, Physicians and Illness,* Glencoe, Ill., Free Press, pp. 528–537.

S. Schulman (1972), 'Mother Surrogate – After a Decade', E.G. Jaco (ed.), *Patients, Physicians and Illness,* New York, Free Press, pp. 233–239.

J. Scott (1979), *Corporations, Classes and Capitalism,* London, Hutchinson.

R.B. Scotton (1978), 'Health Services and the Public Sector' in R.B. Scotton and H. Ferber (eds), *Public Expenditures and Social Policy in Australia, Volume I, The Whitlam Years 1972–75*, Melbourne, Longman Cheshire, pp. 87–136.

R.B. Scotton (1980), 'Health Insurance: Medibank and After' in R.B. Scotton and H. Ferber (eds), *Public Expenditures and Social Policy in Australia, Volume II, The First Fraser Years 1976–78*, Melbourne, Longman Cheshire, pp. 175–219.

M.A. Screech (1985), 'Good Madness in Christendom' in W.F. Bynum, R. Porter and M. Shepherd (eds), *The Anatomy of Madness*, London and New York, Tavistock, 1:25–39.

A. Scull (1977), *Decarceration – Community Treatment and the Deviant, A Radical View*, New Jersey, Englewood Cliffs.

A.T. Scull (1979), *Museums of Madness, the Social Organization of Insanity in Nineteenth-century England*, London, Allen Lane, The Penguin Press.

B.E. Segal (1962), 'Male Nurses: A Case Study in Status Contradiction and Prestige Loss', *Social Forces*, 41:31–38.

R. Sennett (ed.) (1969), *Classic Essays on the Culture of Cities*, Englewood Cliffs, New Jersey, Prentice-Hall.

R. Sennett (1974), *The Fall of Public Man*, Cambridge, Cambridge University Press.

A. Sheridan (1980), *Foucault, The Will to Truth*, London and New York, Tavistock.

E. Shils (1981), *Tradition*, London, Faber and Faber.

E. Shorter (1977), *The Making of the Modern Family*, London, Fontana Books.

E. Shorter (1983), *A History of Women's Bodies*, London, Allen Lane.

M. Shortland (1985), 'Skin Deep: Barthes, Lavater and the Legible Body', *Economy and Society*, 14(3):273–312.

R. Sidel and V. Sidel (1982), *The Health of China, Current Conflicts in Medical and Human Services for One Billion People*, London, Zed Press.

C. Singer (1925), *The Evolution of Anatomy*, London, Routledge and Kegan Paul.

J.K. Skipper and R.C. Leonard (1968), 'Children, Stress and Hospitalization', *Journal of Health and Social Behaviour*, 9:275–286.

T. Skocpol (1980), 'Political Response to Capitalist Crisis: Neo-Marxist Theories of the State and the Case of the New Deal', *Politics and Society*, 10:155–201.

V. Skultans (1974), *Intimacy and Ritual, a Study of Spiritualism, Mediums and Groups*, London, Routledge and Kegan Paul.

V. Skultans (1979), *English Madness, Ideas on Insanity, 1580–1890*, London, Routledge and Kegan Paul.

B. Smart (1985), *Michel Foucault*, Chichester, Ellis Horwood and London, Tavistock.

B.E. Smith (1981), 'Black Lung, The Social Production of Disease', in V. Navarro and D.M. Berman (eds), *Health and Work Under Capitalism, An International Perspective*, Farmingdale, New York, Baywood Publishing Company, pp. 39–54.

J.C. Smith (1986), 'Responsibility in Criminal Law' in P. Bean and D. Whynes (eds), *Barbara Wootton, Social Science and Public Policy, Essays in Her Honour*, London and New York, Tavistock, pp. 141–155.

C. Smith-Rosenberg and C. Rosenberg (1973), 'The Female Animal, Medical and Biological Views of Woman and Her Role in Nineteenth-century America', *The Journal of American History*, 60:332–356.

P. Spicker (1984), *Stigma and Social Welfare*, London, and Canberra, Croom Helm.

L. Srole (1975), *Mental Health in the Metropolis: the Midtown Manhattan Study*, New York, Harper Torch Books.

A.H. Stanton and M.S. Schwartz (1961), 'The Mental Hospital and the Patient', in A. Etzioni (ed.), *Complex Organisations, a Sociological Reader*, New York, Holt, Rinehart and Winston, pp. 234–242.

P. Starr (1982), *The Social Transformation of American Medicine*, New York, Basic Books.

P.N. Stearns (1977), *Old Age in European Society, The Case of France*, London, Croom Helm.

B.J. Stern (1959), *Historical Sociology, the Selected Papers of Bernard J. Stern*, New York, Citadel Press.

R. Stevens (1971), *American Medicine and the Public Interest*, New Haven, Yale University Press.

R. Stevens and R. Stevens (1974), *Welfare Medicine in America, A Case Study of Medicaid*, New York, Free Press.

G.V. Stimson and B. Webb (1975), *Going to see the Doctor*, London, Routledge and Kegan Paul.

L. Stone (1979), *The Family, Sex and Marriage in England 1500–1800*, Harmondsworth, Penguin Books.

W. Stone (1983), 'Repetitive strain injury', *Medical Journal of Australia*, 24, pp. 616–618.

L. Strachey (1918), *Eminent Victorians*, London, Chatto and Windus.

A. Strauss (1966), 'The Structure and Ideology of American Nursing: An Interpretation' in F. Davis (ed.), *The Nursing Profession, Five Sociological Essays*, New York, Wiley, pp. 60–108.

A. Strauss, S. Fagerhaugh, B. Suczek and C. Wiener (1985), *Social Organisation of Medical Work*, Chicago and London, University of Chicago Press.

A. Strauss, L. Schatzman, D. Ehrlich, R. Bucher and M. Sabshin (1963), 'The Hospital and its Negotiated Order', in E. Freidson (ed.), *The Hospital in Modern Society*, New York, Free Press, pp. 147–169.

R.R. Strauss (1957), 'The Nature and Status of Medical Sociology', *The American Sociological Review*, 22:200–204.

P.M. Strong (1984), 'Viewpoint: The Academic Encirclement of Medicine?', *Sociology of Health and Illness*, 6(3):339–358.

E.A. Suchman (1964), 'Sociomedical Variations Among Ethnic Groups', *The American Journal of Sociology*, 70:319–331.

D. Sudnow (1967), *Passing On, The Social Organisation of Dying*, Englewood Cliffs, New Jersey, Prentice-Hall.

S.R. Suleiman (1986), *The Female Body in Western Culture, Contemporary Perspectives*, Cambridge, Ma., Harvard University Press.

A. Summers (1975), *Damned Whores and God's Police, the Colonization of Women in Australia*, Harmondsworth, Penguin Books.

M.W. Susser and W. Watson (1962), *Sociology in Medicine*, London, Oxford University Press.

G.M. Sykes (1956), 'The Corruption of Authority and Rehabilitation', *Social Forces*, 34:257–262.

T. Szasz (1961), *The Myth of Mental Illness*, New York, Harper and Row.

T. Szasz (1970), *The Manufacture of Madness*, New York, Harper and Row.

T. Szasz (1978), *The Myth of Psychotherapy*, New York, Harper and Row.

I. Szelenyi (1978), 'Social Inequalities in State Socialist Re-distributive Economics', *International Journal of Comparative Sociology*, 19 (1–2):63–83.

R. Taylor and A. Gilmore (eds) (1982), *Current Trends in British Gerontology*, London, Gower.

R. Taylor and A. Rieger (1984), 'Rudolf Virchow on the Typhus Epidemic in Upper Silesia: An Introduction and Translation', *Sociology of Health and Illness*, 6(2):201–217.

K. Thomas (1971), *Religion and the Decline of Magic*, London, Macmillan.
I. Thorner (1955), 'Nursing: The Functional Significance of Institutional Patterns', *The American Sociological Review*, 20:531–538.
S. Timpanaro (1975), *On Materialism*, London, NLB.
R.M. Titmuss (1963), *Essays on the Welfare State*, London, Unwin University Books.
P. Townsend and N. Davidson (1982), *Inequalities in Health*, Harmondsworth, Pelican Books.
H. Trevor-Roper (1967), *Religion, the Reformation and Social Change*, London, Macmillan.
P. Trowler (1984), *Topics in Sociology*, Slough, University Tutorial Press.
D. Tuckett (ed.) (1976), *An Introduction to Medical Sociology*, London, Tavistock.
D. Tuckett, M. Bolton, C. Olson and A. Williams (1985), *Meetings Between Experts, An Approach to Sharing Ideas in Medical Consultations*, London and New York, Tavistock.
M.M. Tumin (ed.), (1970), *Readings on Social Stratification*, Englewood Cliffs, New Jersey, Prentice-Hall.
B.S. Turner (1981), *For Weber, Essays on the Sociology of Fate*, London, Routledge and Kegan Paul.
B.S. Turner (1982), 'The Government of the Body, Medical Regimens and the Rationalization of Diet', *The British Journal of Sociology*, 33(2): 252–269.
B.S. Turner (1983), *Religion and Social Theory, a Materialist Perspective*, London, Heinemann.
B.S. Turner (1984), *The Body and Society, Explorations in Social Theory*, Oxford, Basil Blackwell.
B.S. Turner (1985a), 'More on the Government of the Body', *The British Journal of Sociology*, 36(2):151–154.
B.S. Turner (1985b), 'Knowledge, Skill and Occupational Strategies: the Professionalisation of Paramedical Groups', *Community Health Studies*, 9:38–47.
B.S. Turner (1985c), 'The Practices of Rationality, Michel Foucault, Medical History and Sociological Theory', in R. Fardon (ed.), *Power and Knowledge, Anthropological and Sociological Approaches*, Edinburgh, Scottish Academic Press, pp. 193–213.
B.S. Turner (1986a), *Citizenship and Capitalism, The Debate Over Reformism*, London, Allen and Unwin.
B.S. Turner (1986b), *Equality*, Chichester, Ellis Horwood and London, Tavistock.
A. Twaddle (1982), 'From Medical Sociology to the Sociology of Health: Some Changing Concerns in the Sociological Study of Sickness and Treatment' in T. Bottomore, S. Nowak and M. Sokolowska (eds), *Sociology, The State of the Art*, London and Beverly Hills, Sage, pp. 323–358.
P.N. Unschuld (1985), *Medicine in China, a History of Ideas*, Berkeley, University of California Press.
P.N. Unschuld (1986), *Medicine in China, a History of Pharmaceutics*, Berkeley, University of California Press.
F.G. Valle (1955), 'Burial and Mourning Customs in a Hebridian Community', *Journal of the Royal Anthropological Institute*, 85:119–130.
T. Veblen (1957), *The Higher Learning in America, A Memorandum on the Conduct of Universities by Business Men*, New York, Hill and Wang.
I. Veith (1965), *Hysteria, the History of a Disease*, Chicago and London, University of Chicago Press.
L.M. Verbrugge (1984), 'Longer Life but Worsening Health? Trends in Health and

Mortality of Middle-aged and Older Persons', *Milbank Memorial Fund Quarterly,* 62(3):475–519.

L.N. Verbrugge (1985), 'Gender and Health: An Update on Hypotheses and Evidence', *Journal of Health and Social Behaviour,* 26(3): 156–182.

E.F. Vogel (1967), 'Kinship Structure, Migration to the City, and Modernization' in R.P. Dore (ed.), *Aspects of Social Change in Modern Japan,* Princeton New Jersey, Princeton University Press, pp. 91–112.

D.G. Wagner (1984), *The Growth of Sociological Theories,* Beverly Hills, Sage.

H. Waitzkin and B. Waterman (1974), *The Exploitation of Illness in Capitalist Society,* Indianapolis, Bobbs-Merrill.

A. Walker (1982), 'Dependency and Old Age', *Social Policy and Administration,* 16(2):115–135.

J. Walton, A.S. Duncan, C.M. Fletcher, P. Freeling, C. Hawkins, N. Kessel and I. McCall (1980), *Talking with Patients, A Teaching Approach,* London, Nuffield Provincial Hospitals Trust.

W.I. Wardwell (1979), 'Limited and Marginal Practitioners', in H.E. Freeman, S. Levine and L.G. Reeder (eds), *Handbook of Medical Sociology,* Englewood Cliffs, New Jersey, Prentice-Hall, pp. 230–250.

J. Warren Salmon (1984), *Alternative Medicines, Popular and Policy Perspectives,* London, Tavistock.

B. Watkin (1978), *The National Health Service: The First Phase, 1948–1974 and After,* London, Allen and Unwin.

J.L. Watson (ed.) (1984), *Class and Social Stratification in Post-revolutionary China,* Cambridge, Cambridge University Press.

H.L. Webb (1982), 'Socialism and Health in France', *Social Policy and Administration,* 16:241–252.

M. Weber (1966), *The Sociology of Religion,* London, Methuen.

M. Weber (1978), *Economy and Society,* Berkeley, University of California Press, 2 vols.

M. Weir and T. Skocpol (1983), 'State Structures and Social Keynesianism', *International Journal of Comparative Sociology,* 24, (1–2):4–29.

R.S. Weiss (1976), 'Transition States and Other Stressful Situations: Their Nature and Programs for their Management' in G. Caplan and M. Killilea (eds), *Support Systems and Mutual Help, Multidisciplinary Explorations,* New York, Grune and Stratton, pp. 213–232.

M.R. Weisser (1979), *Crime and Punishment in Early Modern Europe,* Brighton, Harvester Press.

A.G. Wernham (1958), *Benedict de Spinoza the Political Works,* Oxford, The Clarendon Press.

J. Western (1983), *Social Inequality in Australian Society,* Melbourne, Macmillan.

D. Widgery (1979), *Health in Danger, The Crisis in the National Health Service,* London, Macmillan.

H. Wilensky (1963), 'The Professionalization of Everybody', *American Journal of Sociology,* 70:137–158.

H. Wilensky (1975), *The Welfare State and Economy,* Berkeley, The University of California Press.

H. Wilensky (1976), *The New Corporatism, Centralization and the Welfare State,* London, Sage.

D. Willcocks (1983), 'Stereotypes of Old Age, The Case of Yugoslavia', in D. Jerrome (ed.), *Ageing in Modern Society, Contemporary Approaches,* London and Canberra, Croom Helm, pp. 104–123.

E. Willis (1983), *Medical Dominance, Division of Labour in Australian Health Care*, Sydney, Allen and Unwin.

E. Willis (1986), 'RSI as a Social Process', *Community Health Studies*, 10(2):210–219.

J.K. Wing (1967), 'The Modern Management of Schizophrenia' in H. Freeman and J. Farndale (eds), *New Aspects of the Mental Health Services*, New York, Pergamon, pp. 3–28.

J.K. Wing and G.W. Brown (1970), *Institutionalism and Schizophrenia*, Cambridge, Cambridge University Press.

L. Wirth (1931), 'Clinical Sociology', *The American Journal of Sociology*, 37:49–66.

D.E. Wolfe (1961), 'Sydenham and Locke on the Limits of Anatomy', *The Bulletin for the History of Medicine*, 35(3):139–220.

S. Wolfe and B.B. Berle (eds) (1981), *The Technological Imperative in Medicine*, New York and London, Plenum Press.

C. Woodham-Smith (1950), *Florence Nightingale 1820–1910*, London, Constable.

B. Wootton (1963), *Crime and the Criminal Law*, London, Stevens.

E.O. Wright (1985), *Classes*, London, Verso.

M. Wright (1981), 'Coming to Terms with Death: Patient Care in a Hospice for the Terminally Ill' in P. Atkinson and C. Heath (eds), *Medical Work, Realities and Routines*, pp. 141–151.

P. Wright and A. Treacher (eds) (1982), *The Problem of Medical Knowledge, Examining the Social Construction of Medicine*, Edinburgh, Edinburgh University Press.

E.A. Wrigley (ed.) (1966), *An Introduction to English Historical Demography from the Sixteenth to the Nineteenth Century*, London, Weidenfeld and Nicolson.

E.A. Wrigley (1969), *Population and History*, London, Weidenfeld and Nicolson.

E.A. Wrigley and R. Schofield (1982), *The Population History of England 1541–1871, A Reconstruction*, London, Arnold.

D.H. Wrong (1966), *Population and Society*, New York, Random House.

W.O. Young and L.K. Cohen (1979), 'The Nature and Organisation of Dental Practice' in H.E. Freeman, S. Levine and L.G. Feeder (eds), *Handbook of Medical Sociology*, Engelwood Cliffs, New Jersey, Prentice-Hall, pp. 193–208.

A.J. Youngson (1979), *The Scientific Revolution in Victorian Medicine*, Canberra, Australian National University Press.

I.K. Zola (1972), 'Medicine as an Institution of Social Control: The Medicalizing of Society', *The Sociological Review*, 20(4):487–504.

Index

Index compiled by Peva Keane